C000147469

FLAT FEET
AND
FULL STEAM

around the world in every way

CHRISTOPHER PORTWAY

summersdale

Copyright © Christopher Portway 2004

The right of Christopher Portway to be identified as the author
of this work has been asserted in accordance with sections 77
and 78 of the Copyright, Designs and Patents Act 1988.

No part of this book may be reproduced by any means, nor
transmitted, nor translated into a machine language, without
the written permission of the publisher.

Summersdale Publishers Ltd
46 West Street
Chichester
West Sussex
PO19 1RP
UK

www.summersdale.com

Printed and bound in Great Britain.

ISBN 1 84024 332 5

Maps by Rob Smith.
Cover illustration by Melanie Barnes.

About the Author

Christopher Portway was born in Essex in 1923. After leaving school he joined the Army and fought in the Second World War. Captured in Normandy, he later escaped from three prison camps in Eastern Europe.

He is married to the girl from Czechoslovakia whom he first met while on the run from the Germans in that country. After 1945, he repeated attempts to reach Anna, though her home was subsequently sealed off behind the Iron Curtain. On one such attempt, Christopher was caught after cutting his way through the electrified fences and crawling over a minefield, to be awarded 104 years in jail. He now has two children; a son and a daughter.

Christopher is a member of the British Guild of Travel Writers and a Fellow of the Royal Geographical Society, as well as being a recipient of a Winston Churchill Award for biography and travel. He is a frequent contributor to various magazines and newspapers and is the author of eighteen books.

Acknowledgements

With thanks to Oxford Illustrated Press for the permission to use extracts from my books published by them.

BOOKS BY THE SAME AUTHOR

Non fiction:

Journey to Dana
The Pregnant Unicorn
Corner Seat
Double Circuit
Journey Along the Andes
The Great Railway Adventure
The Great Travelling Adventure
Czechmate
Indian Odyssey
A Kenyan Adventure
Pedal for Your Life
A Good Pair of Legs
The World Commuter

Fiction:

All Exits Barred
Lost Vengeance
The Tirana Assignment
as John October *The Anarchy Pedlars*

CONTENTS

PREFACE

My favourite method of travel will, I think, always be walking. Yet it came to me, upon assembling my experiences of travel over seventy years of a lifetime, that undiluted walking covered only a fraction of it. Travel with a horse, a camel, a mule, a bicycle; journeying by train, bus, lorry, dinghy, elephant, covered wagon, dog sledge, car, felucca, ship and more opened up the subject considerably and put extra colour into the realm of travel and travel writing.

Being a tidy-minded person I attempted to arrange the order of chapters into journeys made in particular environments and using particular modes of vehicle. But I discerned that my journeyings became muddled with a mass of conveyances that, all too often, broke the environmental order. So, where possible, I have turned the theme to one of geographical settings.

My main problem arising from writing such a book is that of selecting which travelling adventures and experiences to include and which to leave out. In my years I have ridden elephants in Thailand jungles and Nepalese bush, driven Land Rovers around North Yemen, gone dog-sledging in Greenland, tried camping on glaciers in Iceland, crewed tall ships amongst the Canaries, ridden horses in the USA and Mongolia, climbed mountains in Ecuador, Morocco, Greece, Nepal and South Africa, driven trains in India, Russia, North Korea and Jordan, been jailed in Uganda, sampled para-sailing in Wales, flown co-pilot in Alaska, been arrested in Russia and shot at in wartime Normandy, crawled over Iron Curtain minefields, hitch-hiked in Colombia, cycled in Albania and much of Europe and the UK and more. Some of these were adventures; others incidents; though it is hard to differentiate since one man's – or woman's – incident can be another's adventure. So I made my criterion the degree of satisfaction gained, and used my memory – plus a few notes and excerpts from one or two of my earlier books – to narrate some of the more interesting, dramatic and amusing occurrences either at some length or in short anecdotes.

I am sometimes asked *why* I am such a travel fanatic and it is a difficult question to answer. I know I'm not the only person born with this wanderlust; many have it to a greater or lesser degree. Witness the great holiday high-season exodus when those who can get away to pastures new do so with a vengeance – even if many are basically in search of no more than warm seas and a tanning sun. However, an increasing number of us are becoming curious about our fellow *Homo sapiens* around the globe; particularly in the more inaccessible, remote or politically 'awkward' corners of it. Newspapers and television are responsible for both the pros and the cons of this interest. The more discerning tourist or traveller wants to see with his own eyes a territory 'in the news' even though the media is all too often tending to dismiss such territory in the eyes of the less curious as beyond the pale. A regime, however hateful, does not reflect the populace who live under it. Nor do the politics of a nation affect the beauty and character of a country.

I find an easier answer to the supplementary question put to me: why do I like travelling so *uncomfortably?* My wife says I'm a masochist but this is not entirely the case. To me, the most interesting portions of this earth are so often those where life is primitive and to see it requires a certain degree of ruggedness of existence and movement. Likewise to feel how a country ticks it is necessary to live in approximately similar conditions as do the local inhabitants. I remember my first visit to India more than 25 years ago when I spent some weeks existing in a manner as do the vast majority of Indians. This meant sleeping on railway station platforms, eating from curry stalls in the humble end of town, living in accommodations that can only be described as slums, and travelling bottom class on horrifically overcrowded trains. I returned home with my ribs sticking through my skin and considerable relief but the ordeal taught me more about India than have all my subsequent, more tourist-orientated visits put together. And there you have what to me is a *raison d'être* of world travel.

It is a strange addiction, this travel lust, and it is made stronger still for those travellers who have seen or experienced the very worst conditions the world can fling at them. Mishap or disaster never turns them off travel; on the contrary it only increases the fervour. For me, events during the second half of the Second World War have become my nadir of travel experience when, as a captive of Nazi Germany, I was shuttled across occupied Europe locked in overcrowded cattle trucks of trains subjected to Allied bomb, rocket and machine-gun attacks. Later, I was a reluctant participant in the hideous occurences of the terrible 'Death March' of 1945 when hundreds of thousands died of starvation, brutality and cold when herded across eastern Europe before the onslaught of the advancing Red Army in the severest winter conditions for half a century. Though I was luckier than many these episodes should have kept me firmly at home for evermore.

This book has no aspirations to be a guide or 'how to do it' book. Adventuring, exploring and travelling are personal matters and cannot be taught like algebra. My dictionary defines 'adventure' as 'a chance', 'a remarkable incidence', 'a risk', 'an exciting experience', 'the spirit of enterprise'. 'Travel' it expounds as, 'to move along a course', 'to go with impetus'. Put all these aspirations together, raise the will to do something about them and you hold the key to the elixir of a full and satisfying life.

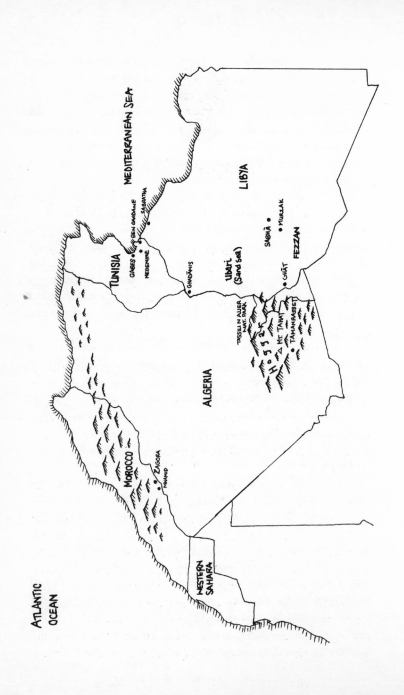

Chapter One

TRAVELS IN THE SAND

IN WHICH THE AUTHOR GRAPPLES WITH A BAD-TEMPERED CAMEL
CALLED PLASTIC CHARLIE, MEETS JEWELLERY-LOADED BEDOUIN
WOMEN, NURSES SADDLE-SORE HINDQUARTERS, PASSES THROUGH
A TOWN KNOWN AS THE PEARL OF THE DESERT, BEFORE FINALLY
ATTACKING A DUTY OFFICER ON THE IRAN-IRAQ BORDER WITH AN
ELECTRIC SHAVER.

Harsh and terrible a desert can be but beautiful and fascinating too. I am not alone in my affection for deserts but, quite certainly, their environment is an acquired taste. The lure of the sea and the mountains is far more universal and conventional. As Quentin Crewe remarks in his In Search of the Sahara, *'Any old fish, as it were, can live in the sea, but it takes a very special fox or gazelle or even scorpion to survive in the desert.'*

I have touched upon a number of deserts and semi-deserts about the globe in North Yemen, the Nubian in the Sudan, the Indian in Rajasthan, the Mojave in California, the Gobi in China and Mongolia, the Kalahari in South Africa, the Syrian and others, but it is the Sahara to which my footsteps return again and again; not only because it is the nearest and most accessible. Three million square miles in size – twice that of Europe – it covers almost the entire northern end of the African continent, from the Atlas Mountains in the north to the beginning of the dry savannah fringe of tropical Africa in the south. In the west it reaches to the shores of the Atlantic and in the east to the coast of the Red Sea. A gigantic desert indeed is the Sahara; one that occupies a

11

sixteenth of the entire area of the earth and is a sure-fire magnet for the traveller with the slightest penchant for adventure.

FOR THOSE WHO come to relax in North Africa the proximity of the great Sahara is nowhere so compelling a draw than in Tunisia. It can be reached by car or bus and, nearly, by rail with no trouble at all from towns and resorts like Sfax, Gabes and Sbeitla. I first took the road to the Sahara in 1969 and having looked upon it was conquered.

A sunset equalled only by the sunrise, a distant sound of barking dogs, the drums and voices of a faraway festivity and the incoherent rumblings of a town relaxing upon the dying day. These are the sights and sounds that greet the first-time visitor to the desert approaches.

It is at Nefza, a township close to the Algerian border, that the Sahara and its strange compelling remoteness and pulsating silence can be sampled even by the most comfort-conscious visitor. The startling significance of a desert unrolling into eternity is a haunting experience in itself.

The Tunisian *bled* is a land of nowhere, a desert with no sand, a flat treeless plain that turns briefly green in spring, is parched in summer and is bleak and windswept in winter. The earth is scarred by *wedds,* dry eroded gullies that suddenly become raging torrents in the rare but violent rainfall. The lunar landscape, its frightening emptiness occasionally broken by sagebrush and wormwood, can be home to few. Yet lost settlements do exist in this land of mere subsistence where a traveller seldom proceeds alone.

Here is also a country of the mirage where the sun and air play games as you look out across the half-world in which you find yourself. A Bedouin tent becomes a clump of cactus. A herd of camels is no more than the ruins of a Berber village. Driving along you shake your head and watch the road run straight into the blurred horizon. And

12

when you get there nothing has changed: the road still runs into the void.

Occasionally a dirt track wanders off the road to disappear into the *bled* towards some nameless community of mud-walled houses and unsmiling people huddled in earth-coloured *jebbahs* and blankets. But the folk most at home in the *bled* – as they are in the sand desert – are nomads.

The Bedouin are not a race but represent a way of life. The men are tall and lean with deep-set eyes, high cheeks and hawk-like noses. The women are often strikingly beautiful with fine features and a poise that would be the envy of a ballet dancer. But like the brief flowers of early spring their beauty all too soon withers under the yoke of work and rheumatism. Their chins, cheeks and foreheads bear tattooed markings and they are loaded with silver jewellery which is the family fortune.

To the Arab as well as the European the Bedouin is a remote and mysterious figure. The townspeople speak of him in wonder, a little fear and probably a lot of ignorance. Tourists are always being offered a visit to a Bedouin encampment which underlines the air of mysticism that surrounds them. But no self-respecting member of the Bedouin community would tolerate this intrusion by a gaggle of gawking foreigners and I suspect that those who do are not typical of their race. The Bedouin women never veil, and all, including the children, keep themselves to themselves, living in ragged tents and, when travelling, never acknowledge you as you drive by. Tales of wedding-night beatings, of vicious customs and pagan rites, if true, tell of a life that is unchanged since the Dark Ages.

Bedouin, Berber, Tuareg. Desert names for a desert people. Their lives – to the outsider – are something of an enigma that, for some, sharpen still further a thirst for knowledge of the vast, terrible and inspiring land behind the *bled*.

At Gabes in Tunisia the Sahara invades the country from the west. Like a tide, via the great salt lakes or *chotts,* it advances to well nigh cut Tunisia in two. It clogs the valleys near Gafsa, brushes the foothills of the high steppes, and rivulets of sand dribble to the sea. Huge herds of camels dot the landscape. Medenine and Ben Gardane are outposts of a lost world. Sabratha, in Libya, is another. Once it was a fine Roman city but today its bones bleach in the desert sun.

During the 1970s I made a journey southward travelling by open Land Rover driven by a local Arab with a life-long experience of negotiating the treacherous conditions of a sand sea. The trip was an experience in itself. In his vehicle we hurled ourselves at ridge after ridge deep into the stationary ocean of sand, the skill lying in an ability to generate enough power to climb up a knife-edged crest, stopping at the top and then digging away with shovels from beneath the vehicle until it gently tips forward and can roll down the opposite slope. Understandably it was a slow journey.

Our objective was the Fezzan, Libya's southernmost province, and, in particular, the Wadi el Ajal containing the records of 10,000 years of man's history. In fact there is probably no other stretch of country in the Sahara so rich in historical monument. And to go with this concentration of history is a concentration of geography whereby every constituent of a true desert are present within one comparatively small area. Rocky uplands called *hammada* give way to the gravel-covered plains or *reg* and vast sand seas of fragile beauty – the *erg* – wash against lofty mountain ranges. All the world's deserts – their drama and their poignancy – are in the Fezzan.

Though the savagery of desolation is all around, the wide Wadi el Ajal valley is pleasant indeed, with strips of green fertility prized from the waterless sand. Small villages add their vivid colours to the eternal yellow of the great sand sea of Ubari that forms one wall of the valley. Five capitals have been nurtured here; quite a number for a desert. Such an abundance

14

of cities is an indication of the importance once enjoyed by this region of the Sahara. And, what's more, Garama, Zouilla, Traghen, Murzak and now Sabha are still very much in existence; living reminders of an evocative past.

But it is left to Mathendous, a gash in the harsh grey clinker of the *hammada,* to tell the story of this barren land and what it was like ten millennia before. I spent two days and nights in this rock-bound *wadi*, westwards out of the desert where no roads run. Displayed for posterity upon the rocks are carvings of elephant, giraffe, crocodile and cattle that roamed the Sahara when forests and rivers covered its face. Wadi Mathendous is the most prolific rock art gallery anywhere and its canvases offer an enthralling insight into the beginnings of time. I wandered at will within this fascinating cleft watching the sun and its shadows bring the zoological collection to life.

Clues to the history of this land can also be found in the Acacus Mountains, where black eroded ridges rise in jagged masses for as far as the eye can see to make a lunar landscape of weird intensity. And within their cracks and crevices and wondrous caverns are cave paintings from 10,000 BC, depicting life as it was then as clearly as if created yesterday.

Living beyond the enormous dunes is a tribe called the Dawada, or literally, the 'worm eaters'. For countless centuries the Dawada have been isolated from the outside world, safe from their enemies but captives of their own security. They live around a miracle of water, a shy timid people who retained their charm even when their privacy was invaded by the likes of me. Approaching with some misgivings I gazed upon their habitations scattered about the sand hills; little huts called *zeriba* made of the fronds of palms set down in the sand. My gaze took in the tiny gardens watered from wickerwork baskets on the trunks of trees weighed at one end by chunks of natron or hydrated carbonate of soda.

Once the people would have fled from such a visitation but now they stood and watched me; nervous, apprehensive but wanting to be friendly. Several women stood in the dank water of the lake netting for *dood,* as the 'worm' is called. Actually it is a sort of brine shrimp, blood-red in colour, that lives in a water heavily charged with natron and comparable in density with the Dead Sea. How any creature can exist in such a strong brew is a mystery as is how it got there in the first place. I watched the women, up to their waists in slime, undertaking their exclusive and soul-destroying task. And the taboo is such that not only must it be a member of the female sex that enters the lake but this only on alternate days. In addition, no woman can enter until 41 days after childbirth and then only after purification with incense. The lake is very deep in the centre; the Dawada insist it is bottomless.

For cultivation and cooking the tribe make do with the same implements that their forefathers used 2,000 years before. I felt as if I had stepped out of the twentieth century back into the Middle Ages, the purity of their way of life guarded by the sand sea lapping at their doorstep. Questions flew to my lips. Where does the water come from? Why doesn't it drain away in the intense heat? Why is the water so cold? But nobody knows and the mysteries give added dimensions to a desert's wonder.

The village headman came forward and bade me welcome. Sitting on rush mats in a compound, we drank tea in the company of the other village elders while being watched by bevies of children whose initial fright soon gave way to raucous laughter. I asked my questions but obtained no answers; only smiles and more tea.

The Dawada own nothing but their *zeribas,* a cooking pot or two, a few vegetable plots, a share of the date palms that surround the stagnant lake and the rags in which they clothe themselves. Yet, so far as I could see, they seemed perfectly happy.

Thus I was privileged to look upon yet another aspect of the greatest desert in the world.

In 1974, a friend of mine attempted a project to attract tourists into the desert on the traditional means of conveyance – the camel. A fortnight-long plod, spending the nights under the stars and living as near as possible to the real denizens of the Sahara, made for a mild adventure with some rugged and uncomfortable moments. But the enterprise never took off commercially; the consensus of opinion being that it was *too* adventurous and *too* rugged for most tourists to consider. But that experimental journey was fun and brought about my initiation to the art of camel travel.

My mount, nameless in the beginning, became known as 'Plastic Charlie'. He was a king of camels; the strongest, fastest and, a rare attribute, almost white in colour. He was also bad-tempered, fierce and afflicted with the habit of leaping to his feet just as I was attempting to get into the saddle. This had the effect of projecting me skywards like a renegade missile; an additional hazard to others that are part and parcel of mounting a 'ship of the desert'.

But I soon got the hang of it. Rising to all four feet involves a three-part zigzag, the first propelling you forward over the head, the second making you tumble backwards over the rump and the third throwing you forward again – if you're still there that is. And should the gurgling, foaming beast fail to catch you unprepared on the ascent assuredly it'll do so when you dismount.

My companions for my circuit in the Moroccan Sahara were Brahim, the resourceful young Arab son of the owner of a camel herd, who spoke fluent French when he wasn't singing bawdy Arabic ditties. And Lute, a bearded, moustachioed, Tuareg usually high on *kif,* a popular stimulant in these parts. With me too was Rene, the instigator of the project, plus a couple of wary clients. With them I was to make a journey taking in the desert township of Mhamid and the Algerian border, returning via Jbel Bani to our start point of Zagora.

Some people insist that riding a camel is positively soporific but I'm not one of them. Being pitched backwards and forwards like a fly on a piston rod is not my idea of an inducement to slumber. Breaking into a trot has you bouncing around until your teeth almost drop out; cantering makes for a smoother ride. 'Grip with your knees,' came a sepulchral voice from afar which sounded remarkably like my long-suffering Pony Club instructor of aeons past. But how the hell can you grip with your knees when they're stuck out in front of you? And the steering gear's all wrong. A length of cord attached to the beast's left nostril is supposed to cater for both a left and right-hand turn, the direction depending upon the angle of pull. Going left was no problem but pulling right simply activated the animal's head which swivelled round on its long neck so that a hate-crazed face glared malevolently at the rider. Since Plastic Charlie always insisted in being the lead camel and I didn't know the way I sometimes found myself plodding in the wrong direction thus requiring a right turn. To undertake this I was forced to institute a left about turn and complete a circle which plainly annoyed my mount who audibly displayed his displeasure. The words of command are 'Ha!' (move, blast you), 'Shshsh' (stop) plus a tap on the small of the neck which is supposed to indicate that you require the animal to sit down (if it hasn't done so already). A series of variously-pitched clucks allegedly effects an increase or decrease in speed.

For those enamoured with the notion of camel-riding for any appreciable distance allow me to offer a morsel of advice. Very early in the proceedings pad your saddle. It won't be of a design you'll recognise as a saddle and it inflicts indignities upon human hindquarters such as you will have never previously experienced. And you'll soon learn why Arabs envelop themselves in so much linen when the wind rises and blows stinging clouds of sand at your exposed parts.

We left Zagora around mid-morning with the sun high, its brilliance severing the demarcation line between the horizon and the sky. And as if to prove that variety is the spice of life the night that followed was freezing. Brahim and Lute together determined the length of the day's plod, the odd waterholes and the time taken to travel between them being the regulating qualification. Between the fry and freeze the pace of progress rarely altered and, that first day out, my sense of values underwent a sharp revision. Life in the desert demands an existence of complete simplicity that releases an instinct for survival. In a Western world suffering from over-indulgence the transformation becomes a remarkable lesson in humility. Stopping only to draw water that is little more than liquid mud and give the camels a snack off the occasional clump of prickly desert shrub, we went right through to evening before Brahim designated a campsite in the middle of nowhere. The evening meal was carrot stew, multiple glasses of sickly-sweet tea and the odd date from a sticky brown-paper bag. New bread baked expertly between hot sand and ashes was full of grit but delicious. The camels were hobbled and left to their own devices.

Our route followed the dry course of the Draa River marked by a few empty *ksars* and skeletons of deserted villages of mud that petered out by the end of the first afternoon. The sombre heights of Jbel Tadrart and a hidden pass led us eventually to a land of dunes eerie with silence. We slept in the open, each of us scooped into an indent of the soft, initially-warm sand, our clothes on and rugs piled upon us.

Four days out from Zagora had us in Mhamid where I became the guest of the village headman who had taken a shine to me. For two further days we remained here and for all of it I was bidden to share his home, his food and his life as if it was the most natural thing in the world (which it was). In the humble dwelling I was content to sleep upon the floor, eat upon the floor and meet members of his considerable family upon the floor, for that is how it is. Together with them I ate *couscous* with fingers that attempted to emulate those of the others by forming the damp warm millet into a firm ball for transfer to the mouth, consuming huge amounts of green tea and, with the nightfall, joining in the Berber dances that had me prancing about like a member of the chorus of the London Palladium.

The third morning we loaded the camels, bade our hosts farewell and lumbered into the wilderness, pitching back and forth in the gait that is peculiar to camels. Flat sand and rolling dunes gave way to desolate rock gullies with the approach to the inhospitable Jbel Bani, a 3,000-foot mountain rising if only to prove that desert is neither flat nor solely sand. Brahmin intoned one of his interminable ditties and Lute, his eyes glazed from a surfeit of *kif,* led without enthusiasm or complaint towards the stony uplands. Even Plastic Charlie dragged his feet. When the going got really tough we dismounted to lead our reluctant beasts over a hard uneven track that had them stumbling and nervous; not at all their former haughty selves when sand was underfoot.

A nomad family, relatives of Lute, sheltered us for the night. We spread ourselves over a none-too-clean carpet in company with an assortment of children, goats and sheep exuding equally powerful smells. Meat – rare on a desert menu – formed the main ingredient of the evening meal and this, as is the custom, was removed from the blackened cooking pot, portion by portion, and handed out according to age and seniority; each fragment, in the handling, congealing and collecting liberal coatings of sand and grit. A watery vegetable stew, followed by the usual endless servings of green tea plus a series of mammoth belches, and we all lay down to sleep where we sat, a young goat just behind me making quite a passable pillow.

In the morning we came down from the mountain to be claimed by the great plain of Zagora which held us in its sweaty maw for two more days until journey's end. Zagora town took on the aura of a metropolis.

My farewell to Plastic Charlie was a private affair between beast and rider. His gurgle was no less musical than the plumbing of a Kensington hotel I knew but the bite he gave

20

me held, I'm positive, an inner meaning – even though it was in the same spot on my left buttock where he had bitten me before. Brahmin hugged us all in turn and Lute became maudlin but I think their verdict was approval of our conduct.

With a new companion, an Irishman named John, I set off from the Libyan Fezzan on a fresh and longer desert journey across a larger fragment of the Sahara. At Sabha we picked up Gamel, a Tuareg guide who had once lived at Siwa Oasis on the Egyptian side of the Libyan-Egyptian border. We would be picking up our camels forthwith while John's associate with his Land Rover would meet us in the weeks to come east of Ghadamis hundreds of miles to the north. At least that was the plan. The popular overlanders' route into the desert's interior is that which leads from Ghardaïa southwards through Algeria's Hoggar Mountains to Tamanrasset, but ours was a lesser-known itinerary and one that ran, eventually, at right angles to the norm, though equally devoid of what we term as civilisation. I had put my trust in the hands of John, Gamel and Allah and their arrangements for our immediate future.

My camel was a moulting, tick-infested animal with none of the attributes of Plastic Charlie beyond the ability to bite. We rode steadily that first day out and the going was faster than I liked. Throughout the morning I had trouble keeping my mount at the trot and trailed badly behind the other two. Then I discovered that if I gave my mount a belt with my riding stick he would, after a protesting snarl, break into a gallop and recover the lost ground. What was more, I found that by crossing my feet over the neck and gripping the pommel of the saddle between my thighs, I could ride at a gallop without feeling too precariously perched.

We had all those miles to cover before we would see the Land Rover again and I had private doubts about whether it would ever find us in the weeks to come. Better, I felt, to stay put in Ghadamis where at least he was sure to find us. However, I held my peace.

21

We met many nomads in the days that followed, for the desert is a surprisingly populated place. Not a day passed without our seeing at least a dozen humans tending their herds of flop-eared brown sheep and we spent as many nights in the company of others as we did alone in our solitude. Either a shelter was raised for our benefit, or we slept in the lee of a nomadic tent. It was the unwritten rule of the desert that we should be fed and housed by these nomads to a degree that made me feel extremely uncomfortable but there was simply nothing to be done about it. Offering money is taken as an insult and money was the only commodity that John and I had to give.

Everything in the lives of the nomads we met was bent towards a preoccupation with food for man and beast alike. Food of every kind was an obsession. These desert Arabs were particularly avid for meat which represented to them the most nourishing as well as the most satisfying form of food. This desperate desire for meat, I soon realised, explained their habit of merely singeing it in the flames of a fire as soon as they had hacked a lump off a butchered animal: they simply could not wait to get their teeth into it.

Upon arrival at an encampment the process of greetings commenced and it seldom varied. Throughout the Arabic-speaking world this begins with 'Selehmoo alaikum' – 'His peace be with you'. But a shorter salutation is used in differing circumstances, such as when two strangers pass and here 'Le-bas' – 'No evil – is the operative phrase.

Again our route and rate of march was dictated by the availability of wells. Gamel must have had a built-in map inside his head for we always came upon the vital source of water even when the track we were following was obliterated by sand storms. The second day we moved from the plain into low dunes, scattered thinly above the bedding of hard rock. For five hours we slogged wearily on foot leading the camels up and down mounds of sand which was invariably soft and that, in the hollows, was never deep enough to prevent our feet bruising upon stone and clinker. A wind arose, blowing grit into our faces, to add to the discomfort. But we had to maintain the pace to reach the well before darkness: a hole in the sand, perhaps four feet wide and 20 deep, which, the thought kept occurring to me, we might so easily pass by, even with the best navigation in the world. The only clues were a criss-cross of tracks leading to it but, again, this could be blown away by the next sandstorm.

We sloshed water into cooking pots so our beasts could drink, and a great deal dribbled back into the well each time they stuck their heads into the containers. After sucking noisily at the proffered liquid, the animals appeared to be satisfied, so we turned to filling our *guerbas*; I was drinking five or six pints a day of unclean water quite apart from the intake from tea and that used in the cooking.

We pressed on into a series of days that became blurred by the thickening haze of weariness. The most eagerly awaited moments of them were those at midday and evening when we drank the first glass of syrupy tea, knowing there was plenty more to come, each loaded with properties that would restore energy to our wilting bodies. But then the dragging agony of movement would begin again, the grinding ache where the left leg joined the pelvis, a sore on my buttock and the pain of cracked and dried lips whipped by blown sand.

For myself, I was happiest when we spent our nights alone, for my nerves became frayed by the sometimes uncongenial atmosphere of the camps. That we were in debt to our hosts who had so little for themselves I was only too aware, but I found the perpetual staring and cadging for items we had to keep for ourselves hard to handle.

We reached the township of Ghat close to the Algerian border on the edge of the Tassili n Ajjer Mountains on the twelfth day. The mud-walled houses, the new but empty hospital, a modern school occupied by boys but not girls and a garish necklace of concrete lamp-standards welcomed us back, for a moment, to modern Libya. The minarets of half a dozen mosques made the only distinguishing feature of a town that fights for existence against the ubiquitous sand.

One of the most substantial dwellings was that of the town hall. An elder received us on the premises and allowed us to sleep and feed in the corridor of the courtyard. We cooked our evening meal of left-overs from our provisions; hardly an inspiring menu but, this notwithstanding, the headman eagerly joined us and appeared to enjoy the fare.

Ghat, served only by desert tracks, has Ghadamis all of 200 miles distant and to the north, and we were uncertain how many of these miles we would have to ride before we were met by our vehicle. Should the condition of the tracks preclude the Land Rover using it then we were in for a long ride. But Gamel was confident that the track was passable to four-wheel drive vehicles at the very least for 50 miles south of the little town.

The first afternoon out of Ghat we had ridden across glaring sand, then over a range of dunes which the wind had carved into a series of strange shapes, full of enormous overhangs that put me in mind of a stilled ocean, its waves frozen solid as they broke over a beach. The dunes were very steep and we were moving across their grain, which taxed both us and the camels to the limit. The beasts grunted with the effort of uphill struggle, which they made in jerky bursts with each of us leaning far forward to put maximum weight over the shoulders of our respective mounts. Frequently we would dismount and lead them over the steepest portions. Riding downhill was even harder, for the camels, moaning softly, ran stiffly in long strides to avoid losing their control while we, leaning backwards now, our arms braced against the sides of the saddle, had our spines and shoulders jolted unmercifully.

A night on our own made for a restful sojourn but our proposed early morning start was confounded by the temporary loss of the camels. Though their forelegs were always tightly hobbled together, they could move extraordinary distances in their search for fodder, proceeding so with the determined shuffle of comical bunny hops. When we were guests of the nomads the children of the family took it upon themselves to rise early, track them down and return them to the camp, but on our own the chore was ours. On this occasion the beasts had broken all records for wandering and half the morning was gone before we could load them and continue on our way.

We traversed more dunes in the days ahead and their negotiation induced in me an alarming sensation of foreboding. In the hollows between the dunes it was as though I was very close to the edge of the earth. There was no vista beyond that undulating ridge just ahead, nothing but flawless blue sky; gain it and I would drop off into eternal space. But at the crest of the ridge a vista did appear, and it was even more intimidating than the illusion of space. A repeated sequence of this and the mind became dazed by the sameness of these elliptical shapes: a sort of fascination that became hypnotic. Don't ask me why I felt such a sensation; John seemingly was not affected by these illusions.

We came out of the dunes at last and moved across a pancake of gravel for all the world as if a village had been here but had been wiped clean from the face of the desert. I shivered but not from cold. Tired though I was I'm glad we did not have to camp there though I can give no reason. Instead we rode for two hours and then, seeing a dark tent, decided to camp near it hoping for the company of fellow men if not their attentions. After a while a woman and a small boy materialised, bringing some milk. While we prepared a fire a man joined us unbidden for our evening meal and we were pleased to have the opportunity to return some hospitality even if it did expend our limited provisions the faster.

The next day was unpleasant. We were riding directly into the face of a strong wind which continued right through to nightfall, the flying sand flaying our faces. The particles found their way into my nostrils and into my system so that I was eternally spitting out the stuff. In fact, after my return home, grains of sand exited from every orifice of my body for weeks. We camped again with nomads, this time in their tent, the only advantage being that we had no need to set up our own refuge for the night. The effort of doing anything was getting beyond me; it was more than weariness for several parts of me had begun not to function properly. I found myself blinking rapidly to bring things into focus, and my limbs were trembling with excessive fatigue.

Once again, our days became a long drawn-out agony of perpetual movement under a blistering sun that never, for a single second, hid itself behind a cloud. Measurement of time became a simple matter of countless obscure hours of movement punctuated by the relief that resulted from a meal or snack stop and, the climax of the day, the events brought about by dusk and the onset of a freezing night. I noticed that John, too, was flagging visibly – and he was younger than I. Looking back, I counted the days of the journey by the differing end-of-day occurrences. There was the evening when we rode up to an encampment where three men lounged and a woman sat apart, nursing a baby. We paused to exchange greetings before riding on, but the men seemed anxious that we should stay and talk. This we did, subsequently accepting their invitation to share their meal, though on closer acquaintance the three of us took an inexplicable dislike to them. They acted furtively which was odd for a nomad. We all resisted sleep that night, including Gamel who was likewise suspicious, but no harm befell us. And there was another evening when we rested with a band of friendlier folk who erected a small tent of hides for our benefit and then entertained us to a musical interlude; their numerous children were still dancing when my eyes finally closed. The meals we were sometimes given were, to me, highly suspect to say the least, though this in no way blunted my appreciation. Fortunately, inside a dark tent, it was hardly possible to see what it was you were eating and, possibly, just as well – particularly when handed an alleged delicacy like a camel's eye which, wrapped in sand-baked bread, had to be swallowed whole while pretending to oneself it was something else! Finally came the evening when we learnt that our vehicle had been seen on the track south out of Ghadamis. Such an occurrence as the coming of a car – even many miles away – was cause for much speculation; the news spreading far and wide.

We estimated that we were now within less than a 50 miles of the town and it had not gone unnoticed that the track had begun to improve and was more pronounced – or was it our fevered imagination? However, the news of the Land Rover had us in high spirits that last night in the wilderness. It was spent with our informants, a ragged bunch of Tuaregs, and we treated them to lavish amounts of our provisions cooked over their fire. Together with them we laid ourselves down under the patched and frayed tent roof in a fog of acrid smoke from both fire and a battery of cigarettes.

The last camp, the last well. There was a small crowd of Tuaregs drawing water, stripped to the waist in the shimmering heat. It was the first time I had seen such men out of their robes which normally left only the eyes and bridge of the nose visible. They were an amicable lot who helped to refill our *guerbas* and speed us towards a village they said was not many hours hence.

A clear morning gave way to a sandstorm in the afternoon and visibility dropped to no more than a few yards. We halted during the worst of the conditions, burying our heads in our sitting camel's flanks to protect our eyes from the flying sand. Then onwards again and although the continuing wind was hot I felt fingers of cold playing about my body as if I had a fever. But I was glad to keep moving through the lacerating void for fear that if I stopped I'd never get going again. By mid-afternoon a line of rocks showed through the haze, no more than a low shelf with a few stunted trees standing by. We settled under a prickly bush and contrived a fire using the saddles as wind breaks. On this we made unsweetened tea with the last of our water as a kind of celebration afternoon tea minus the cucumber sandwiches.

Barely had we resaddled the camels and moved off when we found ourselves in the village: a white village, its street deserted as a result of the storm. Such a community of houses we had not seen for weeks; it was as if we were entering the suburbs of a city. So eager were we to press on that we nearly missed the Land Rover parked prudently in the lee of a wall. John's colleague emerged from a doorway hurriedly wrapping swathes of muslin around his head. His momentary look of guilt turned to relief as he perceived our pleasure at the meeting. For me it really did feel like a 'Doctor Livingstone I presume' encounter.

I never did learn the name of the white village. It was old, constructed of uncemented stone flags to form box-shaped houses and the mosque had a solid square tower that made a bastion out of a church. We spent the night in the guesthouse, a stark building of empty unfurnished rooms.

The wind dropped during the night and, with no camels to locate and load, we were on the road soon after dawn. Gamel stayed behind to spend a rest day in the village with some of his innumerable relatives and these now appeared in a great phalanx of varied humankind to wave us on our way.

The track, washed clean of prints, was hereafter marked at intervals by stone cairns and poles and made effortless driving. By midday we had Ghadamis on the horizon. A Libyan border patrol intercepted us en route but they were exceedingly friendly, even offering us refreshment.

With its white stone buildings within a forest of palm trees, the town likes to be known as the 'Pearl of the Desert', though I would not put it quite so eloquently. However, any oasis has undeniable charm after days in the pitiless outback, particularly when attaining it across an endless plain with green trees and white houses in sight of one's mirage-tricked eyes for miles beforehand.

An hour north out of Ghadamis, very close to the Algerian border, I was again marvelling at the beauty of the dunes now that we did not have to urge camels over them. Just across that border was the fort of Michaguig, one of many French Saharan forts long fallen into disuse, some of which we had passed by earlier. At Michaguig, however, the fort stands proudly on a hilltop, very much alive, with soldiers on its battlements watching the border that is a bare 400 yards away. Below the fort we could discern the remnants of a village and, nearby, a mound topped by a classical obelisk. This was the memorial to the Marquis de Mores who died courageously furthering the Saharan interests of the French a long way from his one-time enterprise in the American West, which I would be involved with later. His death at the hands of a large force of hostile cameleers is the stuff of glory, with the Marquis, outnumbered and outgunned, taking many of them with him to his death.

Somehow this made a fitting end to our Saharan journey.

THE GOBI MUST be the second largest desert in the world yet its borders are not well defined and its composition gives a misleading impression of its character. Situated mostly in Mongolia it overflows into various provinces of China. And the Chinese term *Sha-mo* (sand desert), often applied to the Gobi, covers only small sections of it. Much is bare rock while grass plains and high mountains are included. Animal life is considerable; the *havigai* or Bactrian two-humped camel, the rare *tahi* or Przewalski horse, mountain sheep, antelope, gazelle, marmot and, of course, yak predominate. In the oft cloudless sky soar eagles, kites, cranes, vultures and the Mongolian lark.

I flew by a dilapidated Russian Antonov of Mongolian Airlines in which not only were there no seat belts but no seats. So one sat on the floor amongst the baggage or next to the pilot who happily zoomed down to near ground level whenever a passenger pointed out something of interest to him. Except in Ulan Bator, the capital, with the country's only modern airport, such aircraft land anywhere vaguely suitable. Thus we put down in a field close to a community of yurts or *gers,* the traditional cosy Mongolian tented home, within the Gobi confines.

I progressed unroyally, with the brown, scaly mountains – part of the Altai range – looking deceptively barren and empty from a distance but, as I was to see, hiding verdant valleys and deep gorges peopled by heavily-coated yaks while all-year-round ice lay in the rocky clefts where the sun's rays failed to penetrate. My vehicle was a bus even more dilapidated than my Antonov, that moved at speed over atrocious tracks that had multiplied over the years as drivers found new routes along them. From it I was to observe the *hainag* – a cross between a yak and a cow – roaming in large herds as we collected and dropped off passengers at *ger* villages. In both desert and steppe a wealth of wild flowers bloom, from the homely dandelion to carpets of edelweiss, and in one section I found myself, joining with others, sliding joyfully down the sides of the hot stilled 'waves' of a sand sea on our hindquarters – at the risk of a burnt bum! I was even able to look upon the Valley of the Dinosaurs where 70 million-year-old dinosaur eggs were found.

EVEN AS A child I have dreamed of travelling the fabulous Silk Road stretching from eastern China across Russia and Persia to the eastern shores of the Mediterranean, as well as branching south from the Pamir Mountains to Bombay.

Which is why I eventually found myself in Sinkiang, China's remotest province, and, in particular, Sinkiang's unlovely capital, Urumchi. From here a 130-mile drive by springless bus over a heavily rutted but undeniably Silk Road route through the Tien Shan Mountains brought me to Turfan, again within the rim of the Gobi Desert. Turfan is reputed to be the hottest place on earth though it was no more than pleasantly warm when I got there.

The town, a famed Silk Road caravan halt, comprises an old and a new section though, at first glance, both look equally aged. The bazaar could hardly have changed over the centuries and a number of mosques still stood to give a faint shadow of glories shared by Isfahan and Samarkand. In the hottest months of the year the citizens of the old town retire underground or to vine-shaded courtyards since their mud houses become veritable ovens. Scorpions, big hairy spiders and Turfan cockroaches – two inches long with red eyes – are good reason for the hard wooden beds with no bedding, upon which the whole family sleep, that can be seen in every courtyard.

I was to see row after row of what looked like pockmarks in the desert and learnt that these were the holes through which the men of Turfan descend to clean their *karez*, or underground canals, dug to bring irrigation water from the Tien Shan Mountains. Something like 950 *karez* converge on the region and many date back to the Han Dynasty, when the concept first arrived in Turfan via the Silk Road from Persia. There they were known as *qanats* and it is these underground canals that make possible the oasis that the Turfan region has become; a green island with a fertility that is a complete contradiction to the barrenness of the surroundings and the extremes of temperature to which it is subjected.

Old cities have been discovered in this fiery basin and one to which I journeyed was Kaochang beneath the so-called Flame Hills. Plainly a large population once inhabited this lonely land: the sense of antiquity is strong and the ruins I gazed upon were massive and extensive. But mud cities cannot last forever, though this one was taking an uncommonly long time to die through a complete absence of rain.

TO END, LET me narrate an episode that occurred during the homeward leg of my journey from India, via Pakistan and Iran in 1973, prior to the Iran-Iraq conflict when the two countries were in a state of mutual hate. I had arrived at the Iranian border post opposite that of Iraq.

Before me lay a four-mile stretch of sandy no-man's land. With an Iranian dog snapping at my heels, I strode out across open desert towards a distant speck which I presumed was the Iraqi customs post since there was nothing else in sight. I was alone in a hushed world, thankful that I didn't have a couple of trunks to carry. It felt like the end of a movie: the hero walking into the sunset. Except it was sunrise.

For some time the Iran-Iraq border had been a dodgy area; an air of front-line pervaded it. At the Iranian frontier post the officer had been in bed, but condescended to rise on an elbow to exit-stamp my passport. 'The border's closed over there,' he grunted sleepily from under a bulbous eiderdown, indicating Iraqi territory before reverting to the prostrate position, leaving me to proceed on my way.

My preconceived ideas about Iraq – magic carpets and public hangings – was probably little different from anyone else's, and their border people were to have little to do with any reappraisal when I reached it. A soldier, festooned with lethal hardware, eyed me suspiciously and indicated that I could enter. From yet another eiderdown a jaundiced eye opened and a mouth spoke. 'The border's closed,' it said.

I waited and was steadfastly ignored. I tapped my passport on the bedpost and raised a grunt of irritation. I searched the bedside table for the correct entry stamp with the idea of a DIY job, but my back-to-front Arabic was not up to it.

A commotion outside materialised into a trio of Serbs intent upon crossing into Iran for a day's outing. Their raised voices finally put paid to any notions the duty officer might have harboured of a lie-in. He rose into a sitting posture and surveyed his tormentors balefully. Quite certainly he wanted to refuse the Serbs' request to leave Iraqi territory, but was aware they were folk of substance and members of a fraternal delegation to his country so had to be humoured. A conversation on the telephone produced no ruling that he could comprehend and his charges were exhibiting impatience. The Serbs, decked out in flamboyant suitings in anticipation of decadent pastimes at their destination, Khorramshahr, ignored me too, even when, following a surreptitious peep at my copy of *Lyall's Languages,* I remarked 'Izvinite, koliko je sati?' on the assumption it meant 'What's the time, please?' in Serbo-Croat.

The problem was abruptly solved by a brilliant stroke of compromise. It seemed the stumbling block to transit lay in numbers permitted through the post. Two in each direction was the daily quota. Yet here was a determined unit of four making the officer's life a misery. He glared at me and I perceived a repugnance of things British clashing with expediency – and expediency triumphed. He would swap one incoming Brit for three outgoing Serbs. The ratio, with its implications, plainly stuck in his gullet – as no doubt it would with the Serbs had they understood – but it provided a solution. He banged stamps into all the passports and the room emptied.

Revenge is sweet. The officer, now reinforced by two grinning minions, proceeded to upturn my bag and rummage through the contents. He extracted my portable electric shaver and the discovery of its two batteries had the whole post alive with suspicion. Wasn't this a British infernal machine loaded with pro-Israel consequences? Everyone turned to me for enlightenment. Playing the salesman I obliged with a demonstration of its harmless magic. Hostility gave way to childish delight and, in order of seniority, the personnel of the post went to work on their five o'clock shadows. With the last chin smoothed, the officer demanded the shaver back for a trim of his moustache. But the batteries had become as tired as I was and Iraqi stubble is the stuff of hedgehog quills. The shaver took a firm grip on a sheaf of bristles, gave up the ghost and hung on like a limpet. The scream of agony heralded a return to hostility, but it was also a cry for help. With difficulty I prized the offending apparatus from the man's visage, shovelled my belongings back into my bag, and fled.

Chapter Two

TRAVELS IN THE COLD

In which the author treks across the largest ice cap in Europe, warms up in a hot-water pool in Iceland, goes dog-sledging in Greenland, tries to eat whale on the Faroe Islands, and finally attempts to sleep in the land of 24-hour daylight.

First the heat, now the cold. Though my thin and angular frame is susceptible to intense cold – it prefers to fry than freeze – I have found myself, with a certain reluctance, embarking upon journeys in the more northerly extremities of Europe and the world drawn more by the demands of my job as a travel writer than a deep-rooted attraction. The closest I have been to the North Pole is Spitsbergen, some 500 miles away which, judged by the vast expanses of the Arctic, is no great distance, but quite close enough for me. On several occasions I have also set foot on Iceland and Greenland, both during winter and summer months, and Alaska too. At the other end of the range, looking towards the Antarctic, are the Falkland Islands, decidedly cool and which, likewise, I've visited. Closer to home are such as the Faroe Islands that I looked upon in 1995 while, should one wish to bring the UK into the scheme of things, I suppose the islands of Orkney and Shetland could be included; but a line must be drawn somewhere.

Icelandic landscape has formed the backcloth to the sagas and is a fitting match to the stories themselves. Beyond Reykjavik lie the farmlands, the rivers, the fiords, the coastal townships and, behind them, always the mountains, ice caps, the cold deserts, the everlasting wastelands of black sand, snowbound and deserted throughout the long long winter, but, in the summer, warm under the 24-hour sun.

35

We angled across the swiftly-flowing river like robots, battling against a strong current, stumbling in the glacial water as we attempted to maintain a precarious balance. Packs weighed heavy on our shoulders, threatening to topple each of us from booted feet placed gingerly among a morass of hidden slippery boulders. Before we were halfway across my limbs were half-paralysed with cold as the group, strung out in line, made its slow-motion way towards the opposite bank to emerge onto dry land in squelching boots and in the knowledge that, within the hour, yet another river would have us doing it all again.

The route led across a snowfield, the whiteness sullied by lava dust, and our footfalls changed to a rhythmic crunch. Sodden boots sank into wet snow, gripping them in an icy embrace, and my toes curled with the additional cold.

Above, the clouds were breaking up, and, to the east, low mountains tumbled towards the coast. All around, fading into the horizon's haze, was a serrated alpine outline of incredible brutality and awesome loneliness.

Our small group was trekking across southern Iceland dominated by the huge plain that sprawls many miles wide to the southern edge of Vatnajokull, the largest ice cap in Europe, containing the great Oraefajokull Glacier, one of many. And Vatnajokull itself is but one – albeit the largest – of a quartet of such ice caps.

It invariably comes as a surprise to me that human beings are at their best in such an aura of discomfort and fatigue. And perhaps particularly so when conditions are voluntarily imposed. Right from the start the dozen members of the party became fused into a closely-knit team as the warm glow of achievement suffused minds at the close of a long hard day. Much of the camaraderie clearly blossomed from the sombre remoteness of a countryside that haunts the souls of those who travel it.

Iceland has frequently been termed a land of fire, a land of ice, and a land of contrasts. It is certainly all these and a land of misconceptions too. The island received its chilly-sounding name from a Norse Viking in the ninth century though, without doubt, it would be more appropriate for Iceland to exchange names with Greenland since the latter consists largely of no more than a huge ice cap.

The misconceptions must have gone a long way towards the creation of the notion that the island, newly discovered on the fringe of the habitable world, was a land of challenge too. Eleven hundred years ago this drew men of stature to a coastal belt that, alone, gave a toe-hold for human life; men of the likes of Erik the Red and the resourceful Gnupa-Baror who, having established a new home in the north, suspected that milder conditions might be found on the opposite shore. Constructing sledges for livestock, he loaded them with his worldly possessions and drove south, through unexplored deserts and mountains, among ice caps, and over five great glacial rivers, to put his theory to the test. So, down the ages, we come to modern times, to men like Hannes Jonsson whose duties as postman to the Oraefi district involved him, in 1934, in an eight hour crossing of the Skeidararjokull ice-sheet, with a volcano erupting under the ice cap behind and the glacier moving beneath him, floated up by the force of the melt-waters below.

The Torfajokull region is an ideal snapshot of some of Iceland's breathtaking landscapes. From the small grass-turfed youth hostel at Fljotadalur we walked for three days to Laufafell, climbing steadily, the route hurdled with glacial torrents, lava-fields of hard frozen rock and chasms probed by the chilly fingers of glaciers. We were three women and nine men and, for most of the time, our leader was Jenny, an Australian damsel of considerable efficiency, diplomacy and accomplishment who quite clearly knew her Iceland. Later we were joined by one

Dick Phillips – an exasperating but not unlovable character – whose tour it was. So, since this worthy spent half his life in the country, our leadership was far from unqualified. Above us the skies darkly threatened one moment, turned bright and blue the next, while a wind that never failed to search one out whatever the shelter found or clothing worn arose from nowhere. The adage 'If you don't like the weather, hang on a minute' never was more apt.

Our overnight accommodation was vested in huts of varying amenities – or lack of them. That of Einhyruinger was spacious and well-equipped whilst being conveniently close to the gnarled peak of that name to make a surprisingly easy evening climb unthreatened by the perils of darkness, since daylight lasted the whole night through. The second hut, at Krokur, was primitive in the extreme: no more than a sheep shelter and smelling accordingly, most of us froze on the hard dirty floor that relentlessly released its ground cold to seep through our sleeping bags. Crowding together for warmth and through lack of space our night here was not of the greatest success though, in the circumstances of our journey, part of the general experience. Me, I shivered so audibly that I kept the rest of the party awake. Outside, our sodden boots drained, upturned, on fence posts, and wet socks stiffened into woollen gumboots.

A long day of climbing eternal cols and crunching through snowfields, ever mindful of the towering Hekla volcano which last erupted in its terrible wrath just eight years earlier, brought us to Laufafell and the most comfortable of huts; this one gently warmed by the eternal central heating of a nearby hot spring, all of which tempted us to stay for two whole days. 'Rest days' they were called but brilliant sunshine lured us from the fug and, to the mournful pleas of oyster-catchers and the laughter of arctic skua, we trudged the startling terrain raising a greater mileage than we had forged daily before.

While we did manage to climb Mount Hekla, our slog up a lesser peak, Mount Haalda, made better viewing with eight ice caps and the white eminence of Vatnajokull etched upon a stupendous panorama. Haalda was but a wind-swept staging post to Landmannalauger where another palatial hut – a further youth hostel – brought us into contact with a party of mountain-climbing Swedes. None of us could resist the temptation of prolonged immersion in nearby hot-water pools of varying temperatures the next day. And it is something of a Nordic trait, with Sweden as the main perpetrator, to go in for the eminently sensible nude bathing lark. Except for a hard core of Rock of Gibraltar English ladies who steadfastly retained their knickers, we all stripped and soothed away our aches and pains in water that remained constantly hot.

Food is an all-important element of an Icelandic trek and our appetites were wolfish. A system of advance food caches had been devised by Dick, though this did not preclude the necessity of carrying a certain amount of provisions ourselves. Generally we ate well, the 'cuisine' being basically British with the addition of Russian jam, Czech sugar and occasional dollops of delicious Icelandic *skyr* or curd.

Rivers, bogs, soft snow and a minor blizzard accompanied the walk to Jokuldalir and its hut, an abrupt come-down in the accommodation stakes. We slept, head to foot, in close proximity and, this time, firmly beat the cold. Around us the landscape was uniformly forbidding; dark tangled masses, basalt pillars with a gleam of sunshine striking colours from the garish chemistry of the lava-fields. As a backcloth were the mountain ranges, low, misshapen and disconnected, matching the ungainly heaps of snow which lay on top of them and the lop-sided formations of cloud which hung above them.

The region is a wonderland of birds and flowers. Iceland turns the luke-warm bird-watcher into a fanatic. There is the puffin which dives and comes up with a clutch of fish in its bill, the arctic tern which makes periodic flights of incredible trans-continental distances, the raven that nests in the river cliffs by the Godafoss waterfall, and the rarer white-tailed eagle that soars majestically in the sky. And that's only the beginning. Where the snow has receded a profusion of plants, ferns and wild flowers ignore the cold to grow and often blossom at the very edge of a glacier's lip. Blue sesleria, *Rosa dumalis* and green spleenwort are common.

Twelve days and nights in the wilderness were enough to give us an insight into this amazing land. Discomfort, fatigue, the purgatory of cold, ever-wet feet and an unrequited hunger had been our constant companions, yet one acclimatises fast as lessons in survival are learnt the hard way. Very early in the trek I noticed members scampering off semi-naked in the wickedest cold to the nearest semi-freezing stream, flaunting towels like battle-standards, or accepting the most primitive of accommodations without a murmur of complaint. Iceland does this to one; it makes a man – or woman – of you as do few other destinations in the world. It is a harsh, rugged countryside which can be daunting but always magnificent. There can be few finer leisure pastimes than a week or two here with a rucksack and the freedom to go where one pleases without restriction.

LIKE, I SUPPOSE, many others, I had pre-conceived ideas about Greenland as I had about Iraq. It was a land inhabited by igloo-residing Eskimos angling for fish through holes in the ice. It was a land of eternal night; a land of frozen granite and icebergs upon which seals and polar bears waddled and which occasional eccentric explorers explored. One by one, these illusions came crashing down as, going there, I discovered the facts behind the popular image.

Erik the Red is Greenland's most celebrated son, though actually a Norwegian. He seems to have been a most enterprising person who not only had a lot to do with the early colonisation of Iceland but, possibly, the discovery of Greenland as well with his arrival there in 982. Yet Greenland had been home for a tough little people long before then. Thousands of years ago Eskimos, pushing in from arctic Canada, inhabited the world's largest island to squeeze from the country and the sea around it the resources necessary for survival in an environment as harsh as any on earth.

Enterprise was not Erik's only idiosyncrasy. He was also trouble-prone. His violent temper brought him a manslaughter charge, necessitating a quick getaway from his native Norway to Iceland, where he settled with his family on the north-western coast. A short while there and he was indiscreet enough to kill again during an argument, an act that resulted in his banishment. This time Erik headed west, reaching the south-westernmost shore of Greenland, where he explored the huge fiords and was greatly impressed by the virtually uninhabited but entirely fruitless land.

His period of exile served, Erik returned to Iceland to mount an expedition with a view to permanent settlement of his new-found territory, which he called 'Greenland', more a public relations ploy than an accurate description. In 985 an expeditionary force of 450 men, women and children set sail in 25 sea-going Viking ships. The voyage was hard; storms and the cold took their toll, and only 14 vessels reached land. But with the survivors were enough domestic animals, tools and provisions to provide the rudiments of a settlement. The European occupation of Greenland had begun.

Proof of Erik the Red's endeavours can be seen to this day; yet even in this age of mass tourism, relatively few visitors look upon them. I am not a polar explorer and did not venture deep into the snow-bound interior on my first visit, but what I found on Greenland's outer perimeter was as fascinating as that of the warmer regions bordering upon the Sahara and the Gobi deserts.

A self-governing possession of the Danish Crown, the country has an area of 840,000 square miles, of which more than 760,000 are ice-covered. Its 50,000 inhabitants live along the coastal strip in the south in some half-dozen townships and lonely hamlets among the myriad fiords. A mainly Eskimo population, their attractive Eskimo characteristics have become diluted by intermarriage with twentieth-century civilisation to produce a not entirely happy result.

This revelation was the one disappointment of my visit. It is a similar story among the native Eskimo/Indian population of northern Canada, where our civilisation has seeped into a lifestyle not geared for it, producing an unpleasant veneer of greed, laziness and selfishness.

My arrival was by way of Narssarssuaq, a one-time American air base. This had a reputation as a somewhat hairy airport at which to land; come in too low and the icebergs catch you; overrun the runway and you smash into a glacier. Three hours by motorboat, dodging icebergs, brought me to Narssaq, the second largest town containing a very beautiful church – though its charm lies entirely in the interior. Within easy reach of both Narssarssuaq and Narssaq is Brattahlid, the name given by Erik the Red to the spot where he and his wife, Thjodhild, settled. Today Brattahlid ('The Steep Slope') has developed into a settlement of several hundred souls, yet the relics of Erik remain much in evidence.

In 1961 a tiny church was discovered holding the unmistakable characteristics of a Viking building. It is, certainly, the oldest church in Greenland, built around the year 1000 by Erik the Red's wife, and skeletons unearthed from the graveyard are thought to include those of Erik, Thjodhild and their son Leif. The site is now marked by a low turf mound and is looked upon as the first Christian church outside Europe.

The iceberg-spawning Qoornuq Glacier can, if the ice permits – and it permitted me – be reached by boat through a maze of ice boulders in sensational hues of blue and green, some as big as cathedrals and sparkling like jewels in the crystal-clear water. Subsequently an all-day walk out of Narssarssuaq over a range of modest-sized mountains brought me to the mighty Kiagtut Sermiat Glacier behind a 'doormat' of colourful spring flowers: an impressive sight. Greenland's capital, Godthaab, standing on a headland encircled by enormous fiords, was equally magnificent.

So if a short summer visitation to Greenland succeeds in removing those pre-conceived notions of the country, a short winter one can but add to the allure of this unbelievable island.

Landing from a spruce little eight-seater Mitsubishi air taxi on the lonely air-strip at Kulusuk on the east coast, I was now some 360 desolate miles north of Narssarssuaq. The journey was to continue by Bell helicopter over virgin white mountains to my destination of Angmagssalik, a winter wonderland perched above the frozen waters of the fiord of the same name. In fact Angmagssalik gives its name to many things: the fiord hardly recognisable as such beneath its snow coating, the small fishing town of 1,000 souls with its vessels locked in ten feet of ice, the island of some 20 miles in diameter which, in winter, is an island no more and, last but not least, the cosy hotel then run by a Kelly Nicolaisen at which I initially based myself.

The reason for making this somewhat protracted journey into the cold was to go dog-sledging, surely one of the more original winter pastimes. Though not a winter sports fanatic – my only skiing experience had been over a couple of seasons in Norway – I felt unable to turn down this invitation so accepted it with slight reservation. But the first day's preliminary sledge-ride over the fiord to the tiny seven-family settlement of Ikateq, whose inhabitants live by seal and polar-bear hunting, put me at ease.

Forget all about the word 'mush' so beloved of fiction writers. No dog I know understands it. The only 'skill' needed for sledge-travel seemed to be the ability to hang on, and this becomes apparent on the downhill slides when the sledge, hauled by between eight and twelve Greenland huskies, swings alarmingly from side to side while taking unseen bumps –

ledges and snow-concealed boulders – at speed. The Eskimo driver, standing at the rear, has a braking technique involving a ground scraper iron, or simply inserts his dog-whip handle between the runners, which to me seemed extremely rudimentary and frequently had no effect whatever. Dogs are invariably hostile to one another so that mass-fights are an all-too-frequent occurrence whether on the move or when stationary, while the effort expended on pulling the loaded sledge results in much doggy breaking of wind, the reek of which wafts back to the riders. And on the steeper downhill sections a speeding sledge is liable to catch up with its fast-running dog-team which results in a chaos of tumbling, yelping, sometimes dragged huskies with a driver frantically attempting to untangle a cat's cradle of dog leads. The driver's orders to his dogs is in a language incomprehensible to you and me and is reinforced by loud cracks of the whip which produces loud yelps, though the whipping process is more crack than sting. At intervals on uphill stretches a rider is invited to alight and help the dogs by pushing the sledge which gives a welcome opportunity to stretch the legs, recirculate a sluggish bloodstream and get warm, since the face, hands, buttocks and feet fast succumb to temperatures many degrees below freezing.

I learnt and experienced all this over a period of several exciting days that took me diagonally across the island to the village of Tinitequilaq by way of the Asingaleq Glacier which offered breathtaking views over the Sermilik Fiord. At Tinitequilaq I was to spend a couple of nights based in a snow-bound wooden cabin equipped with basic amenities that included the wherewithal for simple cooking though the only source of water was that from boiled ice. While here I was sledged across the fiord to watch seal-trapping, an industry upon which the villages hereabouts depend for survival. In my presence two seals were extracted from a series of holes bored in the ice, their meat becoming the main item of my evening meal. I found the meat too rich for my jaded palate –

something akin to blubbery venison – but the cold had given me an appetite that ignored individual fads. The views in the fiord were magnificent; even ensconced in their snow-blankets the icebergs displayed their muted colourings that hinted at a true glory reserved for the spring melt of the snow.

Most of the population of Tinitequilaq were on hand to see me off on the third morning. A coloured ring of haze encircling the sun boded an ominous change in the hitherto fine weather, though on the run homeward no cloud appeared in a blue sky. Only back in Angmagssalik did the blizzard strike, delaying by two days my final departure as if to show me another face of a vast territory as yet untamed my mankind.

ALSO IN THE North Atlantic zone are the Faroe Islands, midway between Scotland and Iceland, though they are hardly in the low temperature range of Greenland and Iceland. In fact they are on the same latitude as Norway.

For millions of years these islands stood alone in the heart of the North Atlantic. The first settlers may have been Irish monks seeking a tranquil refuge possibly in the middle of the seventh century. What is better known, however, is the Norwegian colonisation, beginning about a hundred years later, and developing through the Viking age. Viking settlers established their own parliament with local *Tings* in different parts of the islands with the main *Ting* at Torshavn, the capital, on Tinganes Island. Later, the islands came under the control of the Norwegian kings who, in turn, became subject to the Danish Monarchy, though the Danish monopoly ended in 1856.

Today the islands form a self-governing community under Danish suzerainty though the islanders are far from Danish. For a start they have their own language linked to Icelandic and old Norse, the population of only some 45,000 remaining fiercely independent of any unpopular controls to which they may be subjected from outside.

Rumour and supposition have been unkind to the Faroes. 'There's nothing there but fog, rain, sheep and whale-killing', I'd been told. Sheep there are in plenty. Fog – or at least low cloud – does descend at intervals (it delayed my return flight to Glasgow by a day and a half), and rain is no more prevalent than in northern Scotland. The last activity has earned the Faroes some notorious publicity over the years; when pods of pilot whales are sighted, they are driven close to inshore by a massed array of boats, then slaughtered, bloodily, in the shallows. In one restaurant I asked for whale-meat having developed a taste for it early in the Second World War when it was a staple meat diet. The waiter looked hard at me and declined to adhere to my request thinking, no doubt, that I was being sarcastic – which indicated to me that the islanders themselves are touchy about the subject.

I covered the series of islands by bus, hire car and inter-island ferries. The roads are excellent and furnished with miles-long tunnels expensively drilled through obstructing mountains.

The chief town is Torshavn, dubbed the world's smallest capital. It is hardly a ball of fire but very pleasant nevertheless with a picturesque old quarter – Tinganes – where the town was born more than a thousand years ago. Here red-walled, turf-roofed houses glow in the sunshine while the comings and goings of the multitude of ferries in the sizeable harbour ensure there's always something going on.

Directly from Torshavn is the ferry link serving Nolsoy Island in sight across the harbour. An ill-defined path on the steep flank led me up 371-metre Mount Eggjarklettur in a wind that made the walk a hazardous procedure. From the summit, range after range of Faroese mountains offered a superb spectacle.

On completion of my descent I met a farmer whose land I had crossed. He exhibited a desire to chat that gave me the chance to bring up the unpopular subject of whale-slaughter. He was not the least put out by my directness. 'It used to be a shocking business,' he admitted, 'but nowadays we have strict humanitarian regulations with spears and harpoons outlawed.'

'Well, how *do* you kill them?' I asked.

The man looked a shade uneasy but nevertheless launched into explanations. 'The whales are beached and killed as quickly and painlessly as possible – with clubs,' he added, as if anticipating my next question. And it has to be said that the meat and blubber was once vital to a diet made extremely limited by the inhospitable terrain, though today the reasoning seems a mite superfluous. Little strips of salted blubber eaten with the fingers and accompanied by small scraps of dried fish have become a delicacy much prized by the islanders. If there is another excuse I never learnt what it was.

But assuredly the climax of my visit was the boat trip from Vestmanna on Streymoy Island to the towering bird-cliffs and sea stacks and through gigantic sea caves which put me in mind of those on Bressay Island in Shetland. Here, black cliffs of basalt loom over a blacker heaving ocean; the sea is invariably rough and I have to admit to being not only on the verge of losing my breakfast en route but extremely uneasy as mountainous waves rose up before and behind the boat. However, I was calmed in the knowledge that, in the capable hands of Palli Lamhauge – 'old man of the sea' as he was known, with over 30 years of experience of the dangerous currents and counter-flows of these turbulent waters – I was quite safe.

A visit to these lovely, remote and crime-free islands where the air is pure champagne, its people English-speaking and welcoming, should be at least a once-in-a-lifetime attainment.

YOU DON'T HAVE to be a masochist to go trekking in Spitsbergen, but it helps. When I announced to no one in particular that I was going for a walk in this archipelago on the rim of the world I was pronounced barmy. This in itself was interesting since it told me that people at least had some idea where it was. Actually Spitsbergen is but one – albeit the largest – island of an Arctic archipelago known to the Norwegians as Svalbard, 'Land with Frozen Shores', possibly in an effort – highly successful – to deflect the Costa Brava beach hordes.

In August 1991 I flew into Longyearbyen from Tromso on the Norwegian mainland. I found the airport to be a remarkably elegant establishment and one out of tune with the capital it serves. The desolate urban centre three miles away was haunted by the ghosts of a dying coal industry that could still raise enough life to cover everything in a sheen of coal dust. The double-walled, treble-glazed houses were threaded by a skein of heating pipes and dotted with derelict conveyor pylons. Most of the remaining miners, I was told, were on holiday when I arrived – probably on some warm Mediterranean shore to whence I evinced a momentary urge to join them. But around the township soared the snow-streaked mountains and a promise of the Spitsbergen experience I had come to sample.

William Barents, the Dutch explorer, put these arctic islands on the map in 1596 naming them Spitsbergen, the 'Land of Pointed Mountains', though the Norwegian sobriquet fits better. Stretching to not far in excess of 500 miles of the North Pole, it is, to say the least, a chilly spot. For decades the archipelago remained unclaimed since it had little to offer the world. However, in 1925 it was allocated to Norway by international treaty with the proviso that other nations were entitled to exploit the island's sparse resources. Only coal-deficient Norway and, later, the then Soviet Union did so, and today these are the sole two countries operating mines there.

The Isfiord runs deep into the centre of the main island. Along its shores are situated the two Russian mining camps of Barentsburg and Pyramiden. Between them, up an inlet called Adventfiord, sits Longyearbyren. From there a visitor can sample the 'Spitsbergen Experience' in two ways: in a strictly utilitarian boat amongst the fiords or, within a group, on his or her own feet in the permafrosted interior. Germans form the main contingent of trekkers but, this notwithstanding, I chose the latter method. And I was relieved to behold that my small group was graced with the presence of two compatriots even if one had fallen asleep at Tromso Airport and missed the connecting flight to the island – but we can't all be as efficient as the Germans.

Our base accommodation was a tent pitched close to the airport runway. This was titled 'Camp No. 1' and comprised, in addition to the tents, a wooden building that formed a dining room/kitchen, hot-water ablutions and flushing WCs. I was advised to make the most of them for they would be the last amenities I'd see for the next 12 days.

We left, with a German guide, under sunshine and an icy breeze unbroken by any tree or vegetation, the breeze blowing straight off the glaciers. I was surprised that diminutive flowers, deep and bright in colour, could look so radiant in such conditions even where the snow had disappeared on the low-lying coastal strip of land over which we initially passed. Patches of scurvy-grass and a plant brandishing a white flower we were told could be used, dried or boiled, as a protection against arctic diseases provided further distraction for the botanists amongst us.

They called the first day's trek to 'Camp No. 2' a 'warm-up' and it certainly was that. I was soon sweating like a pig, having donned every item of clothing on the assumption that (a) I'd be cold – and it was when standing about, and (b) to make my rucksack lighter, for, even without tentage and only a minimum of provisions, it was heavy enough. Actually the distance to the camp was little more than 16 miles along the relatively flat Advent Valley, though the walking was punctuated by river crossings and muddy morasses reoccurring at frequent intervals.

'Camp No. 2' had been placed upon an ice plateau, or *pingo*, and was no more than a trio of already-erected tents, one of them containing pre-stored food safely packed in bear-proof containers. Though we held emergency rations in our packs, as well as pocketfuls of chocolate and raisins which were deemed adequate for our midday 'lunch', we had ravenous appetites upon arrival.

The camp overlooked a substantial river which, of course, had to be crossed the cold wet way. For this we were thoughtfully provided with fisherman's waders, but the comparatively shallow channel running through deep water was known only to our guide, which made for something of an alarming undertaking as we were led across one by one, the current pulling at us unmercifully. One false step into deep water and the weight on our shoulders could prove fatal.

Though the evening meal consisted chiefly of powdered soup, instant rice and potato mash it went down a treat. Sleep was, for me, spasmodic since the ground was hard, bumpy and cold.

My least favourite breakfast cereal is muesli and it was to become a staple diet for twelve consecutive breakfasts as well as lunch. But it was that or nothing so, whenever possible, I mixed it with instant milk, water, tea, coffee, cocoa, or dry on its own to acquire variety. In such circumstances a novelty of taste is infinitely desirable.

A day based at the camp was enlivened by a ten mile rucksackless walk to observe strange rock formations forged by ice over the aeons. Reindeer were said to be particularly attracted to this area by a comparative abundance of low-growing vegetation comprising a rare arctic birch, arctic willow and a strange Bonsai-like shrub. An animal we disturbed was thought to be an arctic fox; it certainly wasn't a reindeer.

The third day's trek was considerably longer than the first, taking us out of the Advent Valley into another that eventually led to the coast of the Isfiord, Spitsbergen's largest fiord. 'Camp No. 3' was in view down the bottom of the valley long before we got there. We could see it from atop the new valley and it became a mirage that refused to draw nearer as we stumbled through drifts of treacherous snow towards it.

Attempting a short cut on my own across what I thought to be frozen snow I was abruptly enveloped in a white straightjacket as my feet broke through the crust. Encumbered by my rucksack I found it a devil of a job to extract myself from the icy embrace and for a few unpleasant minutes I envisaged the thought that this would be my grave. Having earned myself a fright and a good soaking I thereafter steered clear of drifts.

With the new camp closer at last, a sizeable hill had to be negotiated before attaining it, which at least warmed up my semi-frozen body. And upon finally reaching the small cluster of tents we were rewarded with an astonishing view out across the Isfiord to a jumble of glaciers the other side.

The site was situated on a stony and lumber-strewn beach. The lumber was by courtesy of Russia, it having been washed ashore from Siberian lumber camps and timber-carrying shipping. It was to become a most useful commodity as fuel for any camp fires that the wind or/and rain permitted or for constructing tasteful items of furniture. Since 12 days is a longish time in such an environment as this any gratis additions to general comfort was not to be despised.

Unencumbered by heavy baggage we explored the region. And what a region it is. Across the wide fiord lay the enormous panorama of smaller fiords buttressed by the savagery of glaciers and sharp mountain peaks, their ethereal quality reflected in a myriad shades of colour in the clear water, each sudden change of weather pattern offering a new perspective. Close to the camp a muddy torrent burbled by, spanned by a lumber-constructed bridge that, incongruously, served also as a treble-seated toilet, which we christened the Bridge of Thighs. Excellently drained, it was, nevertheless, a mite draughty. Across it to the north, south and west lay idyllic trekking country bordered on one side by high perpendicular cliffs raucous with roosting guillemots and puffins, and on the other by a range of assorted mountains inhabited by inquisitive reindeer. In between lay a green, marshy plateau sprinkled with clumps of wild flowers ranging from white dandelions to a tiny blue bloom with leaves that tasted of oyster. It was, in fact, a land of sheer – if chilly – magic.

We saw no polar bears on our explorations; mostly they come south from the colder north of the island during the long night of winter. But we took precautions; the camp was encircled by a trip-wire device that could detonate a small explosive charge to deflect unwelcome visitors. We also possessed a rifle.

With several days based at the camp we had time to spare in which to construct rough bed frames out of the heaven-sent lumber; anything to keep the cold ground at bay. I still found the 24-hour daylight a handicap to sleep and a silly couplet by Lewis Carroll kept running through my head:

'The sun was shining on the sea,
Shining with all its might
[...]
And this was odd, because it was
The middle of the night.'

The three-day homeward slog back to Longyearbyen could have been a repeat of the outward journey but was enlivened by two events. A detour to the Jansson Valley, more gorge than valley, to see more strange rock designs as well as the only *scented* flowers on Spitsbergen. And the consequences of an abrupt ending to the Svalbard summer which had, in the meantime, transformed the normally fairly dry Advent Valley into a skein of fast-flowing streams and rivers of sullen brown waters to make considerably wetter walking and wading than had been the case before.

But we had become, as I found in Iceland, a fitter, more experienced bunch of trekkers as a result of our brief sortie into outback Spitsbergen. And a retracing of a route is hardly a bore in a land where colour and circumstances change hourly offering more to see and experience however many times such a route is covered. In exchange for the odd bootful of water, a muddy dive or two face-down in a bog and an over-endowment of muesli, we had sampled the excitement and charisma of traversing territory north of nearly everywhere else on earth.

Across the ocean to the South Atlantic. Though 8,000 miles away
there is a lot of Britain in the Falkland Islands: Dartmoor, Exmoor,
Orkney, Shetland, the Sussex Downs and Northumbria can be
found within their 4,600 square miles.

Arrival at Mount Pleasant Airport, the RAF base, after a 19-hour flight felt almost like coming home with people and weather to match. It was November 1989 and the icy chill of winter was in the air, though these islands are, again, hardly on a par temperature-wise with such as Greenland, Iceland and Spitsbergen so perhaps don't really qualify to be included in this chapter – but let's give them the benefit of the doubt. In fact the climate, the rigours of which tend to be exaggerated, is not unlike that of, say, the Outer Hebrides – though somewhat colder, mainly on account of a persistent wind that blows throughout the year.

The one-hour drive to Port Stanley, the Falklands' diminutive but now historical capital, offers views of Bluff Cove and the hill called Tumbledown, household names since The Conflict, as the short, sharp war between Britain and Argentina, just seven years earlier, is known to the Falklanders. Patchworks of dramatically marked minefields added to the aura of the journey.

Over the years since their discovery by one John Davis of
Britain in 1582, the Falkland Islands have undergone a
series of occupations. Recorded history begins with the
establishment of a party of French settlers on East Falkland
in 1764 though the following year a Captain John Byron,
who had been sent out on a survey expedition, claimed
the islands for Britain and left a small party on Saunders
Island. Two years later the French settlement was
withdrawn under pressure from Spain which later – in
1770 – ejected the British party. Port Egmont was restored
to Britain in 1771 but voluntarily abandoned three years
later. In 1820 the Republic of Buenos Aires, which claimed
to have inherited the rights of Spain, developed a colony

in its name. This lasted until 1831 when it was rash enough to seize three American seagoing vessels which promptly brought a US corvette, the *Lexington*, which, after 'laying waste' the settlement, proclaimed the islands free of all outside occupation. In 1833 Great Britain, which had never renounced its claims to sovereignty, resumed official occupation. The colony lay under the charge of successive naval officers engaged on hydrographic work until 1843 when a civil administration was set up at Port Louis and continued from that time. In 1914 the adjacent waters were the scene of the World War One Battle of the Falkland Islands while, during that war, Stanley became an important naval base and radiotelegraph station.

The town reminded me of Nome, in Alaska, for although there is no permafrost, the multi-coloured roofs of corrugated iron, oft-drunken fences and small garden plots full of hoarded junk awaiting possible future use reflected, to me, a gold-rush township; a sort of South Atlantic Klondike. Standing cheek-by-jowl with the attractive clapboard houses was a throng of Portakabins. When I was there a chronic housing shortage made a strong deterrent to would-be immigrants, so these ubiquitous descendants of World War Two prefabs met a vital need.

One such temporary/permanent home was number 17 Fitzroy Road, occupied by Chris Bundes and his wife. Their original home and farmholding lay within an unswept minefield which, understandably, gave them strong views on Argentinians, who they blamed for the loss of their farm. At 350 miles, Argentina is the nearest mainland to the Falklands, but Chris made plain that he would never consider going there even for a brief visit. Considerable bitterness was still harboured by these sturdy people, or at least this was the case in 1989, though the hatred has no doubt mellowed since.

He was able largely to carry on with his farm duties elsewhere during the latest short-lived non-British occupation, and met with little unpleasantness from the Argentinians.

'Had there been compensation? A pension?' I asked.

'We get a pension, in the same way as you do in the UK, and there are certain old-age benefits. I also get some help with this small house,' he told me. 'It was given me in lieu of the house that my wife and I can no longer live in.'

After The Conflict, people poured into the Falklands: servicemen, contractors, merchants and tourists. The influx triggered an astonishing transformation in the islanders' fortunes.

But though the Falklands were now on the map of the world, not everyone was happy about it. 'We are a small, tight community,' explained Chris, 'somewhat parochial and small-minded. Some of us resented this intrusion of outsiders with their cut-throat commercialism and the threat of some of the cancers of society like drugs and crime. But you can't stop progress – if that's what it's called.' He gave a bitter laugh, adding, as an afterthought, 'Of course we wanted the servicemen for obvious reasons.'

Mount Pleasant base, the keep of Fortress Falklands, was then a larger community than Port Stanley. Few servicemen stationed there bothered to explore the land of their posting during their four-month tours of duty, though an exception was my son, Paul, who, with my old regiment, was stationed there but left just before I arrived. He too has the urge to explore the world. Except for him, therefore, during my nine-day sojourn, I probably saw more of the hinterland than servicemen do in a third of the year.

Pebble Island for instance. I flew there sitting beside the pilot, Andy Allsop, in his little red BN2B Norman Islander aircraft. We conversed on the intercom and he told me that, for the time being, he was the only pilot for the four aircraft available to FIGAS – Falkland Islands Government Air Service

– although reinforcements were expected shortly for this inter-island lifeline. Thus his services were much in demand. A 40-minute flight and we landed on the beach of Pebble Island, a manoeuvre possible only at low tide.

An awareness of the islands' virtual absence of roads, apart from the one that ran between Mount Pleasant and Port Stanley, was brought painfully home to me as I was driven lurchingly between the landing beach and Pebble Island's only hotel, across open country liberally endowed with bumps, tussock grass and bogs.

John Reid, hotel owner and wildlife expert, brought the whole community of – I think – 13 into the front room to meet me. Among them was Cynthia Betts, an alert 90 year old, who had lived on the island all her life. Hale and hearty, she smoked like a chimney. I asked her how she had fared under the Argentine occupation and was told, with a throaty chuckle, that for much of the time she and her family were locked up in the farm manager's cottage with an armed guard on the door. 'They didn't trust us – and with good reason,' she said. Trust, apparently, decreased still further following the SAS raid on the island which resulted in the destruction of 11 Argentine aircraft on the ground. The greatest moment of her life, she added, was watching the liberation aircraft arrive to accept the surrender of the Argentine garrison.

From Pebble Island it was but a short hop, with Andy and his flying bus, to Port Howard on West Falkland. About half the population of the Falklands is spread throughout the sheep-farming settlements in the two main islands and small communities are scattered far and wide among them. Port Howard is relatively large, containing, then, just 13 houses for the 30 people who are heavily outnumbered by the island's 42,000 sheep.

A pilgrimage to the hill called Tumbledown where the celebrated battle between the two opposing forces resulted in the Argentine surrender was, of course, on my agenda, and I duly walked up to its summit still littered with discarded

Argentine military equipment. A fine view over Port Stanley was some small compensation.

A final Falklands port of call was distant Sealion Island for the intoxicating spectacle of a myriad penguins, giant petrels, king cormorants sitting on their eggs and enormous elephant seals grunting and belching, in an environment where neither bird nor beast had reason to fear Man. Wandering along the beach I was literally rubbing shoulders with orange-beaked gentoo penguins as they waddled to and fro in their black-and-white business outfits like lunch-time shoppers on Oxford Street, bumping into each other and moving on without apologies while disdainfully ignoring my presence. But their smell was overpowering.

The wildlife and unspoilt landscape – the legacies of The Conflict apart – are what is special about the Falkland Islands, to which the friendliness of the human inhabitants have contributed. The result is a way of life which is as British as our own islands, yet, in spite of Chris Bundes' forebodings, still largely aloof from the blemishes that now afflict our own society. Long may it last.

FINALLY TO ANOTHER ocean, the cold Bering Sea and northern Alaska.

There is much of the frontier about the far north of North America and this includes Canada's Yukon and Northwest Territories. Here is a land of airstrips, of cold lakes bordered by seaplanes and flat vistas merging into the mists. It is also a land of startling beauty. Alaska throws up unique obstacles to Man, and he in turn invariably finds novel ways of surmounting them. Farmers and builders must compress their year's work into the brief summers; nearly all provisions must be shipped in from the lower United States and Alaskans live with the threat of earthquakes such as the one that struck on Good Friday 1964. They also fly over roadless terrain; take to their boats despite bone-chilling water and rugged coastlines and exist in temperatures that we in lukewarm Britain can barely imagine. It is, above all, another land of challenge holding beneath the surface of its permafrost the vast wealth which first attracted the scruffy hot-eyed miners in 1896.

Alaska's northernmost town is Nome on the west coast facing the Bering Sea, not many miles from the Arctic Circle. I flew there in a Boeing 707 of Wien Alaska Airways in 1979, for there are no alternative ways of reaching it. Spawned by the discovery of gold on the beaches it boomed into a gold-rush camp of tents and frame buildings. Once the community numbered 40,000. When I was there it was about 4,000. The gold rush has passed and mining was on the decline but an aura of those glamorous days lingered on. Touring the ramshackle town was like sight-seeing in a junkyard with most of the tottering houses surrounded by a collection of pipes, boilers, tin cans, old cars and discarded ice-boxes which, as in Port Stanley, form a treasure chest of valuable spares. Telegraph poles and television aerials leant at drunken angles, for nothing holds up for long on the shifting permafrost.

Based in the town I visited the outback of arctic Alaska in a series of flights in a gritty little British-made Norman Britton Islander aircraft – similar to the one that carried me to outlying islands in the Falklands – of Munz Northern Airlines, for, again, the local roads led nowhere. My 'bush pilots' were Eskimos, and for a week I flew in the co-pilot's seat sampling the daily flights to and from a number of tiny communities amidst an awe-inspiring desolation. For this venture I had been invited by the airline's boss who allowed me to accompany his pilots on their passenger and grocery carrying runs between these remote communities.

Our destinations included Little Diomede Island, just 22 miles from Siberia and in sight of its equally desolate landscape where, across the International Date Line, today is tomorrow. Though, at that time, Siberia formed part of the Soviet Union my pilot, just for the hell of it, took me on a zigzag course along the line passing, on each leg, from Monday to Tuesday. I glanced around, periodically, to see whether or not we were being chased by a missile since the practice of entering Soviet airspace was strictly forbidden and, presumably, highly risky.

Another flight was to Shismaref where I watched the local ladies making the mukluks and parkas which are de rigueur wear in such climes. I also visited Wales, this one the westernmost point on the North American continent, where we flew low over the vast jig-saw puzzle of fractured ice-flows covering the ocean. At each location I would help load and unload the aeroplane of supplies, of which Coca-Cola seemed to form a disproportionate part. And, with the pilot, scrape ice off the aircraft's wings so that the inevitable build-up did not endanger flight. Whenever I saw something of interest on the ground we would go into a steep dive for a closer look which did not suit my stomach at all. And landing on airstrips that looked no larger than pocket handkerchiefs had my feet stamping hard on non-existent brakes.

The arctic winter scenery here must be one of the unsung wonders of the world, as it is not just in shades of blue and white, as one might expect, but in glorious hues of red, orange and subtle pink. The wildlife too is spectacular. Witness the overwhelming impact of thousands of majestic snow geese sweeping across the horizon and you will appreciate the magnitude of God. Alaska is a refuge for many endangered species, such as the trumpeter swan and the bald eagle. One million caribou range over Alaska and Canada and I was delighted to observe some of them for myself.

Chapter Three

TRAVELS IN THE MOUNTAINS

In which the author journeys to the Atlas Mountains of Morocco in a clapped-out Bedford lorry, digs for gold before dawn in Peru, shares sleeping space with a litter of pigs, some hens and a dog, and is marched to police headquarters in San Luis by a gun-toting patrolman.

In my time I have had the pleasure – and sometimes displeasure – of trekking in the Himalayas, the Karakorams, the Alps, the Andes, the Atlas, the Drakensbergs, the Pindus and more. I am no climber but have – occasionally through mistaken ardour – reached summits such as 17,000-foot Mount Kenya, 10,000-foot Cathedral Peak in the South African Drakensbergs, and highest of all, the near-22,000-foot Chimborazo in Ecuador.

I have a special affinity with the Atlas Mountains of Morocco. Or that's what I like to think anyway. I have passed through them, round them, over them and along them. I have climbed near-14,000-foot Mount Toubkal – no great feat since it is no more than a multi-hour slog up its northern flank – to stand shivering with cold at the summit on snow that one imagines has no right to fall in Africa.

Actually the Atlas are not just Moroccan. They extend across both Algeria and Tunisia too for a distance of 1,500 miles running more or less parallel to the coast of north-west Africa, bounded on the north by the Mediterranean and in the south by the Sahara. But my travels among them mostly took place in Morocco where they are known by Moroccans as *Idraren Draren* or 'Mountains of Mountains'.

My *original* Atlas journey was made during the summer of 1974 in a clapped-out three-ton Bedford lorry of World War Two vintage along ledges and tracks where no wheeled vehicle had been before. There were, if I remember rightly, nine of us on board. I'm not technically-minded enough to say what model the lorry was but I know it was a wartime baby because it still carried some Eighth Army yellow paint and had a hole in the cab roof through which could be poked a Bren gun.

I was something of a wartime baby myself, being nearly 20 when my first German took a pot-shot at me (and missed). Bedford three-tonners were part of the scenery in those days; I've ridden in them, slept under them and cursed them like everyone else did. So to be joy-riding around Morocco and the Atlas in one stirred a few memories.

We were making our way to Ouarzazate along the main road from Marrakech. Behind us was the Tiz-n-Tichka Pass through which the road had coiled. At the village of Agouim our driver, Rene, said 'I wonder if it would be possible to reach Toubkal from here?' By road it would have been no problem, but Rene wasn't thinking of roads.

At the junction at Agouim a signpost indicated a place called Sour to be 26 kilometres distant; the map assured us that a road of sorts led to it. Thereafter it appeared to expire and even the enlarged inset became vague when it came to positioning the various tracks that led hopefully in the direction of Toubkal.

'Perhaps we would learn something at Sour,' I observed doubtfully. 'We can always turn back.' As I said it I knew we were in for a rough ride. As if Rene would ever *turn back*. Ex-overland driver, soldier, traveller and budding explorer, defeat was a word foreign to his vocabulary.

The road to Sour wasn't exactly the M1. Clouds of dust billowed up behind, caught up and enveloped us all in a grey film. The canvas sides of the truck were furled to allow for extra ventilation under the hot sun and, because of the reduced speed, the exhaust fumes seeped into the buck instead of dissipating at the rear.

We never actually discovered Sour. Two baked-mud dwellings marked a junction of the dust road and a local bright boy sent us rattling along the left fork towards a further couple of dwellings on the skyline. Halfway there a passer-by confirmed our suspicions that we were on the road to Ait-Kalla and that we had passed Sour. So we returned to the junction and took the other fork, which is how we came, eventually, to Tiourar. And we *knew* this was Tiourar because all nine inhabitants were bunched together with nothing to do except enthusiastically affirm to bewildered travellers that this was indeed Tiourar.

The condition of the track had deteriorated further since the Sour junction. Veins of rock stood out on its surface and deep crevices lay in wait for a moment of careless driving. Corners never planned with three-ton trucks in mind had brought our speed down to a crawl. 'Can we get through to Azrou?' Rene enquired of the nine wise men. Solemnly they gazed at our vehicle, went into a huddle and emerged with their findings. 'No,' said four of them. 'Yes,' said five. Encouraged by a majority of one on the side of what we would do anyway, we continued.

Or at least we continued to the river. Small stream if you like but it ran deep in a fissure and required a bridging party to effect its negotiation. Twice the wheels got stuck and had to be dug out; the third time we took it at a running jump, since on our side was a downhill gradient. A small voice asked how we were going to get back over it but was ignored.

The cold of early evening forced the battening down of hatches. Diesel fumes swirled in the buck. Sweat and dust-stained handkerchiefs became plugs for foul-tasting mouths. Smarting eyes cascaded crocodile tears. Choosing to freeze rather than asphyxiate, I balanced myself precariously on the rear of the chassis with warnings against doing just that of wartime years ringing loud and clear in my mind. Standing on the tailboard breathing God's fresh air, I rode out most of the frightful lurches. Then we plunged into a hole and everyone was on top of one another. I suppose I was lucky to escape with a badly scraped thumb and a bruised rib. Thereafter, bleeding profusely, I chose asphyxiation as the old Bedford ploughed on with dusk adding a new hazard.

Each hairpin bend now required three and even four shunting movements to negotiate. Too far to the right and you scraped the rocky walls; too far to the left and your wheels were in thin air over a 40-foot drop. Only one headlamp worked, the other having been extinguished by a well-aimed stone from a small boy in Agouim.

Somewhat the worse for wear we arrived at what purported to be Azrou and bargained for the hire of a room with rudimentary toilet facilities in a stone and mud building. The arrival of a truck-load of visitors from another planet could not have drawn larger crowds and, under their intense scrutiny, we cooked our stew and prepared for bed. With no water available and it being too cold to undress, such preparations were minimal, but certain calls of nature had to be answered.

'Mind the dogs,' warned the villagers and we found out what they meant when two members of the party, ashen-faced and clutching various items of apparel, threw themselves into the room ahead – but only just – of half a dozen snarling, snapping young tigers. During daytime, stupefied by the heat, Atlas dogs are subdued, cringing creatures, but at night more ferocious instincts return. In a state of siege – two of us in the truck acting as guardians – we spent an uneasy, freezing night.

Early next morning we continued to what we termed the Imlil junction. The track narrowed to little more than the width of the Bedford, which was satisfactory on the straight, the complications only arising at the bends. Most of the time I was – thankfully – out of the truck watching the inches between offside wheels and the precipitous edge – and oblivion – of the track and judging whether or not the edge would hold. One of the signs arranged between Rene and I consisted of quick flip of the fingers which meant 'accelerate like hell' because the edge of the track was giving way. Fortunately the innocents in the buck remained ignorant of the reason for the many violent spurts of speed!

The village of Imlil, lying inert just up the road at the foot of Mount Toubkal, had become our destination. Thus our mission was virtually accomplished; Rene had found the answer to his own question. 'We could go back,' he pondered gently, 'or we *could* carry on and try to link up with the main Ouarzazate–Agadir road. It's about the same distance.' Actually it was a damn sight further but nobody was enthusiastic about returning. At least the horrors ahead would be novel.

All around, the great bulk of the mountains loomed threatening and seemingly indignant that a motor vehicle had the nerve to invade their wild domain. Little boys emerged from mud dwellings to stand amazed, then either ran home to mother or excitedly draped themselves along the truck's sides depending upon their degree of boldness. The village elders were coerced into admitting that it might be possible to get to Aoulouz on the Agadir road. On a mule at any rate. It was enough for Rene.

With Toubkal on our doorstep at least we knew roughly where we were. The map showed Aoulouz to be some 50 kilometres distant. As the crow flies. A dotted line linked a number of village names and grew thicker some ten miles before Aoulouz. The carrot before the donkey. In the usual bottom gear we ground out of Imlil and took the left fork. Ten minutes later we came to the trees.

The first – a fine walnut – flung a heavy bough across our path. There was no getting by and no detour. Or so we were gleefully informed by our retinue of young Berbers. We tried swinging round it by going to the very edge of the track but the verge began to sink and we were lucky to escape toppling over. A child emissary was sent back to Imlil and a delegation arrived to ponder our fate – and to bargain the price of tree surgery. Five pounds it cost us and two hours of time before the offending limb was axed to the ground.

Thereafter we were held up by a succession of very large overhanging branches of further trees, these necessitating the three males of the group to lie athwart the canvas roof and bodily lift each branch away from the framework as the vehicle inched forward beneath. Twice we were swept painfully back across the sagging canvas through a breakdown of communication between roof party and driver. But perseverance won.

A river successfully forded, the villages of Assarad and Tanmitert negotiated, despite the mud walls of their houses causing the road to narrow to within inches of the width of the truck. More trees, and then we hit the rock.

To cross a damp patch of sand we had accelerated, got stuck and reversed straight on to a huge partly-submerged boulder. It promptly showed its wrath at being disturbed by up-ending and jamming itself into the rear axle and other vulnerable mechanisms in the belly of the vehicle. Again checkmate. Everyone disembarked, lay flat beneath the Bedford and pushed at the offending obstacle. Nothing happened. Reinforcements arrived from nowhere. Even in the remotest districts of the world there are always people, little people, who emerge from heaven knows where. One, fortuitously, happened to have an entrenching tool with him and soon, like ants in the dust, we scraped a hole into which the boulder could be laid to rest. An issue of cigarettes went round to our Berber working party and we were again on our merry way.

Beyond Tizourine the excruciating track could be seen wandering down the side of the right-hand shoulder of the valley to disappear round a distant spur of the hillside. The scenery was magnificent, the valley green with cultivation –

though it had a startling habit of appearing 100 feet sheer below the verge and but four inches from the offside wheels. Like the man who once held a red flag in front of a Victorian train, I walked backwards ahead of the truck, again guiding its wheels away from the nightmare edge. Ahead, the track wound remorselessly on and, as each rock spur was attained, another lay in wait.

The Bedford was taking ferocious punishment and it seemed to us that something surely must give. Lurching, bumping, skidding, its engine sometimes screaming with pain as we took an incline that would have daunted a tank, the plucky vehicle ploughed on. Surely, if nothing else, we would run out of diesel fuel, a prospect that frightened the life out of us. It was not one that had escaped Rene either but he forbade to take a dipstick reading. Sometimes ignorance *is* bliss.

And so we came to the township of Aguerd n'Ougadir. I say 'township' because it boasted a mosque and a couple of white-washed buildings of officious dignity. More significant, there was a *car* standing in the main square. And indeed the road out of Aguerd n'Ougadir *was* an improvement for a mile or two though it deteriorated again at Tamaout.

Darkness finally defeated us; not any malfunction on the part of the courageous old Bedford. We spent another uncomfortable night, this time on the stony bed of a dried-up river, hoping it wouldn't rain.

In the morning we gained Tasdremt but the thicker line on the map was a fallacy dreamed up by an optimistic cartographer. 'Aoulouz four kilometres down the road,' affirmed a squatting Tasdremtian, and ten kilometres later we reached it.

The hard tarmac that swished beneath the tyres was music in our ears. 'Now we know the odds what about going back the way we came?' announced the indefatigable Rene, but we pretended not to hear.

A more appropriate form of vehicle for alpine travel is the humble mule.

Have you ever contemplated what it must feel like to be a fly walking up a wall? Probably not but the thought arose to me as my beast traversed a route that crawled across an almost vertical face of a mountain. On foot it would be exciting enough but perched atop a mule brought a new dimension in travel experience. And a mule train winding its way through defile and pass has something timeless about it; only the plodding camel trains of the desert can offer the same awareness of one's surroundings to give an insight into a life where speed is an unknown word.

I was with a small group of fellow muleteers – I think that's the word – traversing the all too vertical terrain in the Middle Atlas. Our nights were spent on the floor of the huts of Berber villages or simply under the glorious panoply of a myriad stars. The nights were decidedly cool, the days hot and all the time my accompanying Berbers – who became my friends – infiltrated me into their unsophisticated world. At the end of a long day one of them would jump up behind me to ride the last mile to his home village chanting lustily.

A mule is not a difficult animal to ride, nor is its back so far from the ground as that of a camel's hump. But there are surprises. There is no saddle in the accepted sense but a hard, pack-like device made for the attachment of pannier bags or baskets and any cargo you care to name. It is the cargo that counts and if this is – and it is – an impediment to comfort, then it's just too bad. A mule, as we all know, is a stubborn animal; some more stubborn than others. To compensate for this the muleteer's bark of command (more effective than one's own), together with his stick or boot, produces spurts of acceleration, usually at hairy, precipitous spots that are the last places on earth you desire it.

Our route wound through and around great massifs, alongside raging torrents and bone-dry *wadis,* through stunted undergrowth alive with the chirp of crickets, by mud-brick and wattle villages with each house supporting another in the manner of a child's pyramid of toy bricks. And, everywhere, those chasms and precipices around the next corner.

Meals, as was to be expected, were of the simplest, consisting mainly of *couscous* attained from the villagers, payment being sometimes by barter. Cooking was a communal affair; we all ate together in one great happy family – as indeed it should be, since involvement is the very essence of such a journey.

ANOTHER HIGHLIGHT OF my mountain journeyings took place in the Himalayas of Nepal.

There I participated in a 20-day trek that circumnavigated the Annapurna massif on an ancient trade route that led me by way of the Marsyangdi Valley, Manang, the 17,200-foot Thorong-La Pass, Muktinath, Jomsom, the upper valley of the Kali Gandaki and the Ghorapani Pass.

This I undertook the end of 1979 when the route was little trodden by trekkers. Today, of course, it is all too well-walked.

THE CLIMAX OF my mountain travels, however, occurred in the Andes of South America in 1977 and a portion of these I will relate in some detail. But first it might be of interest to readers if I explain how my acquaintanceship with these mountains came about.

Ever since my turbulent school-days the subject of the Inca roads and the Incas themselves had intrigued me, so, in my more mature years, it was an obvious destination towards which to set my ageing mind and feet should an opportunity arise. Yet the eventual accomplishment of this venture was to come about almost by accident.

Twice, in quick succession during the mid-70s, I became involved in the arranging and planning of someone else's equinine journeyings; first that of a circuit of the globe by an over-optimistic Berkshire horseman and then that of a hefty slice of it by a West Sussex ditto. The first petered out after several months of preparation which included an exchange of correspondence with HRH The Duke of Edinburgh and the then Soviet ambassador in London.

The second came about when the subsequent horseman with vast hacking distances in mind requested my assistance and participation for part of a journey he was planning. This was from the very bottom of the South American continent to Washington DC on the east coast of the United States. The intrepid rider in this case was one Gordon Roddick, an unlikely resident of staid Littlehampton, and, with my financial and practical assistance, this project did actually get off the ground. Prior to joining him in Peru I acted as a sort of base camp, receiving regular reports of his progress through his wife, Anita, who, bored with being alone, had opened a small shop in my hometown of Brighton which she called the Body Shop. Alas, after two months of hacking across Argentina and Bolivia Gordon's two horses bolted one night and ended up very dead at the bottom of a canyon. This abruptly terminated this second enterprise – though, for Anita and Gordon, it brought about a much more commercially remunerative one!

But one can't just stand by and let a venture like that fade away, so into the vacuum came the notion of continuing northward myself from where Gordon had come to grief but, in my case, tracing the historic route of the most famous of Inca highways, the royal road. And this time no temperamental horse need be involved; instead I would utilise my own legs. It was an opportunity that, assuredly, would never come my way again and fate was handing it to me on a plate. Additionally, the then British Caledonian Airways had granted me a gratis flight ticket to Lima, Peru, where I had planned to join Gordon, and I could hardly let *that* go to waste. Straightway I launched into a fever of preparations with the aim of replacing the old journey with the new.

I also had to find a new travelling companion since Gordon had returned home, somewhat disillusioned. My search for a colleague produced David Taylor, of Bletchley, who not only spoke Spanish but had travelled in the Andean countries so could be of inestimable help as a counter to my own ignorance. A dark-haired, slight youth in his early twenties, David was as plainly ambitious as he was enthusiastic. I was a little concerned about the difference in our ages but this seemed a small price for a companion well versed in Inca lore.

To carry out this trek I had little more than three months at my disposal while David had all the time needed since he was currently unemployed. The distance we proposed to cover was well in excess of 3,000 miles, much of it – particularly the 1,400-odd miles between Cuzco and Quito – on foot. Furthermore it was not going to be simply a case of following the remnants of a road but also of searching for those remnants in a vast panoply of high mountains with the strong risk of losing ourselves in such hostile territory. Furthermore, though we did not know it at the time, the embryo terrorist movement *Sendero Luminoso,* or Shining Path, had killer gangs in those areas through which we proposed to pass. The local peoples we would meet deep in the Andes provided another question mark; neither of us could be certain of the sort of reception we might expect from the more primitive communities. Communication, too, would be a problem for we were aware that only in the urban regions was the Spanish tongue understood and spoken. We would carry some basic foodstuffs, as well as camping equipment, but would still have to rely on local villages for more substantial fare.

On the credit side I was as fit as anyone could be for my age – 54 – and David had the advantage of youth. But our optimism and inspiration stemmed largely from the written words of the fourteenth-century Spanish chronicler, Pedro de Leon, whose diary records:

'I believe since the history of man, there has been no other account of such grandeur as is to be seen on this road which passes over deep valleys and lofty mountains, by snowy heights, over falls of water, through the living rock and along the edges of tortuous torrents. In all these places, the road is well constructed, on the inclining mountains well terraced, through the living rock cut along the riverbanks supported by retaining walls, in the snowy heights built with steps and resting places, and along its entire length swept cleanly and cleared of debris – with post stations and storehouses and Temples of the Sun at appointed intervals along its length.'

As expeditionary journeys go ours was absurdly unprepared. But if de Leon wrote the truth and the ravages of time and the elements had not been unduly harsh it was to be hoped that the route of the royal road would still be clearly defined enough to provide, if not a banister, at least an indication of the way to go. With two of my previously-managed expeditionary journeys in ruins, another ingredient for success could have lain within the adage of being third time lucky.

The revelation that we had bitten off more than we could chew struck me as David and I struggled up our umpteenth boulder-strewn ridge; just another of many behind us and countless more to come. But the highway – here no more than a wide grass thoroughfare bordered by stone drainage culverts – remained a hard taskmaster binding us to its course. In the distance, etched against the blue sky, aloof and mocking, lay the enormous bulk of the Cordillera Huayhuash stretching across the horizon in a glorious panorama of snow peaks. The explorer, Colonel Fawcett, might have been standing by my side for, through dulled senses, I heard his words: 'Never had I seen mountains like these, and I was crushed by the grandeur – speechless with the overpowering wonder of it.'

The Spanish conquest of the Inca Empire in 1532/33 by a cavalry force just 170-strong had never ceased to fascinate me. Of course it was the Spaniards' secret weapon – horses, of which none existed then in South America – that was a major contribution to the collapse and flight of the thousands-strong Incan army whose men invoked in these animals supernatural powers. Yet this notwithstanding it was a remarkable achievement since, earlier, the Incas themselves only completed *their* conquest of the hotchpotch of tribal fiefdoms after centuries of fighting.

The Inca empire, at the zenith of its power, stretched over much of western South America. In order to hold the huge realm together and convert great territories of mountain, desert and jungle into a close-knit entity, communications had to be of the highest order. This was where the system of their renowned roads came in; the hub of the enormous complex being the Incan capital, Cuzco.

The complex was based upon two trunk highways, one following the coast, the other, running parallel to it, along the mountain chain. The coastal road stretched from Tumbes (the frontier town now close to the Peruvian-Ecuadorian border) southward through the coastal desert and the entire length of Peru down into Chile. The Andean royal road ran along the spine of the mountains from Colombia's Ancasmayo River, down through present-day Ecuador, Peru, Bolivia and into Argentina. The total length of the former artery was 2,520 miles while the royal road could boast an astonishing 3,250 miles.

The original royal road had been built to connect Cuzco, now in southern Peru, with Quito, then the Inca's northern capital and today the capital city of Ecuador. This was the route that David and I planned to follow.

We actually began the journey further south than Cuzco, tracking the southerly extension of the road from Bolivia northward, using rail and road transport where it followed the route and circuiting the reed-bordered shores of Lake Titicaca. We had spent a hot and humid week in Lima amassing large-scale military maps of our proposed line of march, effecting final research and sightseeing in the Peruvian capital. The remains of its Spanish founder and the conqueror of the Incas, Francisco Pizarro, still lay in a chapel of the twin-towered cathedral in the Plaza de Armas, for Lima feels itself to be a Spanish city and continues to honour the man who, legend has it, was suckled by a sow.

All who go to Peru find their way eventually to Cuzco. It breathes its Incan history as can nowhere else. Founded by Manco Capac it has become a shrine to the Incas, the place where the visitor can do the rounds of its museums and edifices. Almost every central street holds a remnant of Incaic wall that has managed to survive the centuries, the climax being the amazing structure – a third of a mile long – that is the fortress called Sacsahuaman built of monolithic blocks, some weighing up to a hundred tons, yet fitted together perfectly without benefit of the wheel or mortar. Other substantial remains lie in and around Cuzco including Ollantaytambo, Pisac and, of course, Machupicchu, the famed 'Lost City of the Incas', understandably Peru's chief tourist site. For all its Incaic glories Cuzco unaccountably neglects its founder's greatest accomplishment. A dirt track, which we were assured was the royal highway, crept out of the backside of the city and wandered lamely towards a great panoply of mountains shining white in a warm sun. We followed it, shouldering our heavy and unwieldy rucksacks containing the very minimum of survival gear and emergency fodder.

Two days' march had us at Limatambo. The village lay in the frigid shadow of Mount Salcantay which hid the Inca temple and rest station of which little remains. Tahahuasi was once such a *tampo* par excellence, the equivalent of a three-star motorway hotel, that formed part of a chain of rest stations of varying grades of comfort.

Though progressing at no more than a walking pace the geographical changes were discernible but we were still unprepared for the intense dryness as we neared the Apurimac River. Its bridge, that immortalised in Thornton Wilder's novel *The Bridge of San Luis Rey*, was, of course, originally a hanging structure erected by the Incas from cables of braided straw over which many an Inca army poured as did the Spaniards in the other direction. We crossed on a modern steel structure within sight of the supports of the previous colonial one.

The subsequent landmark was Vilcas Huaman, the so-called 'Sanctuary of the Hawk', a celebrated Inca town containing the only one of a thousand and more sun temples to survive almost in its entirety. We had some difficulty in locating it for the royal road in these parts was not an artery of clarity, but our efforts were not wasted.

The temple was magnificent. A great truncated pyramid, it rose in tiers to a small terrace reached by a flight of cyclopean steps while the massive stone doorway which faces the plaza stood dignified and lonely. Framed by the foundations of ancient buildings the immense square offered a sombre sight, accentuated by an oppressive silence. Once 20,000 Indians gave it a spectacle, a colour and a sound that reverberated through the Inca empire.

That the royal road runs through Huancayo is emphasised by its main street, Calle Real, which is actually part of it. The Lord Inca once rode in triumph through the town on a golden litter, preceded by heralds and musicians and attended by Virgins of the Sun who strewed the road with flowers. Today few luminaries visit a town that holds little opulence.

Lake Junin is Peru's second largest lake. The surroundings were bleak but, beyond, was Bonbon, once an Inca command post, and the river that drains Junin led us there across the flat Pampa de Junin, criss-crossed by foot-tracks and laced with ditches half-hidden beneath thick tufts of sharp grass.

Bonbon itself was no more than a scattering of stones but it marked the start of a hundred-mile section of royal road, plainly visible, that accompanied us on a three-day march initially to Yanahuanca. Here we camped on somebody's veranda and restocked with provisions since no further urban centres showed on our maps for many miles.

The Yanahuanca River bubbled through a ravine along the side of which the road had been cut. The road itself was not only emphatically in evidence but was doing duty as a farm track and confined within recently-constructed walls. At the hamlet of Huarautambo we spent a couple of nights at the simple abode of the Spanish-speaking schoolmaster, Valentine Inge, who took us to see a cave-tomb carpeted by human skulls over which we crunched. The tomb had only recently been discovered and was not of Incan origin though the nearby *tampo* most definitely was. Our meals with Valentine consisted of potato with a little *charqui* (sun-dried meat) moistened by one of our package soups, and during the first of these repasts we were advised of an expected pack-horse convoy going our way that could be persuaded to carry us and our rucksacks. The weight of our loads was becoming unbearable and, with the imminent approach of very much more difficult terrain, could be beyond our physical capacity.

While in Huarautambo we came into the scheming orbit of one Jose, whose sole interest in life revolved around gold and the acquiring of it. He thought he knew where a cache of the stuff lay buried, the problem being that his superstitious nature forbade him to dig for it. But for gringos – unbelievers – it was different. Jose was as wily as he looked, a mean-faced little man with a shifty manner – but a persuasive one. Thus before dawn next day he had us out of our sleeping bags; the three of us, armed with two long-handled spades, proceeding in darkness to the base of an escarpment and a small marker cairn of stones. We dug for more than an hour but, as expected, found nothing, so slunk back from whence we had come having risked the wrath of ignorant villagers whose obsession with gold, hidden from the Spanish conquerors by the Incas, led to greed, petty jealousies and, in extreme cases, murder.

The third day the convoy arrived. Our rucksacks were loaded, adding to bulging sacks of potatoes that formed the cargo of a fleet of skinny horses. Only the convoy leader, a *cana*-swigging, ill-tempered Peruvian called Ron, was permitted to ride; the rest of us lesser mortals, including a woman, walked, David and I deferentially in the rear. One of the men was a dab hand with a whip which he intermittently cracked across the horses' backs with a noise that echoed between the valley walls through which we wound our way.

For mile after mile the royal road never let up. Fording ice-cold rivers, stumbling up Inca-constructed steps where high ridges had to be surmounted, and avoiding loosened flagstones laid across areas of bog, we followed it. The width of the road varied between 15 and 18 feet as against the 24 feet of the coastal highway, a discrepancy that was probably a compromise with geography since the former had to be built across very difficult and near-perpendicular terrain.

At nightfall we made camp, the stoic bowler-hatted woman making fires out of handfuls of dry grass over which her menfolk's stew was heated in a blackened cooking pot. She never spoke; her wrinkled Indian features never changed their resigned expression as she went about her tasks. None of our companions was exactly brimming over with the joy of life which, perhaps, is understandable in the circumstances in which they probably existed. As we lay in our sleeping bags directly under the stars David and I slept little, envisaging the distinct possibility of being robbed and having our throats cut into the bargain. Just occasionally Ron had shown a spark of bonhomie, insisting we partake of mouthfuls of his firewater, refusal unleashing spasms of anger and a threatening display of weaponry.

Oro, the word for gold, was pointedly aimed at us once more while passing a complex of caverns, their mouths half-buried in the ground. Ron dismounted and announced that *oro* was to be found here and, of course, David and I had to dig for it while the others looked on. But again in vain and Ron vent his frustration by swigging more *cana* from a seemingly never-empty flagon. Though it meant a return to shouldering our rucksacks we were not sorry to pay off our fractious companions and continue on our own along a still clearly-defined highway that kept changing its surface consistency to suit the terrain.

I suppose we must have covered some 30 miles from Huarautambo with our convoy though it was not so much the distance or the irregularity of the route that affected us as the fact of not being able to undertake it at our own pace. And in the rarefied atmosphere of an altitude that hovered around 11,000 feet this was a major consideration.

And it was all too likely to be a continuous disadvantage of travelling in the company of the locals since Andean Peruvians have greater lung-power than low-altitude Britons. The best solution lay in the possibility offered by the acquisition of a pack animal – either on purchase or loan – though, with the potato-gathering season in full swing, the likelihood of purchase appeared slight, particularly for the sort of money we could raise. Simple hire, therefore, offered the only alternative though this would entail the services of an accompanying horseman over whom we would, at least, have some control.

A heavy frost sheathed our bivouac in clusters of diamonds that flashed and twinkled in the early morning sun. In spite of the intense cold the tremendous sight of the Cordillera Huayhuash range lured us out of bed to watch a procession of clouds like flocks of sheep climb up the ravines between the peaks behind which streaks of sapphire were appearing. We performed the very minimum of ablutions from a water hole that also served as a source of drinking water. Breakfast was baked potatoes we had managed to procure from one of Ron's bulging sacks.

Our campsite for the night had been close to a village that our map indicated to be Gashapampa, a motley collection of mud-and-wattle hovels. The immediate goal was the Inca ruin of Tunsacancha approximately eight miles ahead. Here David wanted to investigate the remains of another *tampo* and former Inca habitation.

Passing through the village our progress was watched by two youths who plainly beheld a source of income out of our stumbling gait for they pursued us and offered to carry our loads to the next habitation. A deal was struck and our cargo distributed to four backs instead of two.

These bearers too hardly inspired our trust. They were equally shifty-eyed and carried sheath-knives which they toyed with lovingly as they walked. One of them, in a combination of Quechuan and Spanish, asked if we carried pistols and I was about to shake my head when David, faster on the uptake, nodded and patted a bulging pocket in which reposed a battered copy of the *South American Handbook*. We had been warned in Cuzco of the dangers of terrorist gangs that were alleged to have bases in the remote villages through which our route was likely to pass, but we had not taken this too seriously. A line of quinel trees, rare at this altitude, gave us the first glimpse of vegetation since we had started to climb in earnest a week earlier. The trees were windswept and spindly but any tree in a desolation of grassland and rock made a comforting sight. The royal road, broad and clear, offered easier walking, though again the necessity of keeping up with our porters exhausted us and by the time we reached the single farmhouse that seemed to constitute a hamlet which might have been Gasacucho our legs felt like rubber.

The *tampo* of Tunsacancha is not of great drama to the layman of the likes of myself but its ruins wore a jaunty air and were set where two valleys met. David roamed the old stones for hours necessitating an early pitching of the tent well before dusk since it was hardly worth going further that day, a set of circumstances that paid a handsome dividend. The householder of the farm, learning of our proximity, invited us to purchase some fresh meat from a recently-killed sheep. This, it was arranged, would be cooked for us that evening.

Presenting ourselves at the house at the appointed hour we were shown into a communal room that served as kitchen, bedroom and slaughter-house occupied by a woman, eight men and a bevy of runny nosed children. In their boisterous company we experienced a veritable banquet, the memory of which we would carry for weeks to come. We ate with our fingers, the fat dripping from our jowls, the darkness hiding the blemishes of dirt and unhygienic handling. Around our legs guinea pigs lunged for the odd dropped fragment.

Before returning to the tent we negotiated the hire of a packhorse and minder for our onward day's journey and retired to bed in a contented mood hardly reduced by the patter of rain on the fly-sheet. Alas, the dry hacking cough I had developed some days earlier was to have me in paroxysms of choking which became most wearing for the both of us. This had followed a spell when I had gone down with altitude sickness, an affliction that can only be alleviated by 48 hours of complete rest. David was to be struck down similarly in the days to come but, in the meantime, his cross to bear was a painful rash on the back of his hands followed by a bout of fever he diagnosed as hepatitis.

Dawn was a depressing one with low clouds spitting rain and hiding the brows of the low hills. Our spirits, so high the previous evening, sank into our damp boots as we plodded dismally behind the horse which looked equally miserable as, indeed, did its accompanying youth. Our morning wash had been taken in a near-freezing stream and was more promise than lick.

The royal road wandered along through broad sweeping valleys of grass and swamp. The stream we followed widened and had to be crossed at intervals while the swamp forced us into detours that, for a while, lost us the route of the road. Large ugly birds soared overhead. They were not condors and were probably buzzards but, to me in my depression, they were vultures.

By midday the sun had poked bright fingers through the stained cotton wool of the clouds to cheer us up as we approached the Banos valley together with plots of cultivated land and crops. We halted to watch a team of peasants hand-ploughing a meadow, working in unison to turn the soil in swift, methodical movements before our presence distracted them.

It was at a point several miles beyond Banos that the royal road finally dropped into another valley, doing so by way of a series of finely-cut stairways, wide and regal. The road remains a thoroughfare to this day, marching across the countryside in arrogant fashion, the only substantial man-made object around. At the bottom of the valley the River Nupe, fast-flowing and deep, barred the way, with no sign of an Incan – or any other – bridge. Eventually we tracked down a modern timber construction a couple of miles upstream, directly beneath the hillside village of Pilcocancha, and made our way towards it, dismissing and paying off our two – and four-legged – companions. Barely had we gained the centre when the heavens opened to send us hastening for shelter in the local bakery.

The prospect of another wet night prompted us to accept the invitation to spend it in what the baker termed a 'spare room'. This turned out to be a bare store with a filthy floor that contained a counter and a shelf of empty lemonade bottles. Ensconced with our baggage in this dreary lodging we were pointedly locked in following a frugal supper of stale rolls and a tin of herrings. Our host turned out to be yet another unsavoury character who reeked of rum and he not only charged us for the room and his stale rolls but also for our own herrings of which he showed himself to be particularly partial.

The night was a dismal one; the windowless chamber stank of urine including our own, the only receptacle for which were the empty bottles on the shelf. Between us we filled more than half a dozen during a night spent trying not to roll off the counter top onto the filthy floor.

Being windowless, the room remained in darkness at daybreak and so we were still abed when the door was unlocked to admit not only the baker but a group of customers. Swept off our counter in the rush we attempted to dress as best we could and collect our scattered belongings amongst a score of customers-turned-gringo-watchers. We left hurriedly, suddenly aware that the bottles we had been using as urinals were being distributed for less utilitarian purposes.

Buying eggs from an emporium in a side street we boiled
them on our Primus stove, a magical piece of equipment that,
of course, drew hordes of new onlookers, many of whom
appeared to be high on rum even at so early an hour. So *that's*
what the bottles were for! But with the stuff cheap by any
standards I could appreciate that living out a life in such poverty,
in damp houses and on a diet of potato and stale bread would
be dismal enough to turn the staunchest teetotaller to the
bottle.

Our negotiations for onward baggage-carrying facilities came
to nought, so we retraced our steps to Banos. 'Banos' means
'bath' and the prospect of immersion in hot water took on a
distinctly ethereal hue. And since Banos consisted of no more
than a series of natural warm springs emptying into Incan-
sculpted stone baths, locating them was not difficult. Our
multi-hour soak in ever-flowing, constantly warm water made
an idyllic interlude.

Thereafter, for us, water was less of an attraction as incessant
rain became a nightly event and, more often than not, a daily
one too. As we neared the township of La Union we gained
another horse and minder to help with our loads. Initially they
were a grumpy pair, but the latter, on longer acquaintance,
turned out to be a pleasant old man, his weather-beaten face
alive with character. When it wasn't raining the lowering clouds
accentuated the threat; but the storm that finally hit us as we
descended an escarpment came without warning. A junction
had deflected us from the royal road which swung away from
La Union to cross the Pampa Huanuco to the Vizcarra valley
ten kilometres west of the town. At the onset of the first drops
of rain we should undoubtedly have taken the old man's advice
and sheltered under the eaves of a shepherd's hut. But La
Union was, we wrongly estimated, only nine kilometres ahead
and its imagined bright lights and culinary expertise
beckoned...

What fell out of the sky as we hurried on was more, much
more, than a mere downpour. It was a prolonged cascade,

virtually a solid sheet of water that soaked us within seconds. The temperature plummeted to zero and the track became inches deep in liquid mud.

The way wound down into a culvert and night merged with the angry black storm clouds. The river, when we came to it, was hidden in darkness. From 100 yards on the old man shouted something, mounted his horse, and disappeared, and when next we perceived him he was on the opposite bank. To reach it he must have waded the river at some point and for a moment we imagined he was abandoning us.

The river was the Guytuc, normally no more than a substantial brook when not a dried-up watercourse. Now, swollen by heavy rain, it had become a raging torrent. Apprehensively we removed our boots, tied the laces together and hung them round our necks, then entered the ice-cold stream. In an instant the water level reached our thighs, pulling at our taut legs and threatening to topple us into the sullen depths. I took a cautious step, lost my balance and floundered into deep water. Out of my depth, I threshed wildly and was dragged forward by a vicious current, my boots swinging against my face. The dark outline of the opposite bank showed close so I lunged for it, grabbed some foliage, lost my hold, tried again, and scrambled on all fours up a slippery shore. Light-headed with relief I turned to help David but he too was safely across the maelstrom.

Our shouts brought back the old man, now leading his horse. He waited, mumbling to himself, as we struggled back into our wet boots. 'Keep moving! Keep moving!' I kept repeating to myself, for the numbing inertia of exposure was paralysing my limbs. Plainly neither of us was in a fit state to reach La Union that night but we had no alternative but to stagger on to keep hypothermia at bay.

Then, miraculously, the dark outline of a farmhouse showed before us, our arrival drawing people from the shadows. Upon learning of our plight the good household swiftly went to work in the rudimentary kitchen to produce a hot meal, while an elderly man helped us spread dry hay on the ground beneath a lean-to roof that partly covered a small courtyard. We peeled off our soaking clothes replacing them with items that were merely wet. The stew of potato, vegetable and macaroni with *manzanilla* tea was disposed of in record time to the accompaniment of our heartfelt expressions of appreciation. Optimistically we hung out our wet garments before settling down in damp sleeping bags liberally encased in stale hay. A litter of pigs, some hens and a dog found their way onto our beds at different times during the night but their warm-blooded presence was welcome and sleep came easily.

A brilliant sun opened our eyes and within the hour we were progressing across a broad open plain, the Pampa Huanuco, stretching in all directions with but a blur of hills on the horizon. Another hour brought us to the edge of a sharp descent leading into the Vizcarra valley, here more a gorge than a valley. An excruciating path of jagged stones brought us into La Union where our ravenous appetites led us straight to the nearest restaurant. It was an unsavoury place and the choice of food limited, but six fried eggs each made a satisfactory start to breakfast after which we paid off our companion before returning for more. The old man had enjoyed his breakfast as much as we had and our parting was warm. We had ignored his advice and paid the price but he bore no grudge. Leaving the restaurant we went in search of a hotel, intent upon a taste of the soft life.

La Union, let it be said, is no metropolis. The little town, divided by the River Vizcarra, was drab, lifeless and smelt of boiled cabbage. We spent three days there, however, after which we ran out of restaurants, while the rats had become too intimate for comfort in the hovel of a hotel. On the second day we retraced our steps, making an excursion to the Inca ruins of Huanuco Viejo which we had by-passed on our way to the town.

And what the Incas had constructed in the middle of the open grassland is truly magnificent. A huge fort-like edifice or *isnu* stood intact, its massive walls – like those of Sacsahuaman – a marvel of construction. We wandered for hours among the substantial remains of old temples, storehouses, barracks and dwelling houses marvelling at the grandeur of the stone arches and staircases. With us were the ghosts of Incan soldiers, priests and the multitude of citizens who once inhabited this lonely, spectacular place.

Horseless, we left La Union intent upon picking up the means of onward baggage-carrying at the point in the valley where the royal road crossed it some ten kilometres north. Our next objective was the township of Huari, which we calculated as about 140 kilometres distant or five, maybe six, days of walking.

And Lady Luck was with us for she produced Manual. He displayed the flattened features and coloured face of the Red Indian though his slanting eyes gave him an eastern appearance. He had turned up out of the blue together with a horse and expressed his willingness to accompany us as he intended covering part of our route anyway.

With him we were on the road by midday. The climb out of the valley was steep, but the new horse was the healthiest specimen that we had seen to date; so much so that Manual was forced to rein it back when we showed signs of lagging. By evening we had reached some scattered adobe dwellings that rejoiced in the name of Chogolagran. It stood at the head of yet another valley, this one that of the River Taparaco, a tributary of the Vizcarra.

It became apparent that Manual was a regular commuter of this route and, accordingly, had contacts at various points along it. Those in Chogolagran were a farmer family who offered us their roof but, with five children as well as their livestock under it, we felt that we would be straining their resources by accepting. The tent, accordingly, again became our shelter for the night but our supper of sardines and bread was supplemented by soup and potatoes which Manual and the family pressed upon us. The family were born of a younger generation than Manual; there was nothing eastern about the young father replete in jeans, black shirt and black trilby while his wife looked older but probably wasn't. Their children sat in a row watching our strange cooking operations, their heads cocked on one side like mystified puppies.

We left early and were on the hoof hardly had dawn tinged the sky. The royal road closed in towards the narrow river leading us easily along the western flank of the valley. The hamlets of Estanque and San Lorenzo de Isco produced their quota of inquisitive citizens plus a garish cemetery, oddly out of place in such poverty-stricken surroundings. At San Lorenzo a friend of Manual appeared with what I thought was a welcome mug of water but which turned out to be some home-brewed firewater to provide an eye-watering aperitif for a frugal lunch.

The road, well-defined and engineered, took full advantage of the contours of the land and seldom was it forced to deviate from the level it first selected when entering the valley. Here the great road of conquest had no need to be guessed at. We were walking over low hills, treeless and bare, the wind blowing in unobstructed from the Amazon jungles to set the *ichu* grass in motion.

By late afternoon, weary but jubilant, we reached a scattering of hutments called by a name – Taparaco, after the river – where a relic of some earlier civilisation was alleged to stand. If so we never found it. But ahead lay the *tampo* of Torococha, some 20 kilometres distant, this one a relic of Inca durability.

Close, but not too close, to the wretched houses we bedded down, tentless, in a mound of last year's hay, strong-smelling, slightly putrid and very prickly. Even here we were invited to share in the evening meal composed almost entirely of the ubiquitous potato provided by a childless couple to whom Manual seemed to be related. The woman wore plaited hair which she modelled into a castle-like structure upon her head; not at all the usual Indian hairstyle of single or twin pigtails swinging free. The man constantly chewed *coca* that produced a most colourful spit.

Two days of fine weather gave way, on the third, to ominous clouds, but no rain fell. We were on the right bank of the river and, by midday, came to a marshy patch of land that had us dodging about between rocks and dry tufts of *ichu*, attempting to keep our feet out of water. We had swung away from the river but the swamp caught us in its slimy maw whatever direction we took. Manual told us that we were between two lakes atop of each wall of the valley and that the swamp was a result of their overflow. We found a decrepit building but its stones were certainly not Incan even to my inexperienced eyes. Any further investigation was discouraged by the depressing swamp and I wondered why anyone should choose to build *anything* at so moist and inhospitable a spot.

I did not have to wonder for long. Further up the valley were definite signs of road drainage stone formations of obvious Incan origin. No doubt, at some earlier stage, the whole area had been devoid of this morass of liquid mud. The ruin that could only have been that of a *tampo* stood, away from the village, dauntingly exposed to the cyclonic winds. It was a square block of a building of substantial stone and without windows. Even David could find no reason for dallying there for more than ten minutes.

The end of the swamp brought a steady climb out of the valley and, somewhere, we left behind our river which must have risen at the behest of the twin lakes. The parting of the ways came around mid-afternoon, with Manual bound for a hamlet called Manca Peque a mile off to the right on a slope overlooking more marshy ground. He suggested we accompany him there to spend the night while, additionally, he would use his good offices to arrange for a replacement horse. This seemed a sensible course of action so we assented.

A lonelier habitation I have yet to see with everlasting hills bucking away in every direction and not even the drama of a true mountain to quicken the pulse. The night meant a return to the tent and, of course, a diet of potatoes this time moistened with our own uninspiring packet soup. All too plainly, the sad remote people of Manca Peque existed at near-starvation level, their pinched faces and suspicious eyes devoid of humour and the milk of human kindness. Manual himself was obviously unhappy at our reception and I wondered what reasons brought him here but didn't like to ask. A clutch of ragged children, to whom we offered some picture postcards brought along for the purpose, had to be urged to accept them; not the vestige of a smile flitted across their solemn features as they gravely made off with their prize.

Manual was as good as his word and procured both a horse and a youth to accompany us. The boy, unused to the sly bargaining of his more money-conscious brethren, was content to let Manual fix the price while Manual himself charged us only a one-way fee.

Once more we left bright and early. Socially the lad was not a patch on Manual though he was willing enough. Communication was difficult as he spoke only Quechuan while Manual had possessed a few words of Spanish. The horse was part-mule and the pace was steady as we walked in near-silence at an altitude of about 13,000 feet, the route firmly sticking to the 4,200 and 4,000 metre contours.

It became noticeable that, as we progressed northward, village dwellings increasingly exhibited more substantial construction that incorporated worked stone taken from ancient ruins and, possibly, the royal road. Most were roofed with grass thatch but the living conditions in these hovels were still surely worse than those of the time of the Inca since, in many cases, entire households slept in one room and generally in one bed made of untanned cattle hides.

A larger village below some great bastions of rock became the end of the marked *Camino Incaico*, the route of the royal road, as shown on the map. Henceforth our eyes and gleaned local knowledge alone would have to show the way. The name of the large village was, as we expected, Huancayoc, but it was good to see the fact confirmed. Where the old road terminated and the modern track commenced we never learnt for the transfer was a gradual process and we had to accept that they were one and the same. Huancayoc was, by past standards, a centre of some prosperity for it possessed a couple of shops and our potato lunch was supported by biscuits that might well have been a leftover from a Spanish soldier's haversack to judge from their antiquity.

If the bigger village indicated a return to civilisation the environment showed otherwise. It fast became more difficult and devious while rock outcrops, steep and black, pushed us from one minuscule hamlet to another. People and houses appeared with increasing frequency and David was forever enquiring in his demanding, no-nonsense voice for the whereabouts of the Inca road. The replies we got from the locals were baffling. Invariably we were given an affirmative; that we were on the right road, corroborated with much head-nodding, but we were well aware this might mean nothing. Gradually, however, we evolved a system by which we could gauge the sincerity of an answer or just the simple desire to please us.

A leaden sky and an icy wind kept us walking hard for warmth. That night we camped on a patch of ground out of range of any village. A swiftly-moving stream offered a water supply and another contribution unleashed itself from above. The thunderstorm that struck during the night hit us soon after we had heated our ubiquitous soup.

We persuaded the lad to join us in the tent rather than rely on the doubtful waterproof qualities of his woollen poncho. This made a tight squeeze but ensured we remained warm and reasonably dry while the thunder rolled among the hills and lightning licked the wet rocks with throngs of fire. Rain hissed down, forcing its way through the nylon of the tent, to finally cease with uncanny abruptness. We lay uneasily listening to the drips.

A morning's walk brought us down from the hills past immense boulders hoary with spongy moss and slivers of eroded rock fallen from sheer sections of cliff as if sliced by a giant cheesewire. The descent led to the village of Pomachaca at the bottom of a three-way ravine where two angry rivers met head on to continue their flow as one. David was delighted when his feverish enquiries elicited the fact that certainly the royal road honoured Pomachaca with its presence, and a villager pointed out the escarpment down which we had come adding that there was now a *real* road to Huari. He was referring, of course, to the dusty street that bore the corrugated imprints of tyre tracks.

A patchwork of cultivation mottled the fertile green valley of the Huari River we now followed and the open landscape beyond made a cheerful consort after the recent geographical hostility. To the east the gigantic mountain complex of the Cordillera Blanca occasionally offered a tantalising glimpse of its highest peaks, evocative with snow and altitude.

Huari is half the size of La Union but its position overlooking the Alpine-like valley was a joy. Impatient to continue on the move and delighted by the improvement in our fortunes and progress we had no thoughts of a prolonged stay. Ahead lay another hurdle in the obstacle course of the Andes and, though we had a broken banister of the royal road, it was all too likely that, added to the exertions of walking it, would be the exasperation of trying to find it.

Like the routine of living, the pattern of our journey emerged and became itself a routine. Stumbling endlessly along rough tracks behind a plodding horse led by a succession of characters from the tediously cheerful to the depressingly morose, our spirits rose and fell accordingly. Rain squalls drenched us, wind scoured our faces, sun drew sweat from our bodies and the bitter mountain cold lay in wait at every nightfall. Our days were not measured in hours but by occurrences that became low spots or high spots in the tedium of fatigue and, occasionally, despair.

A high spot usually evolved from an evening descent from a mountain track for a night amongst the tiniest *kraal* of houses, the simplest community. This was not so much in abeyance to a craving for the amenities of urban living as to a longing for the company of fellow humans. Though neither of us would admit it, we desperately needed this antidote to a loneliness which, in the remoteness of the northern Peruvian Andes, has one by the throat.

But we had not completely ignored the warning of a danger that lurked among such isolated communities. 'Steer clear of bands of armed horsemen,' we had been advised. 'They are not to be trusted and if they think you might report their presence they wouldn't hesitate to dispose of you.' That a guerrilla organisation lurked in these spectacular and intensely beautiful surroundings seemed unreal.

Huari was a high spot for it offered a solid *biftec* for our bellies and an earthen roof over our heads. Our 'bedroom' was no more than the dirty floor of a three-table restaurant but, while there, we became temporary members of the large, cheerful family who unstintingly shared with us the treasure of their companionship.

Prolonged stays in such centres were resisted, for, as La Union had shown, their attractions quickly pall. It was from Huari, however, that we made an excursion; a detour on wheels to Chavin de Huantar, off the royal road but a centre made historic by an earlier culture.

We got there aboard a grossly-overloaded lorry, squatting in the buck clutching our belongings so that they would take up less space amongst the assortment of other passengers and cargo. The road was excruciating, an engineer's nightmare of wrongly-cambered bends and a neglected surface, though the scenery was awe-inspiring. We corkscrewed up one side of a pass and, near the top, found a mountain barring the way through which a quite respectable concrete tunnel had been expensively bored. Its dripping darkness might have been an omen for the storm that struck as we emerged the other side but, if so, we were slow on the uptake. Huddled, compacted together under a few square metres of torn canvas, we were thankful for the soft, yielding paper sacks beneath us until swiftly-multiplying rents in them revealed their contents to be lard. As we wound slowly into the Mosna valley, semi-drenched by rivulets of water through the leaking canvas and greasy from fatty lard oozing from the damaged sacks, I was reminded that walking had its compensations. And it was not as if the ride was free. In the mountain districts of Peru any vehicle serves as a public transport conveyance with fares to match the calibre of comfort. Gringos are, of course, fair game for cash-conscious drivers and tariffs rise with the fairness of one's skin.

There are many pre-Inca cultures; it is recorded that for 2,000 years prior to the Inca there was in Peru a long steady cultural growth but few facts have emerged from the chronicles of time. There are no dated coins such as the Romans conveniently left to posterity; even the Incas had no money, but there is evidence that man was involved with weaving and agriculture as early as 1000 BC. But the first culture of prominence to have been unearthed – literally – is that of *Chavin,* its leitmotif a ferocious-looking cat-god found on pottery and stonework. Here at Chavin de Huantar was the heart of this civilisation and, today, the dusty remains of impressive buildings, characterised by well-laid stone walls decorated with stone-carved human and animal (mostly cat) heads, have been exposed for all to see.

As expected the shabby township of Chavin held a minimum of attractions. All afternoon we waited in vain for conveyance back to Huari so were forced to spend a night on the floor of the police station that appeared to double as the local doss-house. Finally, crammed in the back of a Datsun van with two substantial ladies sitting on our feet, we made it.

The sheer ruggedness of the terrain further emphasised the extent of the Incas' achievements for it seemed incredible that any communication system with the means available to them could ever have been established with sufficient efficiency to control and administer so huge an empire. Since the swift transmission of messages was of paramount importance and the distances over which they had to be passed so enormous, a courier method called *chasqui* was developed. It was not new; the Romans relied on relays of horse-riders, but the *chasquis* could run in relays to better effect than their mounted Roman counterparts. Impossible though it may appear, records show that the *chasquis* could cover the 1,250 miles between Cuzco and Quito at altitudes ranging from 6,000 to 17,000 feet in five days! This meant that runners had to run an average of some 250 miles a day which was considerably faster than the Roman couriers on their metalled roads.

For us the end of a day of severe plodding brought its rewards with the knowledge that for a few blessed hours one's feet could remain motionless. Plainly I was not *chasqui* material even had I the lungs to defeat the demands of altitude. The wear and tear of the passing weeks might have been having its physical effects but, at the same time, it was honing David and I into a team; oft working with irritation, but working. We now knew the ropes and undertook our small tasks and chores in support of our daily existence and survival amongst one of the most terrifying domains in the world. And here, near Huachococha, came the close of yet another day exhaustingly filled. We were asleep before a single star pierced the heavens.

Aldo – as we came to call our latest companion – had not been reluctant to invite himself into the tight confines of the tent or to share our frugal fare. He was the most talkative of henchmen and would blather on in an unmelodious mixture of Quechuan and Spanish. He was, however, full of rural wit and confidence, a humorous figure in his baggy trousers, short white Cordovan jacket and black poncho together with a battered straw sombrero. In the morning it was he who would have us out of our sleeping bags at an ungodly hour with much chivvying and demonstrations of impatience to be off. There was a long day ahead, he would warn, and most of it uphill. They all were and it always was.

The present valley we were following widened into a featureless plateau and the carcasses of sheep and goats littered the grass in unexplained profusion. Most had been reduced to skeletons by the attentions of condors so that only the weathered hooves remained to indicate their origins. We climbed steadily, traversing the broad side of a convex slope, with the horizon in front of us ever receding as if intentionally denying us access to the skyline.

Quite suddenly we gained the top. We stood on the very crest of the pass with the whole *cordillera* becoming the landscape towards which the still higher passes lay in wait. The air was remarkable for its clarity and the magnificence of the view tempted us to pause a while until the cold drove us on.

It was hard to fathom the path ahead. At our feet was a precipice below which, a seemingly infinite distance away, we could see the foam-flecked course of a sizeable river of melted snow. Unquestionably we followed Aldo, leading his horse, along the ridge towards a point where the precipice gave way to a 45-degree slope.

While he halted to adjust the animal's load, David and I set off on our own, anxious to escape the cold of the wind-swept ridge and because the path manifested itself on a downward gradient. The descent was painful. Though we traversed the incline in the professional manner we found ourselves skidding and slipping alarmingly, starting minor avalanches of stones that rattled down the slope.

We were almost at the bottom, breathless and aching, our boots full of pebbles, our eyes full of dust, when we looked back. There behind us, but away over to our right, Aldo and horse were comfortably negotiating the hump of a spur which provided a natural and well-graduated line of descent to the river. With the realisation of how disagreeable and unnecessary our descent had been came a reflection upon the folly of hiring guides and then not letting them guide us. Eventually we were reunited on the riverbank which we followed for a few miles until it sheered away towards a point of the compass not on our set alignment.

Next day, firmly behind Aldo, we made better progress along a line of switchback hills and a route that our man plainly knew well, though for most of it there was no sign of a path. But we had chosen the shortest distance between Huari and San Luis, of that there was little doubt, so we could but presume that the royal road too had made the same choice of course. By early evening the habitations of San Luis showed up in the lengthening shadows of the surrounding heights and a small road materialised from nowhere to lead us by well-cultivated smallholdings into the little town.

Almost at once we were taken in hand by a stalwart of the local constabulary. It was as if Aldo had been in league with the law but, on reflection, I think not. More likely it was our appearance that activated the fresh-faced patrolman of the Guarda Civil. The entry into town of two extremely dirty foreign devils offered the moral obligation of apprehension. Watched by a gaping crowd of citizens we were marched to police headquarters, our escort dramatically fondling his Smith & Weston .38 in its holster. Once inside the door, however, the show of authority was replaced by extreme overtures of friendship and the plain longing for a chat. The unfortunate youngster, it transpired, had only recently been moved from Lima for a two-year stint in the sticks of San Luis without his wife, and so was unashamedly homesick.

Thus, once more, our 'hotel' for the night turned out to be the local nick though, on this occasion, the reasoning was pure compassion – for our host as much as us. For what remained of the day, our baggage safely stowed in an empty cell, we became the constable's guests, and were pressed to endless glasses of beer and a meal at the local pub. No more than a large village, San Luis lay in the shadow of the great snow peak of 19,000 foot Nydo Huandoy, a sobering sight with the sunset ablaze behind it.

Before we turned in – on the floor of course, but a clean one of the guardroom – we made the acquaintance of our host's superior, the chief of police of San Luis. It was in fact that worthy's home-made cream-cheese, a local speciality we had been fast consuming to help down a night-cap of a fiery liquid that followed the beer. Not the least put out, the officer invited us to have breakfast at his home next morning.

Speaking for myself, the night was not as restful as it could have been for not only did David and the policeman snore at varying pitches but a prisoner in the cell below was given to hawking to an extent I never thought possible in a human. But the breakfast, consisting of a whole bull's heart with tomatoes and chips, in the company of the inspector and his buxom wife, made amends.

In such circumstances as these the acquisition of horsepower was no problem. The meal consumed, appreciation shown and farewells effected, we departed from San Luis with some reluctance but with a game little Patagonian mare and a would-be cowboy in tow. If both had been pressed into service on the express orders of the Peruvian Police Force no resentment showed.

Our researches had indicated that the royal road passed close to the town of Piscobamba, our next landmark, some two days hence. The track grew smaller and rougher and though Ricardo, our new colleague, insisted it was the old Inca route, we were far from convinced. At Yanama township, to which the track led, we met an American agricultural technician and a group of Peruvians unloading furniture from a lorry. We offered a hand thus earning ourselves a beer, or to be more accurate, a whole succession of beers, in one of those midget shops that sold everything from transistor radios to hairpins. By dusk everyone was too far gone to know how to start the lorry let alone drive it, so we all slept in the buck amongst bags of cement which I don't recommend as a mattress or pillow. The lorry was destined for Piscobamba where the American had his quarters and we were sorely tempted to accept his offer of a lift. Firm in our rejection we said that we would see him there a day later.

In the event it was another two for, in meandering about attempting to locate definite signs of Inca origins, we wasted precious time and increased the mileage among a confusion of low hills and rivers. We camped the second night in a gorge-like cleft through which the Piscobamba River ran and by the third were within sight of the township. At the first house our quadruped and its owner left us, the latter clearly bemused by our indecisive wonderings.

Piscobamba's construction would hardly win a prize in a town-planning competition. Built in the standard Andean urban mould of a row of buildings grouped round a central plaza, the square in this case was an affair of ugly concrete, cracked and flaking.

In the patio of someone's house we cooked our midday meal by invitation, thus having to share it with its multiple occupants. Released from these activities we went in search of our American friend, running him to earth in his office-flat, the cold bare place of a bachelor's pad. With his help, we raised our porterage to Pomabamba, the neighbouring town on our itinerary. The royal road, we were assured, was on the east side of the valley astride the ridge of the first escarpment parallel to which we had been walking the last couple of days.

Another night in the now empty lorry and we gleefully escaped from Piscobamba, ascending a hill out of town to find a track that was muddier and rougher than the 'main road' to Pomabamba. Our horseman pronounced us crazy from the very start and made it abundantly clear that he did not suffer fools gladly. He was an older man, reserved and spiky, who finally accepted what we were trying to do. So sparse were any Inca-like relics or indications of their highway that he had us doubting our own sanity at times though beyond the valley of the River Vitcabamoa, which forced the modern road into a long detour, we came upon the confirmation we were looking for. Not only did the track take on the authoritative aura possessed of any Incan artery, but here and there it showed the familiar bordering stone and, at one spot, the remains of a drainage system. A line of ruined forts excited our curiosity but these were plainly pre-Inca.

Close to one collapsed and over-grown ruin we set up camp. It was not to be one of our more successful sojourns. A downpour of rain extinguished the stove, our candle burnt a hole in the tent, 'Old Grumpy', squeezing in with us, insisted on sleeping with his dirty feet in our faces and, finally, we lost the horse necessitating a morning spent searching the hillsides.

Our subsequent rest and recuperation extended to three days; such was the calibre of the good people and environment of Pomabamba. Yet again it was the police who provided us with accommodation; not a cell or guardroom this time but a guestroom equipped with two beds. Hardly Savoy standards perhaps but *beds*! We had almost forgotten such items existed. The little room adjoined the police station, the staff of which not only allowed us to use their ablutionary facilities but even provided an old woman to make our beds. But, again, it was the chief of police who became the real friend.

El Jefe introduced himself to us as we revelled in our new-found luxury. A middle-aged man with a neat moustache and greying hair he showed a keen interest in our journeyings. He spoke Spanish and invited us to dinner at his home on the outskirts of town. His wife could speak English, he told us with unrepressed pride, and would be happy to have the chance of airing a language she seldom found opportunity to use. In the meantime would we care for a hot bath and, if so, he would take us there now. We could hardly believe our ears.

Our last immersion in hot water had been weeks before in Banos and, providentially, Pomabamba was likewise blessed with hot thermal springs which ensured that every house in the town could raise piping hot water – even if it was the very devil to get hold of cold. Initially we thought the bath would be in the family home but were taken to the public baths in a depression just behind the town. The huge stone chambers were pre-sixteenth century though it would seem likely the Incas made use of them too, as do the present-day populace of Pomabamba. Wallowing happily like hippos at play in the big vats the grime of weeks peeled off our pink, boiled bodies.

In the evening we accompanied *El Jefe* to his home encircled by massed ranks of fruit trees edged by a guard of honour of funeral lilies. Here we were introduced to a smiling lady, small, intelligent and vital, who straightaway launched into a monologue of English small talk for all the world as if she was having the vicar to afternoon tea.

Dinner was a banquet by any standards. The main dish consisted of as many roasted guinea pigs as we could put down and, rich and indigestible as the meat is, we did ourselves proud. To drink was a hot concoction that had a cherry brandy base and, for the dessert, great hunks of honeycomb fresh from the beehives we had seen at the bottom of the garden. Oranges and tangerines quenched a thirst generated by the cherry brandy and the honey.

We experienced some difficulty in finding our way back to our bedchamber, a state of affairs possibly not entirely due to the darkness. The beds were hard but not uncomfortable and we slept the sleep of the just – and the well-fed – ignoring the scurry of tiny feet beneath us.

Pomabamba town we discovered next morning to be of considerable charm, particularly so when measured against other townships we had encountered. And it was its attraction – human and architecturally-inspired – that held us there for so long. Its scanty shops offered a source of provision replenishment, the few restaurants were a cut above the average, while the little church provided a haven for an interlude of spiritual contemplation. On our last evening we were again invited to dinner by *El Jefe*, a repast rudely interrupted when he was called away to investigate a murder.

The incident again brought home to us the realisation of the dangers from fellow-humans. In this instance it was so-called 'cattle rustlers' who had murdered an innocent bystander, possibly because they had thought the victim had witnessed their nefarious deeds. Upon the police inspector's return the good man added his warnings to those we had already received. 'Be careful when you are up there,' he told us, jerking his head towards the darkness. I thought long and hard about the killers in the hills that night.

Our intentions were to leave the following morning and resume our escarpment route. The map showed Sihuas to be the subsequent township north of Pomabamba though, in spite of her considerable knowledge of Inca history, our hostess had been unable to pinpoint the actual course of the royal road sweeping by above her town. 'It's up there somewhere – as you've discovered,' was her only comment.

Her husband had obligingly arranged for horse transportation as far as Sihuas and, in the morning, introduced us to the new horseman prior to seeing us off from the plaza. Leaving Pomabamba was an undoubted wrench. For the first time on the journey I felt really sad to leave a town that had little enough to offer a traveller other than its kindness. With a strong horse and a burly farmer's lad in tow we returned to the silence of the mountains, climbing each false crest until we had attained the summit of the final ridge and were back onto what we took to be the route of the royal road. It welcomed us with a display of shaped Incan kerbstones edging the wide grass artery, a ghost expressway not evident as such unless you are specifically looking for it.

Fearful of losing it, David continued to ply questions concerning the route of all who passed by. Few even knew of the road, fewer still showed any interest – even if they understood what David was asking which they probably didn't. Children, away from the urban influences, replied not a word to our questions, and sometimes women on their own shook their heads as if not wanting to understand and hurried away. A tiny village school produced a pock-marked schoolmistress of sterner stuff, however, who knew all about it and was as voluble with her information as her pupils were mute in their wide-eyed dumbness.

Between every contact we stumbled on. And here on the flanks of this beautiful valley, the clear air revealing the massive peaks beyond, all life was present. Wild flowers tangled in a riot of colour; peasants on the plots of cultivation below looked like toys as they tilled the soil behind toy buffaloes, and, far away, carried by a soft breeze, came the shrilling of children's voices released from the paralysis of fright.

There were occasional horse tracks to follow and, since no other way northward was conceivable for either road or path, we had no hesitation about using them. Each was hemmed in by valleys which gradually narrowed and became shallower, driving us ever upwards back into violent convulsions of rocky desolation.

We camped where a valley petered out into a horizon full of the magnificence of the Cordillera Blanca. Our replenished stocks of food, including an abundance of oranges and honey, increased the calibre of ensuing camp meals for a while, their very consumption giving added comfort since it was lightening the load. A jar of honey we retained as an emergency item.

Our companion saw fit to leave us next day in sight of a hamlet in which his cousin was reputed to live. He had not been a bad lad but his estimate of what we understood as 'just a few more hours to Sihuas' was something of an understatement. Perhaps he meant days – in the event it took two. Attempting to obtain a replacement lost us hours and by the time we were successful we had mislaid the royal route. Fortunately, the new man knew the whereabouts of the dust road that led north, though it was late afternoon before we were firmly on the march again. The replacement was another morose individual; his mule was better company.

There was nothing at all Incaic about the road that ran from near Chullin to Sihuas. Its tortuous course was as nightmarish as its construction and surface. Potholes and bogs lay in wait for the unwary traveller, while every small village across valley, gorge or ravine, though just a mile or so away, was reached only after a crazed display of spirals and detours around the smallest obstacle. On foot it was often advantageous to take short cuts but, for all its gyrations, the road knew a thing or two and a reduction of mileage had to be paid for in sweat, blood and tears.

It took the full two days to reach Sihuas and for much of the second one we had the township in sight but, maddeningly, out of grasp. A number of unfordable rivers also confounded our efforts, and twice the road was not where it was expected to be which meant an exasperating doubling-back to go in search of the thing. The final miles we accomplished after darkness with the sparse lights of Sihuas laughing at us at the end of the corkscrew road.

The township was assuredly no Pomabamba; a village of few amenities though we saw little enough of it in the dark. In the one and only snack bar a lorry driver offered us his vehicle in which to spend the night, following up the invitation with another to join him on his proposed drive to Chimbote, a sizeable town on the coast.

We had no hesitation in accepting the first. The second we debated for only a moment.

The offer was unturndownable. We had both developed another yearning for the balmy warmth of the seaside and here was a further side excursion to it being presented to us.

The night in the lorry ought to have told us what we were in for. Its buck was half full of crates of Coca-Cola bottles and what space remained had to be shared with a woman eternally breast-feeding a baby (which at least kept it quiet) and a man afflicted with a weak bladder. Sleep, in these circumstances, plus the bitter cold, was elusive.

The 24-hour drive was the most terrifying I have experienced. Andean B-roads are little more than pot-holed tracks at the best of times and the ones we took were buttressed on one side by granite cliffs and by sheer drops on the other. Our vehicle, moving much too fast, relied entirely upon the decibels of its horn and the supposition that no oncoming vehicle would be approaching at every bend of the spiralling, zigzag route. And when something *did* the squeal of brakes heralded a series of reversing operations on the narrow road that often had the rear end of the lorry overhanging space. Landslides had also eaten away sections of road surface while ominous cracks in it further added to the nightmare. The wreckage of vehicles that had failed this motorised assault course littered the ground hundreds of feet below; but travelling in the back of the lorry at least offered a chance to jump for one's life if ours was to follow suit.

Chimbote, when finally reached, was a dead loss. Industrialised, squalid and smelling of fish-meal it offered no comfort except for warmth. A truck travelling north on the thankfully flat Pan-American Highway took us the 90 miles to Trujillo, third city of Peru, which was infinitely more pleasant. What's more it held the crumbling ruins of Chan-Chan, imperial city of the Chimu dynasty. Basing ourselves at the Lima Hotel, an establishment of basic amenities, we set out to explore it.

The pre-Inca ruins consist of nine great compounds built by the Chimu kings whose kingdom stretched 1,000 kilometres along the coast from near present-day Guayaquil to Paramonga. The city was almost certainly taken over by the Incas in about AD 1450 but not looted; the Spanish it was, however, who despoiled its burial mounds of all the gold and silver statuettes and ornaments buried with the Chimu nobles.

What David and I found was a vast mud city – the largest adobe city on earth – fallen into decay, the outer walls nevertheless towering so thick and solid that, after the better part of a millennium, they were still standing eight or nine metres high; only the ramparts showed the erosion of time. The old city stood in virtually desert terrain; no tree or fragment of greenery to be seen anywhere. Inside the adobe walls was a chocolate-coloured world with 15 kilometres of streets bordered by crumbling houses, public buildings, cemeteries, storehouses and pyramids. From the apex of one such pyramid was an astounding view of sea, old and new city and a desert backed by peaked and desiccated mountains.

A second night in the hotel and we began the gradual return to the mountains, an operation that took all of three days and involved the services of a local bus, a Toyota pickup, a Volvo truck, a private car and a massive lorry with sides so high that it became a feat of mountaineering just to get ourselves and our packs in and out of it. All this finally brought us to a point near Corongo, parallel to Sihuas. In Trujillo, amidst much heart-searching, we had taken the decision to jettison a good 50 per cent of our loads. This hurt David more than I since he had carried around with him a number of text books on the Inca civilisation which, though desirable, were not vital to the execution of our project. Thus, henceforth, we could look forward to progressing entirely under our own steam, a method of progression I had always envisaged in the first place.

As was to be expected, the locals of Corongo displayed genuine ignorance of the presence of any Inca relics – roads included – which was, perhaps, not surprising since their township does not lie on the royal artery. However, the track north provided easy walking, rising slowly but producing no great feats of physical endurance. Traversing the broad side of a convex slope, the horizon in front receded while a cool breeze indicated a return to rarer altitudes. Our aim was a gradual return to the line of the Royal Highway.

A cleft in the perpendicular wall of crags and we stood upon the crest of a pass with a whole *cordillera* rolled out like a rucked carpet to the north. A number of guanacos – the most timid but also fiercest of Andean animals – looked up from their grazing and froze as if hypnotised by the sight of us.

Our lighter loads made all the difference to progress; our liberation from the dead-weight on our shoulders initially had us spontaneously rejoicing though all too soon the accustomed exhaustion and shortage of breath set in to blunt the elation.

And now, all around was inspiring viewing to switch our minds from one emotion to another.

The colours of the landscape were everywhere different; slopes of slag-heap grey flanked by others of coral-red rock; peaks of black and blue granite above emerald-green foundations. Only at eventide did the land merge into a single hue when the last rays of the evening sun transformed the cordillera into a rose-red corrugation that would have earned an artist the accolade of surrealist.

We had eaten little all day: no more than a bar of chocolate, a packet of dry biscuits and some over-ripe cheese washed down by cold clear water from shimmering pools among the rocks. Setting up camp close to but below a ridge we made ourselves a substantial supper of macaroni and, because it was a heavy item to carry, a tin of some unidentifiable meat. A kind of blancmange followed but, by a mis-reading of the instructions, it became a beverage.

We had chosen an attractive site, though it offered no presentiment of the turbulent night ahead.

It started with a row; one of those bitter dissensions that break out between humans for no real rhyme or reason. I can't even remember how the fuse was lit – and it matters less. We shouted at one another, blew our tops, then smiled sheepishly. But it triggered the weather to bigger things. The darkness of the night was the more intense by virtue of storm clouds blown in our direction by a wind that, minutes before, was no more than a breeze. We fussed around the tent placing small boulders over pegs and tightening guy ropes, then crawled into our bags to ride out nature's tantrums, still aware of our own. About midnight we found ourselves struggling in the folds of nylon but, in both gale and darkness, could do little about re-erecting the tent. We settled down again with the material draped around us and prepared for sleep. But not for long.

'All we want now is for it to rain,' I grumbled, and the heavens promptly obliged with a stinging torrent. We lay miserably listening to the hailstones striking the rocks, feeling the cold wetness seeping through the nylon and wondering how long the storm would last. I attempted putting on more clothes but was unable to locate them, as rivulets of water leaked their way through those I wore.

Duplicating the form of our own dispute, the rain squall ceased as abruptly as it had started, allowing us to re-erect the tent, don more clothes and crawl back into wet sleeping bags. But sleep had fled.

Morning was a relief and we celebrated its dawning with a breakfast of egg powder and beans; its warmth better value than the taste. Glad to be away after a prolonged study of compass and map, we strode off at high speed, intent on re-galvanising stiff, damp limbs.

Rain clouds still dominated the sky, scudding and changing shape as they headed the way we had come. No more rain fell but what did descend around our ears was a gale-force wind that swept up the valley to engulf us in a cloud of powdered grit. I struggled to don my balaclava, soggy from the night's damping, and promptly lost it to the violent gusts.

We pressed on, collars up and heads down into the gale. Patches of hard, off-white snow lay strewn along the sheltered spots of the mountainside above us, not unlike the clusters of whitened bones of sheep we had passed earlier. The new valley into which we descended widened, the walls became less steep and the rounded peaks soared above our heads. As we neared the bottom, the wind dropped to a whisper and rents in the clouds showed a petticoat of blue sky.

The pattern of the subsequent days changed little. Our switchback progress made clear we were moving against the 'grain' of the mountains, crossing valleys and not following them. The path had petered out the second day and what we now followed became no more than a succession of ridge saddles, each selected by the demand of the compass. The weather remained dry for us, more by good luck, for we frequently observed rain falling elsewhere; heavy squalls deluging the peaks within grey mantles of waterlogged cotton wool. Not another living soul or animal did we come across; it was as if we were alone and fortuitously alive in a dead world. Only the great condors, gliding effortlessly overhead, assured us that life breathed in the universe.

It was while we were atop one of the interminable crests that we caught sight of fellow beings. There were five of them; five men riding horses or mules, leading pack animals. They were a good mile away, had not seen us, but were coming our way. There was something about them that prompted caution; a suspicion that these fellow-humans might not be so glad to see us as we had, initially, been to see them. A grassy dip offered cover so we crouched down in it and watched the band as they moved nearer. Two of them carried what looked like rifles slung over their shoulder and, from the direction they were riding, we judged they would pass no nearer than 500 yards. We remained silent, thoughtful and concealed.

As soon as men and beasts were out of sight we moved on again feeling a little foolish. Maybe they were perfectly innocent riders on legitimate business between villages with whom we could have conversed advantageously. Alternatively, we may have avoided having our throats cut.

A while later we came upon isolated sheep; a sure sign of an approach to human habitation. And not a false sign either since a ragged, poverty-stricken little community hove into view with the onset of evening. We camped out of sight of the place, our suspicions unabated.

We entered the village warily next morning but the suspicions now belonged to the villagers. The first of them we saw took hasty refuge in their houses and even the children – usually more inquisitive than timid – took to their heels. It was impossible to get near enough to any of them to attempt a conversation and, again, it was up to a schoolmaster to come to the rescue.

At least we think he was a schoolmaster though we saw no school. Anyway, the man spoke a little Spanish and, after words of greeting, David probed his knowledge of Incaic matters.

The man pointed to the east, to a low range of hills, grass-covered, almost homely; it put me in mind of my own Sussex Downs. Their crest, he indicated, marked the royal road's alignment. The revelation came as a huge relief and showed that we had not gone too far to the east as David feared. We thanked the gaunt figure profusely, pumping his hand with exaggerated fervour.

Two hours later we stood on the new crest, our eyes searching the rolling land. And sure enough, a grass track of familiar straightness softened by a few nature-formed indentations materialised. Our doubts not fully abated we followed it for many miles until the clarity weakened and the route veered to the west. Still unconvinced of its origins we sheered away where a junction offered a more northerly alignment.

We were reminded again how distances in these parts can be deceptive. Sihuas to Huamachuco may have been 100 miles as the crow flies but as two hikers slogged it – weaving about looking for landmarks and avoiding the more impossible walls of granite – it must have been in the region of two. At times we could see the great Cordillera Blanca with its 22 peaks of more than 19,500 feet, one of them – Huascaran – at 22,205 feet, Peru's highest. Even at our average altitude of between 12,000 and 13,000 we were buffeted and half-frozen by a succession of high winds, bitter cold nights and stinging downpours during the days that followed. Only in the late morning was the sun warm; the ground in the shadows remained firmly frozen. The thin, stony soil gave a minimum of sustenance to defiant clumps of coarse, yellowing grasses and alpine plants – often bearing minute, delicate blooms – hugging the ground. There were no trees; only tall ferns of the slow-growing, cactus-like *puyas*.

In such an environment animals are rare though there are rodents, lizards and tiny birds finding cover in the low vegetation, among rocks or in burrows. We never saw a puma but they exist here, as do the guanaco and the fast-running vicuna. These we had seen, as well as the Andean condor, the largest bird of prey in the world. The bird's great wingspan, which has been known to reach ten feet, enables it to glide effortlessly to 18,000 feet on up-currents of air, covering large distances with little exertion.

How we envied them the freedom of the sky. Our way ahead stretched into infinity, a horrific yet stirring panorama of mountain ranges and escarpments that, we were all too aware, would give us no respite even by the time we had conquered those we could make out in the far distance. But there was beauty too; beauty on a gigantic scale coupled with the compelling drama of isolation. Together they offered a combination that, on occasions, reduced us to a condition of suppressed terror and near-panic; a kind of agoraphobia.

Food, or the lack of it, was, once more, an ever-present concern. Our luxury items, purchased at Trujillo, ran out inside of a week, as did our basic provisions. Whenever we came across the smallest hamlet we would top up with potatoes, the staple diet of the Andean peasant as it became our own. Our emergency foods – honey, oatmeal cake and tins of sardines – were exhausted by the time the environs of Huamachuco began dotting the hillsides with villages and the chequerboard of cultivation.

Before Huamachuco, however, we were deflected off our route by the proximity and promise of a smaller but attractive-sounding town, Santiago de Chuco. Our map indicated but a short detour and we located the place with no great difficulty. But it soon became apparent that the charm of the township was vested solely in its surroundings. For us it became the location of a disturbing incident.

Walking along a street, intent upon re-provisioning our food stocks, we were accosted by a mean-faced individual who flashed a laminated card in our faces. 'Special Criminal Police,' he hissed in Spanish to reinforce his status. 'You will come with me.' Not even a 'please' accompanied the order.

Thus came our introduction to the dreaded P.I.P. of which we had heard; the Peruvian equivalent of the one-time Soviet

K.G.B. With ill-grace we followed the stranger to a building off the main street, speaking not a word.

The interrogation was little different to others I had experienced in similar circumstances in other parts of the world though in this latest instance it was half-hearted. So I turned on the heat a little and demanded our rights which seemed to unnerve him. Though initially threatening we were eventually released with some reluctance and our confiscated passports returned. What the man suspected remained a mystery, maybe he thought we had links with the *Sendero Luminoso* guerrillas that were becoming increasingly active.

The journey to Huamachuco was a two day one, the intervening night spent in a cowshed high in the hills while the second day was spent following the bank of the Yomobamba River which could well have been the original route of the royal road, or so David opined.

One of those impossible sunsets illuminated our entry into Huamachuco but darkness was complete by the time we reached the plaza lit by a necklace of electric bulbs. We bid farewell to Pedro, giving him a great bear hug; straightway feeling lonely and vulnerable without his company and horses.

There was no doubt now about being back on the royal road. The town is mentioned frequently in the chronicles of the Incan conquest while Pizarro's Spanish army is known to have rested here for four days after leaving Cajamarca for its southbound march of conquest in August 1533.

As yet untiring of urban living, we repaired to the best restaurant in town, a sizeable colonial building of large rooms and wooden balconies inward-looking round an internal patio. Most of the rooms were locked and deserted but seemed to form part of some sort of hostel, albeit a superior one of ornate doors and gilded mirrors. The meal was a friendly affair with the few diners and staff joining us at a big table, and everyone helping themselves from an enormous tureen of stew. Invited to lay out our sleeping bags on the restaurant floor we were to pass a further night without the necessity of having to raise the tent.

Before taking to the floorboards, however, we took ourselves for an evening stroll in the small town and had entered a store with the object of acquiring a toilet roll when P.I.P. struck again. The representative of the breed on this occasion was a viciously drunk moron who demanded our credentials and openly accused us of being vagabonds. He produced no warrant card or proof of his calling, so we initially ignored him though some sixth sense told me he was a *politico*. The chap followed us around, weaving a slightly erratic course, then disappeared to return later with a saner colleague as we were enjoying a hot rum punch at a well-patronised bar. The atmosphere in the establishment, all chat and gaiety one moment, abruptly froze into silent hostility the next as the two men scrutinised our passports and went through the contents of our pockets. All the while a barrage of questions directed at David had to be coped with as best he could. Then, once again, we were unaccountably dismissed. But Huamachuco had suddenly gone sour, so, downing our rums, we returned, subdued, to the restaurant and bed.

Forty kilometres away lay Cajamarca, famed for Pizarro's treachery, and from whence his small army commenced their southbound march. The road, fairly straight, ran through groves of eucalyptus, their silvery trunks silent sentinels lining our progress in the opposite direction to that taken by Pizarro's army. We pressed on, with frequent halts in a series of townships astride the road to Cajamarca. At Cajabamba we spent a night in a stable which offered yet another change of venue, though an attack by a dog, saliva dripping from its fangs, had first to be beaten off with a stick and a handful of stones.

The road thereafter took the only practical route by following a wide and ill-defined valley. Imparted morsels of intelligence wrung out of local people showed an encouraging awareness of their Inca heritage, the more so the nearer we approached Cajámarca. At Ichocan we camped in the plaza close to an assured water supply of an erratic fountain that donated a soaking every time we attempted to fill a kettle. No P.I.P. squads here; instead the police were most obliging even to the extent of helping in the erection of the tent on an empty flowerbed. Had we arrived a little earlier I have no doubt they would have offered us the best cell at the local nick.

From Ichocan onwards the landscape deteriorated into one of dry and barren semi-desert made the more disagreeable after days of lush, often cultivated vegetation. At San Marco a kindly lady pressed a cold guinea-pig steak apiece upon us and the townships of Matara, Namora and Llacanora became the final urban stages to Cajamarca, the road unfolding into a ribbon of Incaic ruler straightness. We camped the final night beside it amongst brown hills above the town.

That treachery can become a legend is nowhere shown so eloquently as at Cajamarca; 16 November 1532 is a date made infamous in the chronology of Inca annals. Not only is it that of the biggest double-cross in history but also the point in time when Spanish exploration turned to Spanish conquest. For it was here that Francisco Pizarro ambushed and captured Atahualpa, the Incan emperor, promising to release him for a ransom of a storeroom of gold. The emperor's order to scour his realm to amass the ransom was obeyed whereupon Pizarro had him murdered prior to his army commencing the march of conquest southwards.

For David and I, entering the suburbs of Cajamarca at first light, the town notched an important milestone of our journey.

Tourists were not exactly thick on the ground at Cajamarca but those who had found their way to the little town were left in no doubt as to the amount of treasure resulting from Francisco's ultimatum. The ransom chamber they were shown is, actually, not the original, which no longer exists. But no matter; its bareness conveyed the proportions of the treasure and brought the whole ugly incident to life. A white line drawn round the walls a few inches from the ceiling marked the 'high tide' of the gold and silver accumulation.

Three days we allowed ourselves in this most delightful of Peruvian urban centres. The Hotel Sucre – hardly the best hostelry in town – bore a distinct similarity to an open prison but was perfectly adequate for our basic needs. We had walked in on the royal road but where it left remained, to us, a mystery, as it did to all the citizens to whom we spoke. Our researches revealed the fact that it passed through Huancabamba, 30 miles from the Ecuadoran border, reached today by a devious road of assorted surfaces designated as 'Highway 1'. From the vantage point of Santa Apolonia no trace of an *agger* of the highway could be perceived, so its route could only be surmised.

To add to our problem was the fact that we held no large-scale maps covering the northward route; particularly that of the border area which was pronounced a military zone. Furthermore we had received express instructions, due to the then border dispute that existed between the two countries, not to attempt to cross into Ecuador anywhere except at Tumbes on the coast.

Thus for a period we were destined to come down from the mountains.

On a variety of vehicles including another massive high-sided Volvo truck, its buck full of prostrate passengers; a little Saab saloon driven by a Peruvian of Swedish stock; a stinking fish lorry that had a puncture requiring our cooperation in changing the wheel; and for many miles our own two feet along the dangerous, badly-surfaced Pan American Highway under a blazing sun, we made our way northward following the coast. Our route took us into towns such as Chepen, Chiclayo, Piura, Sullana, Talara, Mancora and, finally, Tumbes. The journey took several days with us resting at intervals, sleeping on deserted beaches and exploring the more interesting towns en route.

Peruvian only since 1941, Tumbes was very much the frontier town. The place was swarming with soldiers and, since most South American frontiers are ferocious affairs, we expected difficulties even though we were bona fide travellers. We both donned spectacles to make us look the more dignified and carried our rucksacks by hand in an effort to give the impression they were suitcases. Together with a letter I held from the British ambassador in Lima which I displayed haughtily to every minion of authority who showed the slightest sign of hostility, these precautions ensured a smooth transfer from Peru to Ecuador.

Aware that Ecuadorian public transport was considerably more efficient than that of Peru we took to the buses initially following the southern shore of the Gulf of Guayaquil, before turning inland to climb through lush, tropical greenery and timber houses raised on stilts around which the deep red, often-flooded soil had excited into growth multicoloured water lilies, watermelons, rice and a startling array of flowers.

All too soon altitude defeated this jungle-type terrain and among the foothills of distant mountains we were back in a customary wilderness of heaving scenery. Santa Isabel, perched on a near-vertical cliff, and Giron, a sizeable town, were the final landmarks before Cuenca, Ecuador's third city and one which, according to our reckoning, should have been astride or adjacent to the route of the royal road.

We arrived at midnight and found a room at a colonial building that housed an establishment labelled the 'Residentia de L'Inca' which, to us, was a good omen. The weather was cold again; all the lovely heat we had been cursing earlier had evaporated.

In all we spent four days in this historic city, a pause in our wanderings that was only slightly marred by a noisy invasion of our room in the middle of the second night. Ordered out of our beds while our rucksacks were searched by men in civilian suits and old-fashioned Homburg hats, that made them look like G-men of 1930s America, we stood shivering while every item of our belongings was scrutinised. Though the usual cellophane card had been flashed in our faces we were unable at first to identify the intruders but presumed them to be P.I.P. again, or its Ecuador equivalent.

'It's the criminal police,' David muttered, 'but I don't know what it's all about.'

Our soap and foot powder was to cause the most suspicion and the senior policeman applied small quantities to his tongue and seemed not to enjoy the flavour while the others watched enthralled. Expressions turned from high expectation of a drugs discovery to downright disappointment as the chief shook his head and, without a word of apology or explanation, the men withdrew from the room.

We made our way out of Cuenca in the rain to trudge over waterlogged grassland, trying to keep off the tarmac of the modern highway which, all too likely, was the exact route of the royal road. The ground was hilly but not exhaustingly so and in this manner, after more days of plodding and nights spent in our bivouac, we arrived at Ingapirca, our immediate objective.

Ingapirca means 'Stone of the Inca' and was, without the slightest doubt, astride the royal way. The squat structure – fortress, temple, royal *tampo* and probably observatory – is well-preserved while being Ecuador's sole remaining worthwhile souvenir of the Inca period. It lay, an imposing pile, upon an outcrop of hill and titivated to a well-nigh ludicrous degree for tourist consumption.

The way to Quito, the Ecuadorian capital and terminus of the original royal road, led through the renowned valley of the volcanoes and, our disappointment arising from the deficiency of Incaic mementoes of that road, was, to some extent, mitigated by close proximity to these mighty peaks. Already in sight – when no rain clouds obscured the view – were the giants of Sangay, Chimborazo, Carihuairazo, Altar and Tungurahua. Not the highest but certainly the most remote, explosive and dangerous was Sangay which, with Chimborazo, was to occupy our attentions to the exclusion of matters Inca but everything to do with mountains for a number of days.

115

Mount Chimborazo, every near-22,000 feet of it, is actually a volcano. In the Indian language the name means 'Mountain of Snow', which is no overstatement. A massif of overwhelming scale, Alexander Humboldt only *nearly* succeeded in scaling it in 1802 while Joseph Dieudonne Boussingault, in 1831, likewise failed; halted at 19,290 feet by 'an impossible ravine'. The summit is the nearest point on earth to the sun.

At that time Chimborazo was believed to be the highest mountain in the world before Everest claimed the distinction. Eventually Chimborazo was conquered by Edward Whymper in 1880 and today it is climbed fairly frequently – but not, I declare, by elderly men in glorified gym shoes.

Our subsequent preoccupation with volcanoes began with an ill-fated attempt to reach the base of Mount Sangay, a 17,500-foot monster that, unlike Chimborazo, was treacherously active to the extent of it having killed two British climbers earlier that very year. One of the injured survivors of the party was Richard Snailham, explorer, author and instructor at the Royal Military Academy, Sandhurst, whom David and I knew quite well. When told that the route of our journey would pass close to Sangay he had suggested that we might care to try and reach it with a view to giving a proper burial to the dead climbers if the lava flow had not done so already.

The actual ascent of Sangay peak is not difficult; the challenge lies in reaching the base of the mountain through an almost impenetrable belt of forest bush. This challenge seemed to be more in my line of possible accomplishment and for days we hacked and tore at the thick undergrowth with machetes, our semi-naked bodies drenched in both sweat and non-stop tropical rain until utter exhaustion forced our abandonment of the attempt.

Physically and mentally drained we returned to Riobamba, the nearest town, and it was here we met Willie, an experienced 29-year-old Bavarian climber, whose single-minded aspiration was the conquest of the highest peak in the Ecuadorian Andes – Chimborazo. To attempt the climb alone, he explained, would be foolhardy, since with what was then but a single refuge cabin at the halfway mark and no mountain rescue facilities whatsoever, even a minor mishap could be fatal. So would we accompany him? The young impetuous David agreed at once; the novelty of a snow-and-ice climb attractive after months of rock and rain plus a defeat inflicted by Sangay. 'No way!' said I, my protestations loud and clear. But when Willie, looking pityingly at me, remarked 'You're too old anyway,' my blood was up. I bridled and swallowed my protest. Wild horses, I affirmed to myself, couldn't prevent me from scaling the confounded mountain, even though 1,000 miles of walking and weeks of semi-starvation had me far from the peak of fitness. It's always the same. Germans have this disconcerting effect on me.

Our initial move was to make contact with the Andean Mountaineering Club of Chimborazo which had its office in Riobamba and this led to an amiable meeting with its president, Enrique Valez, who was all too forthcoming with the loan of equipment vital for making the ascent. But either Ecuadorian feet are characteristically small or my feet are unusually large, for they defeated every proffered climbing boot in his store. A pair of crampons was dubiously offered, however, in the pious hope that I could find a method of fastening them to the canvas-topped jungle boots I had been using for rough country walking. Signor Valez was also lavish with advice and proceeded to frighten the life out of me by explaining that, because of the equatorial bulge, the summit of Chimborazo was the point on the earth's surface that is furthest from the centre and that only experienced mountaineers should attempt the ascent. 'We *are* all experienced climbers of course?' he asked and my attempted denial was painfully kicked into silence by David. The good man then stressed the vital necessity of attaining the single refuge cabin at 16,000 feet before nightfall prior to a pre-dawn assault on the summit. 'Miss the refuge and you will almost certainly succumb to exposure. It's cold up there,' he had added, though tempering this heart-stopping declaration with the comforting fact that the path to the refuge – and there was only one – was easy to follow and should have us at the cabin within three hours. He didn't actually say 'You can't miss it', but this one rosy feature of the whole dismal catalogue of revelations was all I had to cheer me up.

Loaded down with crampons, ice axes, coils of rope, snow-goggles and gauntlets, we caught a bus to Ambato, a further step along the valley nearer Quito. Ambato is described as the Andean version of 'The Garden of Eden', and though I would not put it quite like that, it did exhibit a certain grace. However, we had little time to dwell upon its charms before catching a local bus that passed through the village of Pogyo from whence the path was alleged to start. But nobody had mentioned the place consisted of no more than five stucco dwellings and that it was sometimes known as Poggios. Needless to say we missed it and were finally dropped at a village some distance beyond. The error was to prove our first disaster although upon alighting from the vehicle Chimborazo, hiding its head in thick grey cloud, looked deceptively close.

Our fellow bus travellers had added to my growing unease by loudly expressing the view that we were attempting the climb entirely at the wrong time of year, that we'd assuredly lose ourselves in the virtually perpetual fog and that our carcasses would lie on the hillside for months before being found. However, at the point where we had left these prophets of doom a trail did indeed lead up the side of an escarpment in the right direction and we followed it in the knowledge that there were more than six hours of daylight left us to locate the correct route and reach the cabin. 'There's no problem,' announced the alpine-experienced Willie. 'Keep going and we'll hit the right path.'

Arms of lava soil, softened by gaunt springy thickets, pushed down to meet us before the false track petered out into a morass of volcanic rocks and scree made the more treacherous by isolated patches of snow. It was cold and the cold increased as we progressed upwards.

For a while the way ahead, steadily rising, showed clear, but around mid-afternoon the grey cloud descended to obliterate everything in an icy embrace, moving steadily across the face of the mountain blown by a rising wind. The realisation that we were lost struck even Willie so we fanned out as best we could, like beaters at a grouse shoot, attempting to locate a non-existent track or, better still, an elusive cabin.

Hours later Willie's altitude-meter, together with the emergence of the snow-line, confirmed the fact that we had exceeded 16,000 feet; too high above the level of the refuge, and so switched to a downhill search. My breath was already turning to agonising pants and my movements limited to bursts of a dozen footsteps between pauses. David too was surprisingly distressed having not yet found his second wind, but Willie, born and bred in the Bavarian Alps, was hopping about like a mountain goat.

Above us a local peak abruptly emerged from the mist and, perhaps because it was the only visible ground in the clear light of a dying day, we made for it as one, climbing and scrambling with a certain desperation. My feet were already cold; my socks saturated. Underfoot the ground was solid snow and ice hiding sharp lava rock. One moment all was grey nothing; the next the cloud had parted to reveal a glimpse of a wondrous panorama.

Far below, the valley of the volcanoes was hidden by the grey blanket. Protruding from it were the peaks of other volcanoes and mountains. Directly to the south-east was 16,000-foot Altar and, behind, less distinct but recognisable, was a cone that could only have been Sangay. Their snow-capped glory was tinted an amazing blood-red which turned deeper with every second as the sunset matured and faded. The sight was dumbfounding and eclipsed for a moment the dread welling up within me. At least I could be thankful to my

Maker for showing me a manifestation almost worth dying for.

With the setting sun came a terrible cold and hastily we scrabbled to a lip of level ground. Here we held council, consumed some food and squirmed, fully dressed, into our sleeping bags to prepare, it has to be said, for the 'Great Beyond'. 'It's imperative you reach the hut': I heard again Enrique's warning. Childhood recollections of Captain Oates going out into the blizzard of the South Pole to die assailed me and, as if we had all been struck by the same notion, there began a surreptitious scribbling of last wills and testaments on scraps of toilet paper for the benefit of our next-of-kin and those who would eventually find our frozen bodies. 'Get in close. Hug one another like bears,' commanded Willie. 'We must generate all the warmth we can. It's our only hope.' The German was firmly in control and I, for one, had no objection. I snuggled close to my companions and thought about death. Above, the myriad stars made a heavenly ceiling and I no longer felt the cold. All in all it seemed not a bad way to go.

I came to with a bursting bladder and what appeared to be a fever. So it was to Hell I'd been despatched; I knew I ought to have gone to church more often. I started to wriggle free from the cocoon of bodies and straightway felt the biting wind. But what startled me most was that not only was I still on earth but sweating like the proverbial pig. My movement had awakened the others and gradually David and Willie sleepily inched away from one another content to finish the night in less fetid conditions.

Daylight, clear of cloud, showed us the refuge cabin, a wooden octagonal structure painted a brilliant orange, directly beneath and barely 100 yards distant. It seemed to be laughing at us as we rose sheepishly, screwing up and discarding our paper wills as we did so.

Thereafter everything went more or less according to plan. We spent the new day alternating between cooking and eating in the filthy little cabin which we cleaned as best we could. All around were discarded tin cans and food wrappers; some almost vintage Edward Whymper. The name of the then only refuge was Fabian Zurita, and whoever he was he's welcome to it.

To attain the summit and return to the refuge before nightfall it was necessary to set out by three o'clock in the morning. At dusk we therefore climbed back into our sleeping bags intent upon getting in as much sleep as possible before the pre-dawn start. In the event we spent a sleepless night warding off the overtures of friendly mountain rats that emerged from the floorboards to investigate our cooking appliances and nibble our hair and ears. Willie, in true Teutonic fashion, murdered a couple with his ice-axe and it was he who chivvied us out of bed at one o'clock to laboriously melt snow to make tea before setting off at three. Outside was pitch darkness but the wind had died and the cold not so painful. Our early breakfast of stale rat-nibbled rolls and packet soup had not been appetising but Willie, exerting his mountaineering authority once more, forced us to swallow it. 'Food is warmth. It'll keep you alive,' he pronounced, sounding like a survival manual.

Though dawn was nowhere to be seen a feeble moon illuminated the snow to dilute the darkness. We made slow progress up steep escarpments of more lava rock and across sharp black scree frozen solid in a cement of ice. Ten paces. Stop. Ten paces. Stop. It was the best I could do. At intervals I retched, my head between my knees, as altitude sickness struck. We rested ever more frequently in spite of the gathering cold that crept insidiously through our layers of clothing. Willie and David remained ahead of me so that their halts commenced before I could reach them, a state of affairs which coaxed me into new paroxysms of effort to catch up and so obtain at least some of my entitlement of rest. Two steps up. One slip back. Stop. Ten paces. Stop.

We reached the glacier at 18,000 feet and clumsily affixed our crampons. I had never worn crampons before and they, in their turn, had never had to be affixed to jungle boots. Hardly had we moved off again, when they parted company to slide impishly down the sloping glacier floor with me limping and cursing in hot pursuit. The corrugated ice surface cracked and groaned ominously, putting me into a sweat of terror. Willie tried to be reassuring. 'I think it's safe,' he observed. 'Bending ice is usually safe ice,' a rejoinder that might have been more appropriate for an afternoon's skating on the village pond.

I never thought we would ever get off that glacier. Even Willie showed signs of exhaustion as we finally stepped onto soft snow into which, of course, my boots sank to dislodge anew my crampons. Dawn had broken though we had hardly noticed it. The wind rose again to cut through our long-johns, double socks and gauntlets while, through our snow-goggles, we perceived a grey world instead of a black one. My hair and beard turned me into a caricature of Jack Frost.

Beneath the overhang of a cliff known as 'Red Wall' we paused to eat some biscuits and chocolate. The cold was so intense it had even me raring to move. We circled the base of the great bulwark hung with long icicle daggers pointing down on our heads and swung again upwards. The soft snow turned to hard snow once more, hiding deep gashes of ice. Willie unslung his nylon rope and attached it to the three of us. This is where I really make a fool of myself and let the side down I thought but, heavy slog though it was, I had at last found my own second wind and so made reasonable progress behind David, stepping into his footprints as he did in Willie's. In front the German was moving forward with great care, testing each footfall with a view to avoiding the many awesome crevasses, some virtually invisible.

The breach in the wall was easier to find than expected. I was not to know that Edward Whymper had written into his report the warning: 'Thus far and no farther a man may go who is not a mountaineer'. Thus I was about to trespass into a realm of the chosen few as we started up the steep slope of frozen snow punctuated by outcrops of slippery, ice-coated rock. We moved at a snail's pace partly on account of the necessity for extreme caution on the climb out of Red Wall, but mostly because of the laggard at the end of the rope who could move no faster had all the hounds of hell been snapping at his heels.

The nausea that had slowed my footsteps on the glacier returned with a vengeance. This time it was more than exhaustion. I had been sick earlier but now my condition worsened and I vomited uncontrollably at ever-increasing intervals. The symptoms of the malady were not those described by Sebastian Snow who gained Chimborazo's summit in recent years. He called it *soroche*; it had him shivering from head to foot to very nearly defeat him. With me, as long as I could rest at frequent intervals, I was able to continue. But as with all climbers of this mountain, we were working against the clock and, should darkness fall before return to the refuge, our chances of surviving a second night on a bare mountain above 20,000 feet would be virtually nil.

It was this fact and the fear of risking the lives of my companions that pushed me to the limits of endurance. At times I was even able to keep pace with momentary bursts of super-human energy.

The gradient steepened as we shuffled towards its crest, our heels and toe-caps kicking for holds. All feeling had left my hands and feet, and movement became no more than a mechanical reaction to my will. I had long since discarded my crampons which I had slung around my neck.

Willie's altimeter recorded a height of 19,650 feet when we came to the largest crevasse, possibly the one that defeated the French climber, Boussingault. My eyes saw it but my brain refused to function so that the revelation of the consequences of its existence failed to register. We approached with extreme caution and, keeping away from the treacherous edge, Willie tried to gauge its depth. The width was certainly in excess of 50 feet though the depth of this snow and ice ravine was anybody's guess. Working our way along the fissure we discovered, to our relief, that it narrowed dramatically to an ominous crack no more than a few feet wide.

Willie selected a spot that he considered a reasonable crossing point and, thrusting his ice-axe into the snow, inched forward on the anchored rope to as close to the rim as he dared. Satisfied that the gap was leapable, even if he had to trust to providence that the landing point would hold, he turned to David and me. 'If the lip gives way and I go down, brake my fall and haul me up,' he charged. 'Come on, let's go.' Retrieving his ice-axe he watched while David and I played out a few more yards of rope.

Gingerly Willie stole to the very edge of the crevasse in the knowledge that, in all probability, it was an overhang that could crumble at any moment. He bunched himself, and leapt.

He landed safely with a foot to spare, sprawling forward as he did so. The rope tautened, pulling him back towards the opposite lip and feverishly we played out more to allow him to scramble away. He turned to give a 'thumbs up' signal, intimating that it was our turn to negotiate the obstacle.

David, utilising Willie's footprints, repeated the German's movements and, without a second's hesitation, jumped to land easily on the other side. He scrambled to Willie's side.

I too forced myself to undertake a carbon copy of my colleagues' actions, inwardly blessing the good Lord for having favoured me with a commendable schooldays long-jumping record. Then I too hurled myself towards the opposite lip, landed clumsily and started to fall back but was restrained painfully by the rope which bit into my flesh. We were across the chasm and all still in one piece.

The snow grew softer and deeper. Chimborazo's southern summit – the Whymper Summit as it is sometimes called – was but a slog of a few hundred yards distant. The three of us forged on, each footfall a struggle to remove a leg from the clinging snow.

Reaching the head of the ridge a wind of intense ferocity rose to sear the exposed portions of our faces. Frozen flecks of ice stung my ears and the bitter cold numbed anew my inadequately-covered limbs. The snow grew deeper still; the struggle to free our legs more frantic. Maybe the effort of combating the trapping of our feet served to prevent the cold from overwhelming us; I don't know. All that my crippled mind would register was the necessity to conquer the accursed mountain now that I had got this far. Nothing else – nothing at all – mattered. Life itself had become subservient to the single aim of putting myself on the summit. Never before had I experienced such strength of purpose for so unimportant a reason and I hope I shall never again, for it is a kind of madness; a spasm of insanity that turns the famed champions of geography into an elite of men and women.

But the spasm goaded me to the southern summit. Less than 50 yards separated us from the western peak, the true summit of Chimborazo. Time was inexorably ticking away but all rational thought had been cast aside.

We made for the final ridge in line abreast, still roped together but no longer working as a team. The snow rose to our thighs so that, at times, we were crawling; lying flat on the surface; attempting to avoid having to make a downward thrust on a leg that would only be trapped in a freezing cast. The wind increased to a shrieking crescendo; a sound akin to maniacal laughter at our feeble thrashings.

I have never used an ice-axe before or since but the one I wielded clumsily that day on Chimborazo – reaching out to sink the blade into virgin snow ahead of me and hauling myself bodily towards it – taught me a new method of motivation. Gradually, painfully, it narrowed the gap until all three of us attained the crest. Our combined crazed laughter – a song of triumph – was instantly carried away by the wind. Unable to stand on the peak I could only sit on it. The cold was excruciating; if this was the closest point on earth to the sun it certainly didn't feel like it.

The way down to the base of the Red Wall made for something of an anti-climax; to me the happiest event of the climb. Willie brought his disciplinary measures to bear and bade us exercise the greatest care on the descent which involved less effort but was the more dangerous. Still roped, we returned across the great crevasse and beyond, David and I again slavishly utilising Willie's prints to avoid other pitfalls that lay in wait, hidden by the snow.

Cloud obscured the view below, as it had from the summit, and I did not like the look of the wisps of mist building up and rising from the base of the mountain. I was eager to return to less spectacular altitudes, preferably around sea-level. The moment of triumph had receded and though, years later, I was told by an eminent climber that for my age and lack of proper climbing gear I had broken some sort of Chimborazo record, I retain the firm conviction that mountaineering is not for me under any circumstances whatsoever.

A well-earned day of rest back in Ambato and David and I were on our way again, following our original route as if the interludes of Sangay and Chimborazo had never happened. We had attained Ambato in the back of a lorry loaded with chaff, a pig and ten humans. The chaff got into my eyes, the pig was sick over my boots and, along with the other humans, David and I lay on the floor to avoid being seen at the police checkpoint in the suburbs of the town since, apparently, there was an Ambato bye-law forbidding lifts on lorries.

A further three days of walking a route that may or may not have been Incan and, abruptly tiring of the fruitless footslog, we caught another luxury coach to complete the odyssey to Quito. Above us, lost in cloud, were the peaks of

Catopaxi and Tungurahua; but I'd had my fill of volcanoes. The road was almost certainly that of the route of the royal artery but it lay under tarmac and was now called the Pan-American Highway. Only Incan ghosts might have noticed our inconspicuous entry into the Ecuadorian capital – but I doubt it.

Chapter Four

TRAVELS ON RIVER AND SEA

IN WHICH THE AUTHOR COMES TO THE RESCUE OF A GLAMOROUS PUBLIC FIGURE WITH THE AID OF TWO MARS BARS, NEGOTIATES WHITE WATER RAPIDS IN KENYA, SUFFERS SEVERAL DISASTERS ABOARD THE *ADAMSON* AND SCARES AWAY ELEPHANTS IN HEWANI.

It was, I think, Gerald Durrell who made the statement that expeditioning was for commerce, curiosity or fun – and in that order. Few modern explorers – or expeditioners – can pretend that curiosity and fun did not enter their scheme of things; indeed curiosity must be the fundamental driving power of any explorer.

HOWEVER, WHEN PONDERING upon the activities of the 1976 Tana River Expedition in Kenya, it is not difficult to insist that a fourth criterion be added – benevolence. For it must be said that the multitudinous findings of the scientists and laymen of this expedition were, and were intended to be, for the greater benefit of Kenya, its government and, in particular, the Tana River Development Authority as well as the National Museums of Kenya. And it was the celebrated Richard Leaky who, on their behalf, accepted the offer made by the leader of the proposed expedition, the chief source of which was students of the Polytechnic of Central London (now the University of Westminster), to undertake a journey down East Africa's longest river with the object of making an in-depth study of the environment, its wildlife and tribespeople.

The reasoning behind the project lay with the Kenyan government's plan to place irrigation dams on the Tana River which would be likely to affect life along its banks. All in all an undertaking that, when completed, was to earn high praise from its benefactors.

Thus here, on an unsympathetic waterway, were rewarding tasks to perform that, if it does not sound too grandiose, could benefit mankind. An adventurous waterway, nevertheless, that sprouts on a 17,000-foot mountain, frolics youthfully amidst untamed rapids and courses maturely through wild animal-infested bush far from civilisation – surely the linchpin of any expedition.

When invited to join the Tana River expedition as its author, it was the idea of a conquest of a river that set my non-scientific mind aflame. I dug around in my local library and a number of facts and statistics about the Tana began to emerge. A length of 600 kilometres to 1,200 kilometres, said the books, with variations in-between, which to me indicated that, because of its remoteness, nobody knew much about this particular waterway. 'A wild, inhospitable, disease-ridden, mosquito-laden waterway stretching in a wide arc from the slopes of Mount Kenya to the coast of the Indian Ocean' stated an older volume, while exploration history produced names like Denhard, Fischer, Gregory and a paddle steamer named *Kenia*.

More recently, I learnt, sections of the lower Tana had been covered by a couple of hardy canoeists. But more ominous from a potential environmental point of view was the dam at Kindaruma. Electricity is important to the less-developed portions of Africa but progress so often stalks hand in hand with destruction. I began to see where, how and why our scientific survey and our ecological and medical investigations in the riverine forests could serve a useful purpose.

I found it impossible to pinpoint the source of the Tana. Maps I looked at showed the river with firm determination upwards to Sagana, but thereafter the cartographers had hesitated and moved vaguely away to Mount Kenya. So it was to a 17,000-foot mountain complex, snow-covered, ice-bound and very un-African that I had to travel, to discover how the Tana was born.

It was not all 25 members of the Tana River Expedition who staggered, heavily laden, up the Teleki valley route to the base of the triple mountain. We were just a handful of them, labelled somewhat regally the 'Mountain Team'. And since I was designated the expedition chronicler, I had to go with them.

The expedition as a whole, led by Nigel Winser (today the Deputy Director of the Geographical Society, London), had arrived in Nairobi some ten days earlier, against the unpredictable violence of Black African political upheaval and to the beat of twentieth-century war drums. Delayed by an attempted Sudanese coup in Khartoum, uncertain of the tempo and depth of penetration of hostile Somali nomads towards the Tana River, and following a run-in with Idi Amin's grisly security police in neighbouring Uganda and subsequently being forced to flee that country to highlight the then Kenyan-Ugandan border crisis, we were somewhat doubtful of our credentials until Kenya's Minister for Tourism and Wildlife made us welcome at a press reception held in Nairobi's plush Norfolk Hotel.

So while the scientists pitched their base camp close to George Adamson's lion rehabilitation centre at Kora Rock, the mountaineers made the altitude-acclimatising slog to Lake Hohnel, an oval gem of cold water, from which one lone stream emerges. But it is not the Tana that goes tinkling joyfully down the valley protected by ranks of giant groundsel. What maps there were called it the Nairobi River, which is an unfortunate name for so slender a stream that withers away until, infused and transfused by tributaries, it re-emerges as the Tana.

Being of an age when one is not ashamed to take the easy way out, I was quite prepared at 15,000 feet to call it a day and backtrack with the river to lower climes, for we had accomplished our initial task of pin-pointing the source of the Tana. But I was forgetting that I was with real climbers. Captain Harley Nott, RE, with much climbing expertise beneath his belt; Captain Robert Williamson of the Royal Green Jackets, a fanatical newcomer to the alpine suicide club; and young, 23-year-old Richard Matthews, the expedition stills photographer, who, like me, had to cover all the expedition activities – all were made of sterner stuff. Only the planting of a mythical flag on Batian and Nelion, the highest peaks, could offer a consideration of leaving the mountain.

Anyway, we all climbed Lenana of 16,300 feet – even me – to show how easy it was, though the weather conditions made the climb quite a treacherous undertaking. And as I expected, the mountain's third highest peak simply put pep into those suicidal tendencies of the others. My only ally was 'Doc' John Richardson, the fourth member of the team, who suffered vertigo as badly as I suffered lack of breath. On the way to the refuge hut at the base of the trio of summits I was accompanied by a good-looking girl who, in the rarefied atmosphere, was in some distress and to whom I sacrificed two of my precious Mars bars to alleviate her hunger. It was not until later did she reveal the fact that she was Caroline Kennedy, daughter of the late president of the United States.

The Tana is put to work, like many of its peoples, at an early age. When still a child and meandering through Kikuyu Country, it becomes, unromantically, a drainage source for the little mud-and-straw hut villages along the way. From the virgin forest that girdles Mount Kenya, the river scenery changes to that of sparsely-spaced trees and brown bush that choke all efforts by other plants to grow. The lush grass banks give way to sand, soft and powdery and burning hot.

At Kindaruma the first of the planned complex of concrete dams deflected the Tana into slavery, there to drive a budding hydro-electric scheme that would, eventually, send its reverberations outwards to the distant corners of Kenya. Even in 1976 its repercussions were not entirely composed of blessings for those folk who dwelt along the river's banks. The Tana emerged from these indignities a different river. Gone was the placid stream; instead, a sullen waterway, dark with anger, drove into a harsh territory of solid rock. The battle of water against rock began and, metaphorically speaking, the Tana lowered its head for the charge.

Of course we had a team for this subsequent section of the river. The 'White Water Team', like that of the 'Mountain Team', was composed of alleged experts, enthusiastic amateurs and those, like myself, whose expedition task required a presence. Another soldier, Captain Paul Turner of the Queen's Own Hussars, had been a member of the support team of the Zaire River Expedition, while Richard Matthews, with me on the mountain, had undergone experience of rapids-shooting on the West Ethiopia Expedition of 1974. Each was therefore designated captain of our two Avon Adventurer inflatables, *Adamson* and *Thesiger,* with the former, under Paul Turner, taking the lead. The total complement of each boat was four. Our support team of two, in a radio-equipped Toyota, was to meet us downstream at the first scheduled rendezvous some 40 miles and two days from where we put into the river not many miles below the dam; an inspired piece of over-optimism as I had ever come across!

Our first rapids negotiation was of no great feat of accomplishment. Both boats took it in fine style and though the greener of us watched the swift approach of a four-foot drop into a cauldron of boiling water with some trepidation, the mental relief and physical exhilaration of coming out the other side unscathed got our adrenalin going. It was my baptism of fire. Adorned like the others in crash helmet and lifejacket, I even managed to persuade myself that I enjoyed it. As we progressed downstream, nosing into and out of what I was told were no more than moderate rapids, each hour of alternate terror and exhilaration was exhausting to say the least.

'The golden rule is to keep the front of the boat straight towards the tongue,' repeated Paul. He never wasted nautical terms on his landlubber crew, and by 'tongue' we had come to learn that he was referring to a 'slipway' of water by which one attempted to enter the maelstrom. The trick was to choose the right tongue. Some led straight onto huge boulders that could tear the bottom out of the boat; others directed a movable object straight over a horrific drop. The choice lay in the captain's judgement; sometimes a split-second judgement when racing water launched the boat straight at a subsequent set of rapids before recovery could be affected from a previous one. Usually it was possible to stop and assess the gravity of the obstacle and even select a theoretical route through it. Paul had also overflown the tortuous route of the middle Tana by light aircraft a few weeks previously. But it all seemed a dicey kind of game to the likes of me as the rapids became ever more violent.

By last light we had covered fifteen miles and were, on occasions, sweeping down angry waters in every position except forward – a novel but not-to-be-recommended procedure – so we called it a day and spent the night under the stars listening to the enraged growlings of a hippo whose pad we had usurped.

The next day became 'the day of the portages', when we had to hump the boats and our gear by land round unnegotiable obstacles – by which I mean full-scale waterfalls, narrow chasms and the like which even Paul saw fit to avoid. Portaging is the most exhausting and dispiriting of occupations particularly when, having finally reloaded the boats, one rounds the next bend to find the whole operation has to be repeated again. The strain of humping the loads across a jumble of huge boulders showed in our subsequent performance over one particularly hairy set of rapids. In one horrific pitch and toss *Adamson's* cargo, which included a 100 lb outboard engine and a five-gallon drum of petrol, took off six feet into the air! In all we accomplished no more than five miles that day.

Day three was an unmitigated disaster. A small but surprisingly violent rapid shook us out of our early morning lethargy and then we were back to portaging again. At one point we were swept into a cul-de-sac from which we had to extricate ourselves against the strong current. This bit four hours out of our day. Two sets of rapids later and the Tana fell over a cliff into a gorge. Another portage over a near-vertical wall under the usual blazing sun and the two boats were ploughing into a nightmare of chaotic water. Sideways on, *Adamson* smashed against a boulder, filled, and stuck fast, her crew clinging to the side or striking for the shore. We managed to get the boat on to dry land just as *Thesiger*, equally out of control, arrived to collide with the same rock.

Unfortunately, this time, £200 worth of photographic equipment was lost before her frenzied crew could make her fast. The portage that followed was made along half a mile of cliff face upon which a fly would have disdained to settle. How nobody managed to break a leg or their neck I shall never understand. With the boats reloaded at the far end of the gorge, Paul announced, 'Just one more shoot and then we'll camp for the night so let's make it a good one.'

Adamson went first. We caught the tongue head on and were in the grip of untamed power. Our frantic paddling and Paul's barks of command had not the slightest effect. The boat gyrated, spun sideways and bucked madly against the thrashing torrent, tore over a hidden boulder backwards, spun again and hit a solid bulwark of water. The thick rubber walls of the inflatable buckled and the bow shot skywards – Paul and I were ejected like spent cartridges from the stern; the others managed to retain a hold on the upturned craft. In the vortex of a whirlpool – probably the only whirlpool in the Tana – I was sucked under, spinning, into deep water. A roaring in my ears, an eerie calm and darkness enveloped me. 'So this is what it's like to drown,' I told myself, even applauding the method as not a bad way to leave this earth. But the Tana seemingly disapproved and spat me out, whereupon reaching the surface I battled for my life in the thrashing water, finally managing to crawl ashore some way downstream. Paul too emerged, shaken but unharmed and, still further downstream, the other two crew members succeeded in beaching the deflated and torn boat before it could be swept away with its now doubly-tied down cargo. *Thesiger,* wisely, made no attempt to follow though her reticence cost her crew yet another portage.

But the tribulations of the 'White Water Team' were not yet over. With another and larger gorge and more wild rapids to follow, the way ahead was barred. One boat was now out of action and our two-day rations were virtually exhausted leaving us stranded and lost in the remote bush. After a night's sleep in a clearing, scavenging parties succeeded in making contact with the local Wakamba hunters – a bow-and-arrow tribe – while the fishermen of the crews began pulling catfish out of the Tana. At least starvation could be averted.

In the meantime the support group, concerned at our non-appearance at the arranged rendezvous, had raised the alarm. A light aircraft was despatched carrying Nigel Winser which, flying down the river, eventually located our encampment and dropped food and messages. At last, appreciative as we were of the Wakamba's hospitality, we were relieved to see that Land Rovers had fought their way through impenetrable bush to evacuate us.

Coming from the cold of the mountains and acute discomfort of the rapids to the idyllic sanity of the Scientific Team's initial base camp at Kora was a balm. To me it was, without doubt, the finest of the half-dozen main camps later to be established between Kora and the mouth of the river. For three weeks the scientists had been here so there had been time to improve its amenities; later camps were of no more than a week's duration which gave less time for improvement. If there was a village called Kora I never saw it. There was a Kora Rock, an immense granite boil on the face of the flat bush country, but that was all. As both a terminal and terminus it indicated the end of the Tana's youthful tantrums and the beginning of a more serene adult progress through the riverine forests. From Kora onwards the civilised world would seem not only non-existent but nearly impossible to envisage. Life's usual mundane preoccupations were to be completely replaced by the most sensitive attention to noises and movement. We too would become creatures of awareness, attentiveness, quietness and not a little fear.

Though I was at Kora for just a few days it gave me an introduction to the nature of the work of the scientists and to life in the bush and jungle. Birds, bugs and butterflies all came under close scrutiny as did the larger beasts of the forest. Of particular interest was the use of the image intensifier, an expensive piece of equipment that enabled their operator to observe and photograph animals at night. In retrospect I will always look upon Kora as a 'safe' camp; I never saw a 'dangerous' animal there except for the odd crocodile and hippo in the river. At night, however, I lay awake in my sleeping bag gazing at a sky ablaze with stars, listening to the unexplained noises of the living jungle with the recognised growl of a lion. The only threat came from human sources. Local inhabitants were few and far between and what natives there were consisted of roving Somalis, and in Kora and elsewhere we would see these scowling nomads, with their endless herds of camels and goats grazing their way past our camps. Many were *shifta*, a kind of bandit/guerrilla, for this north-east corner of Kenya had long been a breeding ground of strife.

My few days at Kora went by all too soon. Many geographical authors had referred to the Tana as a faunal barrier. This the expedition hoped to disprove. Accompanying the scientists on their business in the forests at first had me somewhat nonplussed. Taken individually the tasks appeared insignificant; almost childish in their simplicity. How could the examination, collection and occasional dissection of a little furry creature or pretty butterfly help mankind to delve into the complex and massive problems of the development and harnessing of a great river? But gradually over the months that followed I could see that our mission, in fact, was that of bringing tiny chinks of light where before there was only darkness; small beginnings where there had been next to nothing.

Our boats were a 15-foot Avon Professional and two 12-foot Redshanks as well as a lame jet boat that had failed to operate properly and so had to be propelled by hand. My craft was initially *East Midlander,* one of the Redshanks, captained by John Richardson, with Alison, one of the four female members of the expedition, as my fellow crewman. Our first objective was the tribal village of Saka, some 50 miles downstream, where our vehicle support team were to meet us.

The bush drew closer to the river as we paddled our way steadily downstream; that both offered life as well as death was emphasised by the sight of buck coming down to its edges to drink. They made a beautiful sight; so gentle and delicate, yet so aware of the close proximity of predators.

With the jet boat leading the way and locating the most advantageous currents and channels we advanced upon the first hippo herd in the full knowledge of their presence. We could see their low foreheads and protruding eyes above the water level some distance away so had ample warning. We proceeded quietly and the beasts, assured we constituted no great threat, continued their cavorting until, one by one, their heads submerged. Being at first ignorant of the ways of hippo, though fully aware that they were one of the most dangerous animals of all, we imagined them to be approaching in the manner of hostile submarines and this fallacy was given impetus by the optical illusion created by a twig sticking out of the moving river and creating a furrow of water, a tiny bow wave seemingly making for the boat. Only when we were well beyond the group did the heads re-appear, their eyes again upon us with curiosity and distrust.

The voyage to Saka was scheduled as two days but in the event took four. The up-river dams had lowered the water level, necessitating hand paddling in the one narrow deep channel which, as in most large rivers, follows the outer or further bank of every bend. And the bends of the Tana have to be seen and paddled to be believed. More often than not we were all in the water ourselves pushing and towing boats stuck hard on sandbanks and it was surprising how quickly we came to terms with the crocodile menace in these circumstances. For crocs there were in plenty; long glistening bodies sliding into the water at our approach and their luminous eyes upon us in the night as we lay down to sleep during overnight sojourns at the water's edge. But it was the hippo that constituted our chief concern those first days. Their concentrations became more and more numerous and to bypass them we often had to press close against the bank, our inexperienced boat-handling projecting us painfully amongst thick foliage plentifully endowed with thorns. And at night on the sandy shore that formed our beds we were conscious of the fact that we might be lying on a hippo track and so at risk of being trampled on by two tons of animal as it headed towards the safe haven of the river.

It was the hippos too that gave us a fright the third day out when, without warning, *East Midlander* sailed right into the middle of a herd and, worse, into the classically wrong situation of between the young and their parents.

'Paddle like hell,' growled John, suddenly aware of the danger.

I hardly needed the warning and plunged the blade of my paddle back and forth through the water for all I was worth. But Alison, paralysed with fright, made no such move with the result that we simply went round in a circle. John was occupied removing the igniter from a thunderflash used to frighten creatures away from us in such circumstances so was unable to correct the manoeuvre with his punting pole.

Low squeaks of terror emerged from Allison, but my grated 'For Christ's sake *do* something, woman' sent her paddle back into the water and we swung the other way.

All this must have been very confusing to one papa hippo who abruptly lunged at us, making a beeline for the boat to disappear beneath the water just before he reached us. I raised my paddle with the vague idea of giving him a crack about the ears should he appear at the side of the boat but nothing happened. Considerably shaken, we made faster progress than we had all day but not before a couple of baby hippos, hearing the commotion, leaped into the water from the bank at a spot where our boat had been but seconds before.

On a less fractious note the birds of the Tana made a joyous sight. Varying in size from the black-and-white fish eagle with its plaintive cry and the solemn lawyer-like figure of the marabou stork to the flitting multi-colour kingfishers and tiny yellow weavers and their strange hanging nests, they made exotic companions down the corkscrew waterway. We also saw our first buffalo about this time; enormous, head down, he stood preparing to drink. Come upon unexpectedly, they are exceedingly dangerous, for they have alert, sharp senses, are extremely cunning and kill without mercy or reason. They were to become the one animal that put the fear of God into me.

We reached the second base camp at a place called Mulanjo on the fifth morning where the first of a series of one-week scientific surveys was to be carried out. The straggling village of that name was but a mile away within the bush and, though a few inquisitive souls came to visit us, we were, again, very much on our own. Camp life at Mulanjo therefore became somewhat similar to that of Kora.

The subsequent base camp, attained following more days of paddling and interludes with hippos and crocs, was Korokora, characterised by an increase in big game, notably elephant, though, alas, many were dead: victims of the poacher's greed. Distant sounds of lion, leopard and hyena made a discomforting background to our own nocturnal meanderings and once, near the river, we disturbed a herd of hippos in the undergrowth who ran in all directions though, fortunately, not ours. Base camp life, once more, began running to a well-regulated pattern with the non-scientists, when not involved with the doings of their scientific brethren, undertaking a variety of chores such as water-treatment and the care of body sores made sceptic by the cruel barbs and thorns of the bush.

Korokora to Kipendi was a four-day voyage and as we progressed the environment of the Tana began to change again. People were more in evidence on the banks, their faces alive with curiosity and excitement. Children ran, chattering, their shrill voices echoing those of the birds. Small *manyattas,* the beehive-shaped huts covered with hides, mats and foliage, showed amongst occasional patchwork squares of cultivation while the shiny green of banana plantations took over where the forest had been before. The site of one of the overnight encampments was plainly a favourite place for elephant; the sandy plateau, backed by groups of trees, was liberally sprinkled with their tell-tale droppings. As we settled down to sleep we heard them crashing around in the undergrowth sending each of us edging surreptitiously nearer the protecting campfire. With the dawn we saw herds of them on the other side of the river, which made all the difference to one's peace of mind. They made a superb spectacle as 14 of the huge beasts tiptoed down to the water's edge to drink close to where our boats were drawn up.

At the base camp of Kipendi we were to meet the good citizens of Wenje, a district centre. These Pokomo people were friendly and welcoming, allowing us into their simple homes to meet their families. That they were concerned about the state of the Tana and of the threatened future development was made plain to us since their livelihood and indeed their

141

lives depended upon the outcome. We could but sympathise with their concern, but the point of our survey was to lay bare the problems for man and beast, not to solve them.

For the subsequent leg of the journey three of us – John Richardson, Sandy Evans (the youngest member of the expedition) and myself – chose to walk the sixty-odd miles to the next base campsite at Hewani, our special assignment being the location of two rare brands of monkey and the scarce Pels owl. That I was not at my walking best I was aware – one ankle sprained and the other poisoned – but a spell away from the boats was an attraction I was unable to resist.

Hardly had we set out, foolishly unarmed but laden with bulging rucksacks, when we bumped into a herd of elephants with their young. Our presence seemed to upset the equilibrium of one mother to the point when we had to beat a very hasty retreat. But this small incident cut a new notch in my yardstick of African experiences. Here we were, just the three of us, alone, weaponless, intensely ignorant of the hazards of the African wilds. All around, unseen but undeniably present, was an unbroken frieze of beasts of the jungle, river and bush. Here was the most abundant and varied life still existing on earth. We were surrounded by imminent death: the horns of rhino and buffalo and elephant, the teeth and fangs of crocodiles and snakes, the claws of the great cats. A score of emotions licked the pit of my stomach: excitement, insecurity, alarm and, yes, fear.

It was, however, a day hence before I experienced my own private close encounter with giant beasts. John and Sandy had gone off to spend the evening with a game warden who had a base nearby and I volunteered to stay behind and hold the fort, albeit our small bivouac.

Left to my own devises I built a fire and waited. And I have never felt so alone in my life. Lonely no; alone yes. Loneliness is a gradual melancholic emotion; being alone in such circumstances can build up into something approaching stark terror. Tripping down to the river to refill a bucket with water

I found a monster crocodile leering at me and a quartet of hippos staring fixedly before they reluctantly sunk out of sight with expressions of now-there's-only-one-of-you on their faces, before I returned, chastened, to the tent.

Throughout the hot day the elephants had been musing and swaying in some cool recess of the forest, but now they began to rouse themselves and drift to their feeding grounds like great grey shadows, their bodies moving through the undergrowth so gently that the only sound was like the faintest whisper of leaves rustled by a tiny breeze.

But if those elephants moved quietly towards their source of dining this was not the case with their evening's banqueting activities. A herd of them grazed their way in line abreast, now like a fleet of battleships, towards me, munching raucously and pulling great chunks out of the bushes. Additional to this the nocturnal noises of the jungle turned to full volume, each howl, squawk and scream a drumbeat of menace. The hairs on my neck rose to attention.

The trouble was I couldn't see anything. I searched the night shadows till my eyes ached, but nothing moved. The fire shrank to a glow; to replenish it would mean a lone walk towards those evil noises which was out of the question. Frantically I blew on the dying embers and raised a tiny flame to kindle a spark of courage within my breast. A military maxim from my past came to the rescue with a clarion call to action. *To attack is the best form of defence.* The first of the elephants loomed out of the darkness. I picked up a glowing faggot that had burst into flame, wielded it about my head, uttered a banshee howl and hurled myself at the oncoming foe.

The big tusker was too intent upon stuffing his face with trunkloads of fodder to notice me at first. Then it looked down, perceived a miniature King Kong figure emitting strange sounds fast approaching, opened wide his eyes in disbelief, turned turtle and bolted. A thunder of hooves, a smashing of undergrowth and, what's more, the whole herd was routed. To consolidate my triumph I flung my smouldering faggot at the retreating elephantine rump and had to spend the next hour extinguishing the jungle fire I had started.

I would say here and now that my reactions are not to be recommended to anyone in a similar situation. Remaining quite still would have been a wiser course. John and Sandy's return long after midnight was like the commuting of a death sentence.

Our ensuing night, or what was left of it, was anything but tranquil. We lay, zipped into our tents, listening uneasily to the elephants grazing right up to our guy-ropes. Any moment I expected a great foot to descend through the nylon onto our prostrate bodies which goes to show how little I know about elephants. In the morning we discovered that one of them had sucked dry a whole bucket of water that we had positioned by the tent flap in readiness for our morning tea. Regrettably it was the treated water, strained and dosed, which meant we had to go through the whole process again – though not before I had accidentally consumed a whole bottleful from the other untouched bucket: the stuff straight out of the disease-ridden Tana.

We left following a delayed breakfast and a first-aid session in which John had the odious task of extracting about a pint of puss from my poisoned ankle which hurt abominably. We moved south via an ox-bow, where the river had changed course, with commendable rapidity but still with some caution. Here and there were small communities of Pokomo peoples living in stockaded acres of cultivation and *chambas*. Twice we were provided with an armed escort: a fellow-traveller of the jungle who insisted upon accompanying us carrying his spear at the ready, appalled at our own lack of weaponry.

We would have been more than appreciative of their protective measures one early afternoon when we made the brief acquaintance of a wounded rhino. It happened in a thick-set portion of jungle bordering the Tana. The thicker the undergrowth the more care we applied to our progress, and the three of us had dutifully – and to expeditionary instructions – noted our respective climbable trees in case of buffalo attack as we entered the forbidding gloom. Rounding a giant bush we found ourselves looking up the backside of an outsized rhino with a spear-wound in the rump that was likely to have made the animal particularly unsociable. John, in charge, shouted 'Quick, drop rucksacks and up your tree. Hurry!' This put the wind up me to such an extent that I was unable to disentangle myself from my harness and, while I was all struggling to do so, failed to make the silent getaway intended. Like the cymbals of a military band my tin mugs and mess tins, strapped to various buckles, clashed as if for the opening bars of 'The British Grenadiers' and the rhino, not surprisingly, wheeled about with some rapidity. Finally shaking off my rucksack, glimpsing the great beast's head lower for the charge and the huge horn pointed at me, I turned and ran.

The crackle of flattened undergrowth and low-pitched impatient snorts drove me forward on winged feet oblivious of the others. My private tree became the single goal at the further end of a vortex of my life. Rhinos, I knew, could run faster than a man. Heavy breathing came from my left and from my right and, the next instant, the three of us were struggling up the same tree trunk. I had beaten John to it by a short head to scramble into the slender boughs neck and neck with the agile young Sandy.

From a safe height we looked down to see the bewildered animal hurl a ton of itself beneath us. The black rhinoceros – which it was – is a solitary beast and a vegetarian, but will charge and overrun anything, even a train, that its poor eyesight is unable to make out.

The danger past we descended a little sheepishly, reshouldered our discarded loads, and moved off in the opposite direction to that the rhino had taken. And in this manner, blundering from one minor disaster to another, we amateur trackers progressed through the riverine jungle to finally meet up with the rest of the expeditioners at Hewani.

The two species of monkey that had been our quest we had observed in plenty but the Pels owl evaded us – until it came to light sitting on a tree above the new base camp!

The Hewani camp was not without its shortcomings. Mosquitoes for instance. In spite of elaborate precautions and all manner of Heath Robinson defences, their insidious attacks struck home. Snakes were another, the only lethal one we saw appearing in my tent. And our lavatory beside the Tana. Romantic perhaps, but perilous, too, if you were in a hurry at night and missed the cliff path leading to it.

The site was a clump of mango trees amongst a bristling sea of palms, their trunks grey and straight like factory chimneys. It was also in close proximity to a community of a new Tana tribe – the Orma Galla – though our first visitors were waterbuck. A family of them took a wrong turning and found themselves among the tents. Realising their mistake they leapt the slop pits and vanished. Otherwise our visitors were black and two-legged, emanating from Hewani village, some two miles distant.

The Orma, a part of the Galla tribe, live intermingled among the three Pokomo subtribes. They are tall and slender with thin faces, long noses, long narrow skulls and narrow shoulders – all vertical dimensions it will be noticed – which description fits, of course, the Masai to whom they are related. These representatives of their tribe were, again, immensely friendly and, during the week we were at the Hewani base camp, I spent much time with them.

This was the penultimate base camp of the expedition and the week went by all too fast as, again, came the time to leave. We were nearing the end of the journey, and with all of us back on the river, the boats were soon drifting into the mangrove swamps below Ozi. And I say 'drifting' because the current had become noticeably stronger as the mouth of the Tana drew us relentlessly forward. And there, at the place called Ozi, we were among a whole range of beasts including elephant, leopard, buffalo, hippo and crocodile, as well as myriad crabs and mosquitoes. At night we could hear the sound of the rollers of the Indian Ocean signalling the end of the voyage. Disease was rampant in the tiny muddy creeks of the mango swamps while persistent rain offered us yet another side to the Tana's character. This failed to dampen our spirits, however, for, after all, water had become very much a part of our lives. The heat was sticky but an occasional sea breeze offered relief.

Nigel Winser and I cut short our stay at Ozi to journey down the last miles of the river sitting astride bags of rice in a dugout canoe paddled by local tribesmen. An elephant, taking a morning drink, flapped its ears at our approach and withdrew. Two hippos blew jets of water into the air, snorted and submerged. We hardly noticed them. Abruptly the Tana widened to impressive proportions and around the thousandth bend the coconut palms and thatched-roofed houses of Kipini village appeared, together with a handful of *dhows* drawn up on a beach that belonged to no river.

We swept into water that slowly turned from rusty brown to a universal grey as the Tana's blood stained this tiny corner of the Indian Ocean and was lost forever.

MY CALIFORNIAN RAPIDS, run two years later, came about through an assignment in that state to investigate the Sacramento region.

Close by the town of Colman ran the American River, placid here but in the canyon a mile or two distant, a foaming torrent with the right mixture of thrashing white water interwoven with serene stretches for pleasurable contrast. These rapids were not all that violent, the inflatables' crews of Sobek were experts, and it was all great fun. Each rapid bore a name like Slick Lucy and the Devil's Cesspool and were, assuredly, less dangerous than the odd rattlesnake and clump of poison ivy that mingled with the riot of flowers on the grandiose banks. I suppose it was worth getting a soaking so as to be able to send a postcard home reading 'I've just ridden Slick Lucy'.

IT WAS IN the United States likewise that I had two further river voyages of note; both, fortuitously, devoid of water rodeo-bucking. The first was in Montana to whence Northwest Airlines and the Montana Tourist Bureau had invited me in 1979.

The peak of my tour of the state was the two days I spent meandering down the Missouri River from Coalbanks Landing to the new bridge at Judith Landing, with one Bob Singer of the Missouri River Outfitters in Fort Benton.

Bob loved his river passionately. Together we camped out near Sentinel Rock, just past the White Cliffs Canyon of strange weather-eroded shapes, beneath a sky of star-studded majesty that beat the pants off the most luxurious of hotel bedrooms, and dined on Montanan steaks of immense proportions. In the silence of our glide downstream we witnessed the miracle of osprey, crane and eagle, of delicate, cautious deer and the glory of the sun's reflection on the placid water, broken only by the splash of a fish as it jumped to catch a fly, or a beaver's wake as it swam towards the bank. And all the while Bob described to me the doings of Lewis and Clark as if he had been a member of their expedition of discovery himself. 'We fly across America in a few hours, drive it inside of a week yet those two explorers and their party started out in St Louis in 1804 and returned in 1806,' stated Bob with awe. 'And if we get to thinking we are men, we might remember that in two and a half years of pushing through wild and unknown territory to the Pacific ocean and back, only one man died. Yet we grumble like mad if our commuter train is late by a few minutes or the postman is behind with his delivery.'

This insignificant voyage with Bob alone would have made my visit to Montana entirely worthwhile.

APPROPRIATELY, IT WAS the great Mississippi, from whence the Missouri stems, that gave me my third insight into a United States river and a paddle steamer to evoke a slice of American history. This was in 1988.

148

Few phrases of the nineteenth-century North American life had so wide an influence on the region and people around it as the Mississippi River steamboat. For 50 years, from 1820 to 1870, this 'swimming volcano', as some passengers called it, dominated the economy, agriculture, commerce and social customs of the middle area of the United States.

These 'palaces on paddle wheels' – another epithet – made possible the golden age of the Mississippi valley and determined the direction of development of other cities, towns and rural areas. They made fortunes for their owners and for the plantation masters; they brought much of the Old South in touch with the world and aided in the growth of slavery as well as the cotton economy.

Steamboat pioneering began in America in 1789 when John Fitch of Connecticut made a successful trial, but not until 1811 was a vessel built especially for the lower Mississippi: the *New Orleans*, constructed at Pittsburgh. Disasters ensured thick and fast, but the vessel survived and this led to Robert Fulton and Robert R. Livingstone running a steamboat service between New Orleans and Natchez, the boat travelling at eight miles an hour downstream and three miles an hour up. Within two years the *New Orleans* sank, though the engine was saved.

In 1816 Henry Miller Shreve of Shreveport made history by launching his *Washington* and making the trip from New Orleans to Louisville in the phenomenal time of 25 days. From then on the people of the Mississippi valley and tributaries turned to the steam vessels for river transportation in ever-increasing numbers. New Orleans, near the mouth of the river could, in 1814, count 20 steamboat arrivals but within 20 years the figure had reached 1,200. Cotton was spreading over the South and sugar had become the major crop of the area below New Orleans. For the South a new age had dawned.

They are gone now, these evocative craft, as have their mournful whistles and the splashing paddlewheels. Yesteryear they were toting their bales of cotton down the muddy banks from the bluffs of Minnesota to the warehouses of New

Orleans, carrying emigrating families, pretty young ladies in silks and satins, diamond-studded dandies and down-to-earth traders towards the fulfilment of their hopes and dreams. But the river remains.

'Father of the Waters', 'Spine of the Nation', 'Old Devil River' and even 'The Great Sewer' are just some of the names given to the sometimes treacherous Mississippi, the world's longest river. Bordering more than a dozen states, the waterway has outgrown the era of the steamboat sternwheelers of the nineteenth century. But not quite. A few of these 'ladies of the river' have survived to continue thrashing down the brown waters carrying trippers on afternoon, and longer, excursions; they alone keep the legends alive.

For one company the century-old romance with the river has never faded. The Greene family, who began the line which would become known as the Delta Queen Steamboat Co, lived through many of the steamboat years, from the time they bought their first boat – the *HK Bedford* in 1890 – until their purchase of the *Delta Queen* in 1946. Headed by Captain Gordon C. Greene, and his wife Mary – who was also an accomplished river pilot and steamboat captain – the couple and their sons owned and operated 28 different steamers, with the family living on the current flagship of the line. After Gordon's death, it was their son, Tom, who envisaged a 'bigger and better' steamboat for passenger travel, and so eventually acquired the *Delta Queen*, now one of three such twin stern-wheelers in service.

In 1976, the company built the country's then largest and most luxurious steamboat, the *Mississippi Queen*, capable of carrying 400 passengers on seven gleaming white decks, combining Victorian charm with the ultimate in comfort and modern-day conveniences.

When my wife and I received the invitation to join the sumptuous vessel for a seven-night round-trip cruise from Minnesota's chic capital, St Paul, I was not sure what to expect. I could hardly visualise myself bursting into melodies like 'Old Man River' as we thrashed our way into the sunset. Nor, when my wife and I arrived at the departure quay in the city, could we have expected such a spacious and well-equipped craft.

The vessel was a floating palace. Amenities included a gym, theatre, library, gift shop, lifts, beauty salons, as well as 're-freshment points' – tea, coffee dispensers (with a dozen varie-ties of tea), hot-dog stands and snackeries – at strategic posi-tions about the decks in case hunger struck between the ample main meals. Accommodation ranged from lavish veranda suites to cosy state-rooms, complete with brass fittings and showers. Up on deck I spent much time at the stern of the boat watching and being part-hypnotised by the thrashing paddles flinging water around in a permanent display of angry displeasure.

Our cruise ran along the shores of Minnesota, Wisconsin, Iowa and Illinois: part of the American Mid-West. Unlike the highways, no indication showed when we passed from one state to another; nowhere did I see a board announcing that we were entering Wisconsin or wherever and proclaiming their individual uniqueness and qualities as do the road signs.

However, airing my infinitesimal knowledge of Minnesota, I remarked to my wife that this was the land of 1,000 lakes and was immediately corrected by an eaves-dropping fellow-guest who lived hereabouts.

'No, it's not the Land of a Thousand Lakes as it's widely advertised. A recent recount puts the figure at more than one thousand five hundred.' And warming to his subject he went on to air his seemingly encyclopaedic familiarity with the startling revelation that, since everybody ran out of different names to call individual lakes, there were 150 of them called 'Long', 122 'Rices', 91 'Muds', 83 'Bases', 72 'Twins', 70 'Rounds', 51 'Clears' and 46 'Sands'.

Remarking to my informant that the only bit of Minnesota I knew was its capital St Paul, the twin of Minneapolis, where I had briefly stayed on a previous visit to the United States, unleashed a further fusillade of facts.

'Ah, but capital cities seldom reflect their state. Minnesota is a rural territory with two thirds of it rolling prairies together with dense forests, vast grainfields, rich pastures and one of the deepest mines in the world.' He sounded like a living tour brochure. 'You must come and stay and let me show you everything,' he added, handing me his business card from which I noted that he *was* a tour operator!

I suddenly remembered the question I wanted to put to him. 'What sort of mine was it you mentioned?' but the chap had gone.

One of the many things I like about the Americans – amongst a few I don't – is their intense patriotism. Pride in one's country is no shame as it sometimes would appear in ours. Many a house in an American town or countryside displays a large Union flag from a pole in the garden without the slightest sign of embarrassment. But when do you see the Union Jack flying high from private houses in Britain outside of the rare great international sporting event?

So Minnesota is the land of 1,500 lakes. I must remember that. One of them formed part of the Mississippi which becomes well nigh a sea at this point. Yet, on an earlier visit, I had stepped across the little stream that is the infant giant emerging from Lake Itasca in the north of the state.

The first stop was at Prairie du Chien on the Wisconsin bank. Named by French settlers after an Indian chief called Dog, this small town was full of interesting items like the Villa Louis – an example of the bucolic luxury a fur trader of the time could afford. It was here too that the British won a battle against the Americans in 1812 – only to lose it in subsequent negotiation.

I could discern little geographical difference in Iowa to that of Wisconsin; the same rolling hills interrupted by occasional bluffs and a scattering of riverside communities.

But my suppositions were corrected by another stalwart of the region. 'You are now in "The Beautiful Land" as the Sioux called it, and one that is a horn of plenty which pours forth the fruits of golden harvests from this, the very heartland of American agriculture. Additionally, you are now in the land of the Indian warrior Black Hawk and the birthplace of

"Buffalo Bill" Cody and Herbert Hoover.' He added a sheaf of further names of apparently well-known personages of which, I fear, I'd never heard, but chose not to disclose my ignorance. The poetic outburst, though stimulating, failed to alter the fact that, to me, the countryside around still looked all the same whichever of the quartet of states we were in.

Our Iowa halt was at Dubuque, a former lead-mining town of considerable character with the aura of French Canada – perhaps not surprising since a French Canadian, Julien Dubuque, founded the place. From it we were taken on an optional excursion to Galena, a town almost too good to be true that basks in its adoration of a famous son, U. S. Grant, who came home here triumphant from the Civil War. And so back to St Paul by the only way possible – by river.

UNDOUBTEDLY THE HIGHLIGHT of my second visit to Thailand, again in the 70s, was the nine days I spent in the jungle beyond the country's second city, Chiangmai. My goal was the township of Mea-Hang-Son, not far from the Burmese border and within Thailand's so-called Opium Triangle.

With half a dozen companions I trekked through the primeval glades beneath great moss and orchid-laden trees where deep layers of decaying vegetation generated a clammy warmth. Sometimes on foot, sometimes on the back of lumbering elephants, we made our way through the eternal gloom, wading leech-infected streams and spending our nights with primitive Mao and Karen people who insisted we sampled their opium, sucking at the stuff through long-stemmed pipes – though all I got out of it was a sore throat! For a couple of days we were sped downstream on the swift current of a brown river aboard a bamboo raft, trying to keep the thing upright in the rougher reaches. Much of the voyage took place under a solid deluge of rain, which actually mattered not at all since our bodies were permanently drenched in sweat.

Today, of course, these activities have become commercialised; they can be found in many tour operator's brochures.

Thus I was fortunate to sample this corner of Thailand when tourists were virtually unknown.

EGYPT WAS THE venue of a Nile voyage I made in 1980 when my vehicle was anything but luxurious: a strictly non-tourist felucca.

There's only one satisfactory way to see the antiquities of ancient Egypt and that's by boat down its famous river. But I was damned if I was going to join a great army of camera-slung, souvenir-hunting tourists on plush river steamers offering the high life at high prices. So, at Aswan, towards the southernmost extremity of the country, I negotiated with a local family for the hire of their felucca and a crew for a northbound voyage to Luxor. With me were three travelling companions – a New Zealander, an American and a compatriot – whom I had picked up earlier on a southward-bound train.

This ill-assorted quartet gathered on the jetty to be met by our crew. The skipper was a dark-skinned, moustachioed figure, handsome in a superficial way in his *jelabah* and headdress, whose name was Sayed Mahmoud Ali. And Abdel, the cook and general factotum, a youngster afflicted with a hearing defect that disorientated him to the point where his conversation (mostly to himself) emerged as a series of rhythmic bubblings. Whatever accomplishments he might have possessed, cooking was not one of them, as we were soon to discover.

Our floating home was barely six metres in length and bore the name *Yournni* painted on her stern. Like all feluccas she possessed a keel that could be raised or lowered for use in shallow or deep water and a single sail that could be swivelled to catch the wind from whichever direction it came. *Yournni* plainly had seen better days, for what remained of her paintwork was faded and scoured, while her sail was patched and ragged. With six people aboard, living conditions were going to be cramped. Foam rubber mattresses and rugs littered the deck.

We set off from Aswan in bright sunshine with a light headwind that had us tacking from side to side of the half-mile wide river. The wind was to remain head-on for most of the voyage, though fortunately the current was with us. By dusk, however, the wind had dropped, necessitating use of the clumsy oars by us all in turn for the considerable distance to Kom Ombo, where we hove to on an island opposite the well-known temple.

A lunch of sardines, tuna, egg, cheese, tinned meat and salad that was classed as 'light' was supplemented for supper by a feast of overcooked Egyptian vegetable stew and rice, followed by oranges and bananas. Vegetable soup, we were soon to learn, was the one dish Abdel could produce – and that only badly.

Next morning, unwashed but well breakfasted, we crossed to Kom Ombo to spend a cultural hour visiting the Ptolemaic temple in the company of a battalion of freshly laundered tourists from a luxury cruiser. The edifice stands on a lofty knoll half-encircled by a bend of the Nile to give the effect of a sort of acropolis against the desert skyline. Dedicated to two gods, Sobek and Haroeris, the former a crocodile god, it contains a small chapel stuffed full of mummified crocodiles.

We left Kom Ombo beneath the bows of the cruiser with tourists enthusiastically photographing and throwing coins at us under the impression that we were colourful locals. Again the wind died, and Sayed decided to accept the indignity of being towed by one of many passing barges that swept by in both directions. This involved much shouting and gesticulating between the two vessels before a barge captain indicated his acceptance of the terms offered. Sayed skilfully brought the becalmed felucca close up against the gigantic motor-barge where a line was secured and our little boat positioned behind the huge stern, close – too close I thought – to its thrashing screw.

Behind the barge we made a fine rate of knots and were dropped off at the town of Edfu after nightfall. The sound of the throbbing engines faded and a blessed silence fell. We went ashore to locate a beer or two – but Edfu by night is no more ball of fire than Edfu by day. We returned disconsolately to 'bed', meaning laying ourselves out sardine-fashion, smothered in rugs athwart the deck. Janette, the only woman, made the mistake of sleeping alongside the skipper and fell victim to his amorous gropings.

But Edfu by day did show us another Ptolemaic temple, a far grander affair than that of Kom Ombo. Described as the most perfect of Egyptian temples it is, astonishingly, almost complete, and towers over the adobe dwellings of the twentieth-century citizens existing around it.

Driven by a freshening wind, our craft soon was heeling over at an alarming angle and, under orders from the slightly worried skipper, the four of us were changing sides at every tack to help counterbalance its tilt. The water repeatedly came over the edge of the deck, once soaking our bedding, so that eventually Sayed played safe and took shelter close by a sandy beach.

We waited in vain for calm, then returned cautiously to midstream there to await another tow. A gravel barge signalled its willingness to oblige so long as it did not involve a change of course, but this time our crew missed the rope flung at them. However, aware that he was about to lose a useful source of added income, the barge captain swung his huge vessel round. Both vessels thereupon circled each other, executing a ponderous ring-o-roses with the respective skippers screaming obscenities at one another. Ultimately we got a line across and were pulled into towing position – whereupon we received a dousing from the madly thrashing barge screw. The financial hagglings concluded, we made good progress through the choppy water and a sheen of spray to reach Esna, the next town, as a golden sunset melted the desert horizon to turn the Nile to blood. Tying up to the barge that had been our tow, we were invited by the captain to join him and the crew for a night-cap of hot sweet tea and a turn at the communal bubble pipe.

We rose early next morning to walk into town to see, in advance of the tourist hordes, yet another temple from Ptolemaic times, on a par with that of Edfu.

Returning to the *Yournni* we were to witness an altercation between Sayed and Abdel. The cook bit the skipper, the skipper twisted the cook's nose, the cook threw the raw stew destined for lunch at the skipper. When Sayed drew a knife, we intervened. The row subsided in oaths and bubbling insults. So angry was Abdel that, emerging on deck, he missed his footing and fell overboard and had to be dragged out of a particularly oily and polluted patch of Nile. In the kerfuffle the boom of the sail swung round to knock me overboard likewise, which at least provoked a mirth that defused the hostilities.

Taking advantage of a captive barge in a lock, we hitched another ride, so left a good deal faster than we had entered. But the towline snapped, and we were again adrift in the middle of the wide waterway. The water in the locks was more heavily polluted than elsewhere – greasy with dead cats and unmentionable debris – though this never dissuaded Abdel from using the foulest water for tea-making. It was in one such lock that I ended up myself when I tripped over the cooking pot, but the further ducking seemed to do me no harm.

We did manage a number of intended swims in the cold water of the open river, our only gesture to personal hygiene. The cook did better by twice falling in fully dressed, the second time again dragging me with him. There was exercise in plenty when, becalmed again, we rowed in turn to attain an anonymous mid-stream island. We reached it after midnight and dined on catfish washed down by local brandy purchased by a still-awake fisherman. Banana Island, as it was called, became our anchorage for the night.

Next morning we were off again with a fair wind in our sail enabling us to make up much lost time. It was stew again for lunch but, bubbling with pleasure, Abdel presented us with an end-of-voyage dinner: fried banana hash, banana fritters and bananas, neat, for desert. He never knew how close he was to going overboard again.

We were now but a line's throw from Luxor where, amongst the haughty luxury boats at anchor, we took our leave of Sayed and Abdel, trading our last affectionate insults as we walked the gangplank for the last time. The enormous temple complex of Luxor and the stupendous pillars and edifices of neighbouring Karnak turned us into tourists once more. But even stronger than the drama of 1,000-year-old archaeological marvels was the memory of a six-day voyage by a battered felucca on a river that continues to influence and guide the destiny of Egypt.

IN THE 1960s, one Peter Deilmann saw the potential of the long-distance waterways of Europe and formed a river cruising company, thus bridging a gap in the tourism market.

Over the last two decades I have partaken of cruises on the Rhine, Danube and Elbe. That of the Danube was from Passau in southern Germany to Budapest with ports-of-call that included Vienna and Bratislava. The vessel was the *Danube Princess,* constructed specifically for this particular river and carrying a crew of 60 to look after 215 passengers housed in elegantly-furnished, air-conditioned cabins. This was in 1984 when long-distance river-cruising was in its infancy. From Budapest I had continued on my own to the Danube Delta and the Black Sea in Romania.

But my most recent long-distance river cruise was aboard the ultra-comfortable MV *Dresden* on a voyage from Hamburg to the Czech Republic – which was Czechoslovakia at the time I made the journey in 1996 together with my wife. And it was Peter Deilmann's Elbe cruise that particularly drew my attention since here was a great river, not so well-known as the Rhine, Danube or Seine, that had only been navigable – in the tourism sense – since the collapse of European Communism.

Forging a diagonal course across Germany, taking in much of the former Communist-ruled German Democratic Republic – East Germany – and running through long-neglected cities and towns, such as picturesque Tangermunde, industrial Magdeburg, Martin Luther's Wittenberg, porcelain-famed Meissen, still-scarred Dresden, the palace-park of Pillnitz and the delectable mixed rock and forestland of the so-called Saxon Switzerland, it made for a voyage of distinction and rediscovery.

The vessel itself was, again, no less than a floating palace with gourmet meals to match; three of them a day plus mid-morning bouillon and afternoon tea, together with ever-available fruit and bonne-bouche snacks. Thus, except for the odd stroll in the ports-of-call, the consumption of food was the only activity.

The voyage ended at Dresden – or ours did anyway, though the journey can be made in either direction and that includes the onward voyage to the Czech Republic and back. The best introduction to MV *Dresden*'s namesake city is to arrive at – or depart from – it because, from the river, one obtains the finest view of its resurrected skyline that was the inspiration for Canaletto's famed painting. Utterly destroyed by the Allied triple bombing raid of February 1945, parts of the heart of Dresden to this day remain a fire-blackened ruin.

Though, as readers might have envisaged, luxury travel is hardly my vogue, disembarking for the last time was a wrench. The trouble with pampering is that it is addictive.

So, FROM RIVERS to sea. And at the very outset I must declare that I'm not a sea-going enthusiast; I'd rather be *in* the sea than *on* it, so ocean cruising is not for me. In fact the only sea voyaging I have experienced are the more localised sort with the shore within easy reach. For instance, one of the Swan Hellenic Mediterranean cruises where the guests spend more time on shore than being at sea, or the Norwegian coastal voyage where, again, the ship sails close to the shore.

A Channel crossing hardly constitutes a memorable voyage but when the year is 1944 this does add a certain *frisson* to such a mundane journey; this one made from a south coast port – I think it was Southampton – to a bare Normandy beach called 'Gold'.

Memory is a fickle phenomenon. Some things stick out a mile with every detail as fresh as yesterday; others, however dramatic, tend to blur into insignificance.

For days I, together with half a million other bewildered and discontented soldiers had been literally imprisoned in a vast leaky encampment under incessant rain and surrounded by belts of concertina wire guarded by strong posses of armed military police with orders to sheet anyone attempting to leave without authorisation. And I'm sure I was not the only one who felt like a criminal instead of potential liberators of an enslaved continent. That this was a preliminary to going to war was grudgingly accepted and the essential details – or at least those that affected one tiny component of the grandiose endeavour allotted to my infantry battalion – had been revealed to us by our officers. Food was basic, our tented accommodation was basic; in fact life became so basic it was a relief to pile aboard a ship in the harbour which was, appropriately, a civil cross-channel ferry called, I seem to remember, the *Invicta*. And if we deemed the camp to have been basic then conditions aboard that ferry dressed as a warship were rock bottom with, it seemed, half the British army compressed into every nook and cranny of that unlovely vessel. I lost out on the hammock issue so, at night, ended up on the floor curled up like a cat through lack of leg-room. And there we remained for a further 24 – or was it 48 – hours before this floating barracks put to sea. With rain still pouring down and each of us festooned with weaponry and accoutrements that we were instructed not to let leave our sides I never did get the chance to gaze wistfully at an England fading into the murk.

With nothing to do and with the realisation that we were really on our way came the thoughts pulsing through my head in a steady mixture of fright and anticipation. Could I, aged 19 and barely more than a schoolboy, kill a man with whom I bore not the slightest personal animosity or hatred? It was a question I was unable to answer though I supposed it would be easier to do given the fact that he would be doing his best to kill me. And, with the coming of action, I began to rue the day I had volunteered for this unsavoury project I had looked upon as a great adventure.

My father's oft-described experiences of warfare in the First World War Gallipoli Campaign had poured into my receptive boyhood ears with 'Johnny Turk' – the then Turkish foe – a jolly and sporty type of enemy with whom he had great respect bordering upon affection. It all sounded rather fun, though the scar of the shell-splinter wound on his thigh and the Military Cross he won told a different story. Would the new German enemy be equally sporty? I doubted it.

But there were crumbs of comfort to be gained to bolster my uneasiness. We were not going into battle alone; other well-loaded ships in their scores and hundreds had come and were coming to join the fray. A few days earlier an optimistic general had spoken to us of the support we were being given by the guns of the Royal Navy and the bombs, rockets and cannon of the RAF. Some 11,500 aircraft would be pounding the coastal defences and inland lines of communication. There would be little resistance to our landing, he declared; how could there be with such a titanic weight of firepower destroying everything that moved or threatened? The battle for Normandy, he affirmed, would be a piece of cake. It all sounded rather jolly.

As the hours plodded by we were lulled into uneasy dozing by the rhythmic thud of the engines, though real sleep was impossible. Some of us played cards; others re-cleaned their weapons; most just got bored and wanted to get the whole thing over.

A clanging of bells concentrated all our minds. Were we being attacked by U-boats or E-boats? Reports of an E-boat attack on ships at anchor the previous day had filtered through to us. What if the *Invicta* was to hit a mine or stop a torpedo? With her lower and upper decks crammed with soldiery there would be carnage. But nothing happened and the card-playing, weapon-cleaning and general boredom continued.

I thought of my parents and wondered if they had guessed where I might be going. For months our outgoing letters had been heavily censored; no mention of anything that alluded to the much clamoured-for 'Second Front' had been allowed to appear in the correspondence. Father was far away commanding a native battalion in West Africa; my younger brother was in the process of gaining a commission in the Essex Regiment; only my mother was alone in our rural Essex home. But Father, being a colonel, expected his sons to be of military prowess likewise though, in me, he was doomed to disappointment. I was too individualistic to make a good soldier and I hated discipline. Over nearly two years I had been trained to kill by participating in large-scale exercises which veterans of earlier campaigns judged to be tougher than the real thing. Exercise code-names such as 'Spartan' and 'Tiger' flickered like fireflies in my memory where, for days, I had lived and slept within the cold, wet confines of a God-forsaken slit; trenches where, in similar conditions, men had actually died of exposure, since in wartime a percentage of fatalities was tolerated.

Our ship-board meals were issued, luke-warm and congealed, in greasy mess-tins; for exercise we were permitted, in batches, to pace a few yards of open deck though I could see little of the great armada of shipping that we presumed to be all around us somewhere in the greyness of the dawn. On the last such occasion the sounds of battle assailed our ears: the sullen roar of guns, broken momentarily by the crack of mortars, the whoosh of rockets and the stutter of machine-guns emanating from directly ahead.

And then the rhythm of the engines ceased and even down below decks we could now hear the thunder. A pause, and came the screaming of orders to prepare to disembark. Men rose to their feet in abrupt silence, all banter at an end, as we struggled with our packs, entrenching tools and weapons. Our junior officers fussed and fretted around, gathering their flocks and hoarsely whispering words of encouragement and advise dredged from the training manuals. We gazed fondly, for the last time, at the refuse we left behind on a deck that had become a kind of home. My heart thudded and my lips felt dry as we trooped noisily to the open deck.

All down the sides of the ship scrambling nets had been lowered and, at the bottom, bobbing up and down in the heavy swell, were rows of LCAs, the flat-bottomed craft that, when fully-laden, would take us ashore.

The noise was awesome, a great smash of sound that dulled and confused the senses, as we clumsily swarmed down a rope stairway that refused to stay still and jigged sideways and unsteadily with each foothold while pieces of equipment kept jagging in the mesh. Near the bottom of this fiendish ladder we leapt, with a certain desperation, across a widening and narrowing chasm of tossing water into the rocking smaller vessel, sometimes on top of other men in a tangle of bodies. Our exposed limbs were cut and bleeding from scrapes inflicted by sharp items of equipment. One man fell between the two vessels and was never seen again.

Hunched in rows we were pushed into a semblance of orderly ranks of squatting, shivering, seasick men, vomiting from both the movement of the sea and sheer terror, as the new craft angled away from the stationary *Invicta* and, in company with a fleet of similar vessels, sped towards a smoke-shrouded shore.

Almost imperceptibly I emerged from youth to manhood as we made our way to war.

FINALLY, WE COME to my only experience of crewing a sea-going sailing ship. And what a hash I made of it! My downfall came in the Canary Islands to whence I had been invited – or cajoled – into spending a week on a barque. Even when it was explained that she had three masts – fore and main, carrying three square sails each, and a mizzen carrying a fore and aft sail (I think these were the terms used) – it took me a while to realise that we were discussing a *ship*; a nineteenth-century sailing ship no less with nineteenth-century discomforts. What was more, this particular vessel was the ill-fated *Marques* (subsequently lost with all hands in a storm during a Fastnet race), alias the *Beagle* which played the central role in the BBC television series *The Voyage of Charles Darwin*, as well as lesser what might be described as 'floating-on' parts in *The Onedin Line* and the current version of *Dracula* – programmes which were all the rage in 1980.

I saw her first standing proudly offshore from the little Gran Canarian fishing port of Rada de los Nieves and I have to admit to being instantly smitten by her fine lines and trim figure. A golden sunset was dropping down behind her masts turning the restless sea into liquid fire. But my poetical emotions were doused very shortly after I had stepped aboard the inflatable dinghy sent to collect me and my baggage when everything was swamped by a very liquid wave. The outboard motor promptly packed up, only reluctantly coughing itself into life again as we were about to be pounded to pieces on volcanic rocks. I was assured that, usually, a new arrival is afforded a drier welcome; I always knew that my middle name should have been Jonah.

I arrived on board in a somewhat bedraggled condition and was straightway sent below to change out of my wet clothes into something 'suitable' which, judging from the semi-naked characters around me, seemed to be swimming trunks or ragged shorts. Going down the companion way I bumped my head on the roof and then again as I entered a doorway made for a dwarf into a recess they laughingly called a cabin. Attired in my denim shorts I emerged to stub my toe on the doorstep and bump my head again as I climbed the companion way. My education on living aboard a ship was proceeding the hard way.

We spent the night gently rolling at anchor and I found the slight motion surprisingly restful. And yet given the same movement on a cross-channel ferry and I'd be leaning over the rail in misery. The crew and my fellow-voyagers were a cheerful crowd and it was difficult to tell one from the other. Everybody, I noticed, appeared to know an awful lot about boats. We would all meet at mealtimes which was invariably a time of much levity while the meals themselves were hearty; that first evening I put away a good half a chicken, a mountain of spud, and a blancmange the size of my head. I was astonished at myself as I listened to the creak and groan of our timbers and watched the horizon quietly dipping and rising with all the phlegm of a born sailor.

The skipper, Robin Cecil-Wright, was a genial and extremely capable sort of chap who gave me a 'first day at school fatherly' on things to do and not to do. Playing safe I said that maybe my ignorance of nautical matters might jeopardise the ship. 'We'll see to that,' he replied, with just a trace of threat in his voice.

Other members of the regular crew consisted of one 'Plum', designated as engineer, a rotund Cornishman sporting a great bush of a beard. At 44 he was the oldest hand and knew more about marine mechanics than I don't know about ships – and that's saying something. Dick – or 'Dabler' – was younger than 'Plum' and better proportioned and wore a perpetual villainous look and nine o'clock shadow that turned him into the perfect pirate though his ambitions were more set on popsys than pieces of eight… Still younger were the trio of Chris, Dave and Chip, though only in age were they at all similar; a mixture of public school and the local primary but all three could do anything with a rope, a chain or a chart. In the galley – kitchen to land-crabs like me – Wanna and Mary were the two incumbents whose glamorous looks belied their capabilities as cooks able to produce repasts from a bellicose and invariably heaving Aga.

It was only when we moved off next day that my new-found confidence begin to ebb. An authoritative command from Robin on the poop deck had the ship in a confusion – to me –

of rope-hauling, of monkey-like figures swarming up rigging to dizzy heights, and of the unfurling of square canvas from spars to catch the wind that, almost surreptitiously, set the ship in motion. I ran about the deck trying to look as if I knew what I was doing.

Gently sailing upon a sun-kissed ocean, the wake curling phosphorescent astern. The sails showing white in the morning light and billowing in the sudden gusts. The bow-wave rushing past and the timbers creaking. That's how my eclipsed poetical other self might have described it, but alarming manifestations were occurring.

It was blowing like hell. All hands were called up to shorten sail. The wind was howling through the rigging. Spray lashed across the deck and shouted orders were like cries for help above the wind. There ensued a more urgent hauling on ropes and a faster ascent up the cat's cradle holding up the masts to frantically refurl the sails.

The sun was obscured behind ominous clouds and the rippling sea had become a great heaving body of grey water frothing with anger, sending great white-horse-capped waves straight at the flanks of our tiny vessel. The ship dipped down into the enormous troughs as if to bury itself for ever, and then, at the last moment, rose again to triumph against the unfair competition. I beheld all this with mounting apprehension, made for a corner of the poop deck and donated my breakfast to the fish. 'Whale on the port bow!' sang out an excited voice but I was in no mood to care. And when I did show interest I looked in the wrong direction.

We ran before the storm all day, first within sight of the shore and then out into the vast heaving ocean edged by smudged, then empty, horizons. I tried to fix my mind on nice solid things like footpaths and railway lines but failed miserably.

'You're on watch, aren't you, Chris. Take the wheel for an hour will you. Keep her on a course of one hundred and eighty and don't let her deviate,' came Robin's instructions, shouted against the gale. I think I replied 'Yes Your Honour' instead of

166

'Aye aye Skipper' but if so, he let it pass. Thus I found myself alone with a madly spinning wheel on a deck that kept sliding from under my feet.

The compass just laughed at me. Almost at once the needle swung back to 170 degrees and I couldn't remember whether to turn the wheel *against* the direction one wanted to go or vice versa. I took a chance and spun it three times against the swing of the needle but only made things worse. I swung it further, realising that, because of the slow reaction of boats in general, I may have been right all along. Then I funked it as the confounded needle passed 150 so I boldly gave the wheel a whole dozen turns in the opposite direction with no apparent result whatsoever. This brought the needle back to 180, edging towards 200. I began to go through the same motions again and nobody seemed to notice our zigzag course across the Atlantic. At intervals I was forced to run to the rails to evacuate more breakfast so leaving the wheel to spin where it liked.

At least all this activity took my mind off the sorry state of my health and, thereafter, I flung myself into a whirl of useless movement, pulling on every rope in sight and 'making shipshape' every loose item of equipment. I was up most of every night on watch, though what I was watching for was not made clear. When not prowling the decks looking into dark bilges for reasons that escaped me I was with the others in the cramped saloon consuming coffee or/and Scotch.

Becalmed – a state of non-movement which pleased me immensely – the *Marques* was forced to use her engines and the rhythmic thud of her diesels was music in my ears. In this manner – sometimes under sail, sometimes under mechanical horsepower, occasionally a combination of the two – we threaded a course from island to island and you could be sure it was always me who was first ashore to stand, happy and content, on blessed terra firma.

You can be sure of another thing too. I'll never make a sailor.

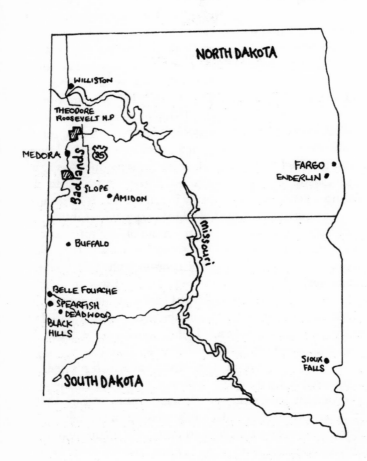

Chapter Five

TRAVELS ON HORSEBACK

IN WHICH THE AUTHOR SADDLES UP WITH A HARD-DRINKING, HARD-SMOKING COWBOY, GETS DRAGGED BY THE ANKLES OUT OF MEDORA, NORTH DAKOTA BY A NERVOUS HORSE NAMED BEAUTY, AND FOLLOWS A TRAIL ONCE RIDDEN BY GENERAL CUSTER AND HIS TROOPERS.

My days as a fledgling horse-rider are but a half-forgotten memory of irksome restrictions at a Pony Club gymkhana and occasional meets of the East Essex Hunt. I was never a horseman by ambition; come to think of it I was never a horseman at all, but my parents were of the opinion that I should go through the motions since, in those days, they gained a certain social standing from the fact that their son could sit correctly in the saddle. Today, many children of all walks of life are equestrian-orientated but in the 1930s this was not the case. And it could have been no later than the year 1941 that I last galloped my uncontrollable Arab pony across the Essex landscape. Thirty-two years later – in early 1973 – had come the invitation to renew this tenuous bond with the horse and to ride one across the wild territory of North and South Dakota in the American Mid-West.

In the meantime my only other equestrian experience had been a couple of days cantering across the rolling Inner Mongolian steppes on a spirited little Mongolian pony and attendance at a horse show at

Huhehot, the Inner Mongolian capital, where riders ended the display by charging down the course, standing on their saddles, blazing away with machine pistols held in one hand; an event that puts the somewhat staid proceedings back home in Hickstead in the shade.

It was not, however, so much my anxiety to renew this aquaintanceship with the horse as the chance to assuage a curiosity that prompted my acceptance of the Dakotan project.

The United States is full of 'trails' and, though the word there has more literal connotations than it does in Europe, the idea of tracing such historic routes as that of the Santa Fe, the Oregon and the Butterfield was irresistible. White-topped wagon trains, herd-riding cowboys, buckskin-clad trappers, grizzled prospectors, dust-raising stagecoaches – all are part of the image of the nineteenth century, an image that still stirs the hearts and imagination of millions of Americans, and not a few Britishers – including me. I was hooked from the very outset. Already I could hear the crack of whips and the strain of harness in my romantic soul and the fact that the trail on offer was no more than an obscure stagecoach line of some 215 miles founded by a little-known French marquis in 1884 mattered not at all.

The end of May 1979 found me at Fargo, North Dakota, at 3 o'clock on a raw morning where my host, Mike Martin, met me at the station to drive me to his farmstead home at remote Enderlin, some three hours south across a dead flat empty countryside that is part of the granary and meat larder of the United States. From there, we were to follow the old Medora-Deadwood stage line, established during the economic boom of late-nineteenth-century Mid-West America.

With the peace that followed the war of 1812, the tide of migration moved the American frontier steadily westward. The 'movers' came by foot, on horseback, in wagons and by river. But it was land as well as gold that lured most migrants to the great Mississippi and Missouri rivers and beyond. Canals, stage lines and, later, railways sped the pace, and, within a generation, industrial cities were thriving – Cincinnati, Detroit, Milwaukee, Chicago – where not so long before Indians had hunted and fished.

For those in the American cattle business the years of the late 1870s and early 1880s were a heady, wildly optimistic time. The profits that could be made raising livestock on the grasslands seemed unlimited; if anything, the money multiplied at a faster rate than the animals themselves. Ranches in the West, some of which covered areas as large as whole states, were the feeding grounds for hundreds of cows, steers, heifers and bulls and even if most of the millions of acres on which these animals grazed were the public domain – which would eventually be carved up into homestead plots – few people at first contested the ranchers' claims to the land.

During these brief halcyon years when shares in vast spreads were selling like stock in diamond mines, the ranchers benefited from a rising market. Year in and year out the steers brought higher and higher prices, for there seemed to be no limit to the world's appetite for American beef.

Reports of sudden riches circulated throughout the West, spread to travellers heading east, and found their way into the clubrooms of London, Edinburgh and Paris. It was hardly surprising that financiers from both Wall Street and Europe (particularly Britain) were eager to pump an unprecedented infusion of capital into the Great Plains. They formed joint stock companies to buy out and combine ranches, bring in new breeds of cattle, and recruit managers and cowboys to run their projects. Grizzled old ranchers with the smell of cow dung embedded in their skins suddenly found themselves near-celebrities, as eastern dudes and European dandies hung on their every word and marvelled at their business acumen.

Many foreign investment syndicates sent representatives of their own to oversee their vast American properties, but some Europeans came in person. Most spent money with incredible prodigality to establish themselves as cattle barons, while at the same time reproducing as near as possible the luxurious lifestyles they had left behind. Among these was a titled Frenchman, the Marquis de Mores, who settled on the Dakota Badlands with twenty servants to staff the mansion he had built in the town of Medora (founded by the marquis himself and named after his wife, New York heiress Medora von Hoffman). The ambitious Frenchman's interests included beef and sheep ranches, a stagecoach line, a refrigeration company, a slaughterhouse, and a firm that specialised in shipping Columbia River salmon to the dining tables of New York's wealthy.

The discovery of gold in the Black Hills increased the pressure of the migrants to occupy the region, notwithstanding a treaty obligation guaranteeing the hunting rights of the occupying Sioux Indians. There were no established trails, much less roads, leading to the Black Hills, and Deadwood – the centre of the new and frenzied excitement – was more than two hundred miles from the nearest railway or water route.

With the tracks of the Northern Pacific Railroad now crossing the Missouri River, people naturally sought a shorter route from the goldfields to the railhead, and government surveying and reconnaissance parties were sent out to determine the shortest and most feasible route from the Black Hills to some town on the Northern Pacific extension west of Bismark. Thus several townships were soon bidding for the very worthwhile freight and passenger service to the hills and it was within this aura of frenetic development that the Medora-Deadwood stage line came into being. Since the marquis's meat packing and refrigeration plant was already established in Medora,

North Dakota, his opening of the stage line to Deadwood was but a logical extension of his enterprise.

Throughout the route, stage stations were erected approximately every 10 to 15 miles. The line out of Medora led south, then east up Sully Creek, thence south again to Rocky Ridge. From this point the trail continued southward by Robert Springs and Cedar Creek, thence to Cold Turkey Creek and onto Crooked Creek near the North Dakota-South Dakota state border. With the station at O'Dell, the route carried on to Bull Creek, Macey's, South Moreau, Belle Fourche, Spearfish and Deadwood, again with stations at convenient intermediate points. Four coaches were put into service and were christened respectively 'Kittie', 'Dakota', 'Medora' and 'Deadwood'.

The modern individual can have little conception of the strength and durability of the old Concord stagecoach. The driver sat at the top with tight reins, his feet braced against the dashboard in the front boot, usually with a fellow passenger by his side. Mail, express and light baggage were carried on top, held in position by an iron railing adapted to the purpose. Heavier items and express packages were carried in the rear boot and sometimes inside, if passengers were few. When crowded, those who could not be contained inside rode on top holding on as best they could to avoid being thrown overboard. The leather compensating rocker springs produced a motion not unlike the swell of the sea. These coaches often carried a two-ton load and stood up under the weight while moving at a good six to ten miles an hour over the roughest of trails.

The company's stock included about 150 horses while each of the stations had a tender whose duty it was to take care of the incoming teams and have the outgoing ones harnessed and ready to hitch with the least delay. The time allowed for changing teams was ten minutes.

A coach left Medora every day of the week, the 215 miles being covered in 36 hours. Departure was scheduled for the early morning, arriving at Deadwood the following evening. On the more level portions of the route four horses were used on each coach and, over the rougher portions, six. A passenger ticket for the full journey cost $21.50 or about ten cents a mile and the cargo fee was ten cents a pound with, on occasions, the coach carrying as much as 2,500 pounds of express freight.

Competition was intense. Medora's location was not such as to give the company a monopoly of the business of carrying freight. Gradually a combination comprising the heavy grades in Badlands territory, loss of freight, a slump in the express business and a sharp reduction in passenger traffic signalled the beginning of the end of the Medora-Deadwood stage line. Economics which cut down the horses' feed and the paying off of employees failed to sustain the company. The end was in sight.

Operations ceased sometime in the winter of 1885-6. The stock was sold for what it would bring, and was scattered across the territory. One of the coaches is now at Miles City, another at Mandan, both museum specimens of the days that were. The remaining two coaches have been retired to Karlsbad, Minnesota. If any could speak, they would find no audience to take time to listen to their garrulous tales. The Marquis de Mores, his other business ventures collapsed around his ears, moved away to invest his remaining money and initiative to finally depart American shores for the friendlier climes of his native France. Medora declined to what it had been originally and today few people even know the approximate route of the one-time stage trail I was proposing to follow.

All this I learnt from Mike as we drove across the featureless plains of North Dakota, a land of a green, brown and yellow-ochre chessboard laid out in numberless rectangular sections. The pattern overwhelms its details, even such recurrent motifs as the silver silos and dark red barns. But it is the pattern of

174

the old America, of the Protestant English farming stock who defeated the Indians, cleared the forests, broke the prairies with the plough, defeated the British Empire and won a civil war.

The story and Mike's obvious pride in his Dakotan upbringing brought the impending ride of ours into sharp focus. It was he who, backed by a master's degree in American history, had undertaken most of the research of the stage line and its route. The previous year he had attempted the journey alone but his horse had fallen lame after 50 miles and he'd had to give up. I had simply drifted into the project, accepting an offer to join Mike in his fresh attempt. He was a young farmer of 25 with a satirical sense of humour that hid his generous heart, yet I felt no concern over the disparity of our ages (though I wasn't, perhaps, so happy about being reunited with a horse). A third member of the team extended the age differential. During our brief stay at Enderlin I met Steve Traynor, a gruff, hard-smoking, hard-drinking ex-soldier and railway worker of 58 years, some three years my senior.

Everyone in the small town of Enderlin knew of our project and were not slow in offering advice and opinions. Many thought we were crazy and, since Englishmen in Enderlin were hardly two a penny, these opinions were expressed loud and clear in the local newspaper. Not the slightest discouraged we departed the third morning in two cars trailing horseboxes containing four horses – Duke, Bill, Trixie and Beauty – the fourth being the pack carrier. Our destination: Medora.

Medora has refused to die completely and it stands, vaguely defiant, at the gateway to the Theodore Roosevelt National Memorial Park. The town's other famous son had a ranch there and the legacy of his hunting lodge competes for tourist patronage with that of the de Mores' chateau and the remaining chimney stack of the meat-packing factory. With a day to spare we had toured the township now slightly self-conscious of its cowboy image and the strange import from France that sits, as a museum, high on a nearby hill. I had also successfully managed to remain aloft during a few circuits on Trixie's back though I foresaw trouble from the excruciating cavalry saddle I'd been given that made riding akin to sitting astride a bucking railway line.

The venture opened with a minor disaster when Beauty, designated as packhorse, took fright at her substantial load. She bolted while I was leading her and my desperate hold was simply on account of the lead being wrapped around my leg. She repeated the performance with Mike as ringmaster, nearly running him down in her frenzy and strewing our provisions over a wide area. Damage amounted to a plethora of broken eggs, a fractured bottle of syrup, scattered packets of noodles and a dented panier. Aware that Beauty was not destined to become the packhorse of the year the honours were transferred to the more stolid Bill.

North Dakota is a land of prairies, rich river valleys, huge ranches and vast stretches of wheat. Its wealth is still in its soil – agriculture, crude oil and lignite. It is a land through which Colonel Custer's men rode with range grass growing up to their stirrups. It is the state in which to trace nineteenth-century frontier history, while at various times Spain, France and England laid claim to the territory before it became exuberantly American.

With the grizzled Steve, suitably attired in his film-set cowboy outfit and ready to play his part in North Dakota's latest epic, we clattered out of town to become the unrecognised, unsung guardians of a stage line's centenary.

The Badlands are aptly named by the Indians who once roamed this rock-studded territory which can be remorseless and dangerous for the unprepared traveller. The land was formed from volcanic ash and swamp vegetation after which a myriad streams cut through the soft strata to sculpt a lunar-like formation of flat-topped buttes and deep fissures.

A dust road led us to Gully Creek where an oil company track pulled us southwards over untamed craggy outback. An antelope bounded gracefully across our path and, from a safe distance, halted to stare. Minutes later I found myself spreadeagled on the ground having been pitched over Trixie's head as she stopped abruptly. The reason for this sudden reaction was the rattlesnake that lay sizzling and throbbing – a coil of hate – barely a yard away. The reptile and I gazed, half-hypnotised, at each other. But it failed to strike and my luck continued to hold when I took the opportunity to incautiously take a close-up photograph of it staring into the camera lens. Later Steve told me off with almost as much venom as the snake was capable of wielding and I learnt a further lesson of life. The route continued across a series of valleys and gullies laced with rocks and streams that made uncomfortable walking for the horses.

Initially we were following another, very much more famous, trail; that of George Custer and his troopers who passed this way in 1876 according to the preserved graffiti of two of their number inscribed upon a large boulder. Clumps of yellow and mauve daisies splashed vivid on the coarse, burnt grass that was the home of bull snakes and rattlers. By late afternoon the sun had dipped below the western hills.

With an estimated 12 miles behind us since our midday start we were content to doss down for the night beneath a clump of skeletal dead trees in Davis Creek, a short distance from where we estimated the first stage station to be. For supper we re-heated our beans left over from lunch, which, though uninspiring to the palate, were adequately filling, and it was while I was bringing in Trixie from a patch of grazing, changing lead reins as I did so, that she escaped. I listened to the diminishing drumbeats of hooves in the gathering gloom and fell into the depths of despair. To lose a load, a horse and possibly nearly one's life to a rattler the first day out was shame indeed and Steve's gruff comment, 'She'll never come back, you know,' hardly raised my morale. But she *did* come back of her own accord and seldom have I felt so relieved. Lesson three – never let go a horse's rein even for a moment – I learnt that day. Lesson four materialised in the night when the top fold of a fly-sheet I was using as a combined groundsheet and cover blew off to expose my sleeping bag to an extremely dampening pre-dawn dew. Lessons were learnt by others that night too. When placing my bedding I had noted the precarious angle of the nearest dead tree under which we were lying, particularly the beaver-gnawed trunk, but the others hadn't. Thus when the wind rose and the offending limb overhead produced a series of groans and cracks it was Mike and Steve who felt it expedient to move. I already had.

Steve had elected himself to the position of cook for which there was no contest. His breakfast offerings were ash-covered omelettes and burnt bacon on which Mike and I aired no comments in case he resigned. Our ablution and washing-up water was one and the same. We had slept intermittently, listening to the fidgeting of the horses and the creaking of the skeleton trees as the wind played amongst their bones.

The new day's ride began by following a dirt road that paralleled the original stage route and about a mile out of Davis Creek we changed course into the swell of hills to determine the possibility of there being anything remaining of the stage station. But nothing showed so we returned to the road. The countryside flattened out as if the exertion of raising even the suspicion of a hill was too much for it. Occasional vehicles passed in balloons of dust, their drivers invariably stopping for a chat. One kind fellow donated three cans of beer; from others we received offerings of water and even a bag of oats. Half-empty creeks grudgingly gave up water for the horses and with temperatures mounting into the high eighties they needed it. Bull snakes squirmed purposefully across the roads as did big jack-rabbits who leapt up from beneath our hooves, momentarily frightening the horses, to lope across the pastures like bloated hares. For miles we ourselves walked in a sheen of sweat to give relief to the horses, a mode of progress that also gave relief to my buttocks if not my feet.

Our second night was almost as disastrous as the first. There was no water source whatsoever until it rained and because we had not bothered to raise tents we spent the small hours huddled together clasping wet sleeping bags around us and trying to re-kindle a dead fire. An early morning start was all too welcome but we lost much time wandering aimlessly about attempting a short cut that wasn't. To add to the debacle, Beauty, shying from a jack-rabbit, shed her load atop a windswept knoll.

We were now but 18 miles from Amidon, a village on Highway 85 and, breakfastless, we set out confident of attaining it for mid-morning brunch by virtue of our enforced early rise. Another dirt road stayed with us all the way to the township but our progress was baulked by the frequent lack of a rancher's 'gate' at points where cattle grids and fencing barred the way. Over much of the Dakotan ranchlands a grid of barbed-wire fences divides the land and where a road or public right of way crosses such a 'border' a cattle grid is positioned. Usually a gate or moveable section of fencing is positioned close by since a traveller on horseback too has the full right of transit. However, in spite of a law that insists upon such an arrangement, not always does such a gate exist. This was the case beyond Second Creek and because the horses were unable to negotiate the grid we had no alternative but to follow the fence up into the low hills in the hope of finding one. Further fences then deflected us from our course and when finally a gate was discovered it led only into another wired compound. Exasperated beyond measure with playing a kind of mounted snakes and ladders and, hopelessly lost, the last straw came when we had to re-pack Bill's load which chose such a time to part company with its bearer. Had it been the nervous Beauty acting as packhorse I dread to think what might have happened but Bill, bless him, stood docile while we painstakingly sorted things out. Upon eventually regaining the road the whole business of zigzagging about the low hills had to begin again as further impassable gates were encountered. All this added at least half a dozen miles to our day's total.

The last two to Amidon were by way of Highway 85, a traffic-laden artery but blessed with no gates and wide grass verges along which, for short spells, we were able to break into a trot. Another rattler caused Trixie to shy and gave me a near fall and heart attack prior to our entry to the village.

Although 'capital' of Slope County the place gave little indication of so high an office, but among its few dwellings were three vital components: a rodeo stadium, horse pens and a bar. From the office of administration – a room at the back of a bungalow – we obtained permission to bed ourselves in the stadium and the horses in the pens before, with the mounts attended to, making tracks for the bar.

Virtually the entire male population of Amidon hung out in that smokey little saloon. The arrival of three strangers – one of them a Brit – caused an unnerving silence, broken, when our project was devulged, by intense competition to supply us with booze, each of us ammassing a line-up of Budweisers. Few of our benefactors had even *heard* of the stagecoach trail and those that had had no idea of its whereabouts. Running out of thirst we dined on hamburgers.

It rained again in the night but the morning dawned dry if a mite chilly. A tap made a convenient water source for the horses but, when our turn came, it ran dry just as we had smeared our faces with soap. Breakfast was thick glutenous porridge and strong milkless tea and, before leaving for the open country, we called at Amidon's only shop for supplies.

The track we followed lost us amongst a series of narrow valleys veined by rivers and streams objected to strongly by the horses mainly on account of the marshy ground into which their legs sunk. Trees with low-slung branches did their best to unseat us but by dint of much urging, thrashing and cursing we got through the morass with nothing worse than wet feet from the occasions where we had to dismount. The weather continued cool and breezy with dark clouds scudding across the sky. Our location had become a mystery and with thickly-timbered hills and more fencing hemming us in we were forced to retrace our steps back over some of the waterlogged territory we had taken such pains to traverse in the first place.

Farmers in the outback were more knowledgeable and by closely questioning those we came across we succeeded in getting back to and maintaining the approximate route of the line and made steady progress. Once more Beauty shed her load and time was wasted as we retrieved it from sundry ditches and puddles.

Under clearing skies we made exhausting but rapid progress along a dead straight grassy route that sped towards limitless horizons. Jack-rabbits, prairie dogs and the occasional antelope bounded across the pastures. In the far distance, almost out of vision, we could see strange hillocks protruding, like boils, from a now flat landscape.

Now that we had gauged the walking and trotting paces of our respective mounts we had developed a formula for our order of march. Trixie, I found, liked to lead but, once in front, needed constant urging. Mike, now on the nervous Beauty, was inclined to lag. Thus Steve or I usually led; though sometimes Trixie moved better as Tailend Charlie. Everyone took turns to lead the designated packhorse for the day.

We made camp late in the evening beside a brackish pond that formed part of Buffalo Creek and close to the only two trees on view within a five-mile radius. Supper was a hurried affair of ham and eggs made in competition with darkness, which won hands down.

Mike and I, remembering the downpour of the previous night, pitched our lightweight tents while Steve put his trust in the open sky. The sunset was one of those that inspire artists but we weren't putting our cards on its promise.

Dawn was equally sensational but freezing. Daytime temperatures were becoming progressively warmer so that the contrasting cold nights put me in mind of the Sahara. Through chattering teeth we forced down a spoonful or two of milkless, lukewarm porridge and called it breakfast, before continuing on our way aware that our campsite was at Cold Turkey Creek where, once, another stage station had served its quota of travellers.

In the township of Bowman the entire press corps turned out to intercept us for our story: a lanky cub reporter who had heard about the pilgrimage on the village grapevine. From Bowman onwards Highway 85 took us by the hand providing litter-strewn verges though, since it had been laid over the original course of the line, there was no alternative but to follow it, off and on, for several days hence. The verges had become receptacles for discarded beer cans and bottles, broken and unbroken, while mileposts taunted us as we struggled on under an increasingly hot sun. We drew some encouragement, however, from passing drivers who kept stopping to ask the reason for our journey and donate refreshment, once even a full bottle of rye whisky. The sores developing on my backside and the strain on my calves when attempting to alleviate the pain of the former became agonising. To dismount and proceed on foot for a mile or two was a huge relief.

At the North/South Dakota state border we thankfully swung away from Highway 85 into the Flint Hills to locate Crooked Creek, another stage station. A series of false trails and the usual deflections caused by fences led us astray but at least we were away for a while from the hated 85. A herd of playful bullocks mock-charged the horses causing them some concern; Trixie took violent objection and I had to keep her under a tight rein. A river, winding and deep, had us meandering along its course in all sorts of directions before a fordable crossing-point could be located.

We came upon Crooked Creek almost by accident. Here the halfway stage station had once been, but my pleasure at being there was stronger for the simple fact that we were to hove to there for the night. And it was during the hours of darkness that Beauty cut her fetlock on barbed wire and, consequently, went lame. In the morning Mike bathed and bandaged the wound but this all caused delay and, when we finally moved off, our speed was much reduced. Trotting was out of the question for plainly the leg was painful. With sinking hearts we reverted to the 85 as the most direct route to Buffalo, a fact that had been taken into account by those who had forged the route of the stage line.

By the time we had plodded into a hamlet called Ludlow we knew the worst. Beauty was limping badly and was not going to stay the course. Furthermore it would have been cruel if we had tried to make her do so. We therefore decided to leave her in the town of Buffalo, a destination at which we had planned to award ourselves with a rest day, maybe two.

Ludlow was no more than a church, a bar, a garage, a confectionery shop and a post office. We made use of all these facilities except, I regret to say, the church – though maybe a word with the Almighty would have helped. With every mile the sun became hotter with the hump-backed Butte Country shimmering in the heat. For the last six miles of the day we were able to divert to another dirt road into Buffalo which was as refreshing as the squall that caught us before we reached the town, serving to cool our shoulders with a sprinkle of water.

Buffalo has the distinction of being the geographical centre of the United States and, for us, the halfway point of our journey. The temperature was rising to the high nineties so we rested here for a day and two nights, residing in a cattle market warehouse containing tables that we utilised as beds.

The next day was a Sunday and not a soul made a move in the town until midday so it was well into the afternoon before we succeeded in obtaining relief for Beauty and arranging for her care. This was through the good offices of the curator of the town's museum who was also a mine of information on the subject of the stage trail. Our arrival in the town had slowly sunk into the minds of its citizens and later in the day we were besieged by the local press who insisted upon taking photographs of us in the company of the mayor. It was if suddenly our project had caught the imagination of the Dakotan populace.

On Monday morning the heat really came on and by nine the day was sweltering. Somehow we attached bed rolls, spare garments and vital stores that had been the cargo of the packhorse to our saddles and ourselves to proceed, looking like overloaded gypsies, into the shimmering horizon along the ubiquitous 85. Without a packhorse we made better progress though speed, in the new circumstances, meant broken eggs which dripped depressingly down saddlebags and horsey flanks. The loss of the eggs brought our rations to the bare minimum; a few tins of beans, an apple or two, some wads of pre-cooked buffalo meat and a supply of tea bags.

Snakes, including rattlers, were once more much in evidence, slithering through the grass of the verges to upset the horses. Trixie suffered a severe attack of nose-fly for a while and became very difficult to handle. A golden eagle spiralled in the sky and coyotes, racoons and deer made fleeting appearances to add a faint aura of menace to a burning land of strange, unreal hillocks, devoid of succour.

At Redwig – no more than a service station and a post office – we were befriended by the proprietor of the former who bade us join him for a fine supper of fried egg sandwiches, potato hash, coffee, lemonade and cold tea, which was a vast improvement on our midday repast of half an apple. We were also given permission to spend the night in a set of sheep pens across the road but our slumbers were rudely terminated by the most frightful storm I have ever witnessed. It struck around midnight and immediately raised hurricane-force winds that promptly blew away the corrugated iron sheets that formed the roof of our boudoir. No rain fell but the initial formation of tornado 'twisters', spiralling downwards in the not-too-far distance had us wakeful and apprehensive for the remainder of the night.

Breakfastless, except for tea, we took to the road once more and two hours later passed Crow Butte, a flat-topped rock rising from a dead-flat plain, a landmark visible for miles and the site of a famous battle between Crow and Sioux Indians. Today it is no more than a source of Indian legends and a breeding ground for rattlesnakes. For us, however, it was where we finally turned off 85 onto a country road that followed the alignment of the stage route. Its dust surface and grassy crown made for more pleasant hacking while traffic was virtually non-existent. The road crossed numerous river-beds, the water long evaporated.

In spite of the storm, the heat increased with temperatures nudging 100 degrees and we were visibly wilting. A brief halt to view O'Dell stage station was a pleasure, though not because of the dilapidated structure with no roof that formed the only standing memorial to the marquis's stage line, but simply for the excuse for a lie-down in its shade. At an isolated ranch house we needed no second bidding to accept the offer of freshly-squeezed lemon juice; the family there had heard of our approach on the local radio. Our host also gave us the name of his nearest neighbour some ten miles distant where he judged we could camp for the night.

General Custer supposedly made the sometimes quoted comment that the Badlands look like 'hell with the fires put out' and we were inclined to agree with him – though not so sure about the fire. Yet there was no denying the delicate beauty of the strange buttes and a barren labyrinth of pinnacles and bizarre shapes washed into existence first from the high levels of the ancient Black Hills, and then carved by the elements. Today a land almost devoid of water, this region must once have had ample moisture, for it was initially a haunt of the three-toed horse, the camel, the rhinoceros and the sabre-toothed tiger.

Our latest but as yet unknowing host's ranch house lay at the end of an imposing drive but nobody was at home when we arrived so we took it upon ourselves to lay out our sleeping bags close to a garden lake that must have been fed by an underground stream. At first sighting it made an idyllic site for a camp but a vicious breed of mosquito made painfully aggressive bedfellows. Our supper consisted of beans eaten with the blades of our penknives, our cutlery having been mistakenly discarded at Buffalo. A tap at the back of the house produced luke-warm water.

During the night we heard the return of our unknowing hosts but, being out of sight of the house, remained where we were and set out early next morning to avoid being run for trespass. We were now in missile country, passing by any number of well-guarded Minuteman silos which only served to accentuate the remoteness of the territory. All too soon the sun was belting out its heat which, together with a hot wind, made conditions insufferable. Slumped on the horses like drunken men we made slow progress back to the despised 85 which we thought we had left forever.

But hope lay on the horizon. A faint swell of land all but lost in the heat haze proclaimed the Black Hills. Between them and us lay the town of Belle Fourche, a sizeable place by all accounts and allegedly well-stocked with bars. We determined to reach it by nightfall.

The town slowly materialised as we pressed on, counting milestones and telegraph poles. At midday we halted in a glade of long-dead trees to sit out the worst of the heat and consume some cold beans and buffalo meat, but clouds of biting insects drove us out of their domain. In all it took eight hours to attain

Belle Fourche when a car could have covered the same distance in minutes. The shadows were perceptibly lengthening as we finally clattered noisily into its urban heart.

'Bell Foosh', as the natives call it, was once the scene of a range war between cattlemen and sheepherders and its annual rodeo is looked upon as one of the finest in the West. Otherwise I would call it a place of no great distinction but plenty good enough for us. We lay out our bedrolls in a deserted meadow close to the arena, obtained water and oats for the horses, then made a beeline for the nearest bar to replenish some of the liquid our parched throats craved.

The night was well nigh as hot as the day – we were told the day temperature had risen to an unpreceded 111 degrees – but the cool fresh smell of the Black Hills was in our nostrils. Breakfasting on no more than a swig of water – heat nullifies hunger as nothing else – we trundled out of town after restocking provisions at an early-opening store.

The new road was a delight when compared with the ruthless 85, a country lane that switched playfully into a scenery that reminded me of lowland Switzerland. Furthermore, it was also the stage route. As soon as we began climbing gently the surroundings became imbued with clumps of trees that, mile by mile, blended into ever-thickening forests of Ponderosa pine clothing granite slopes. Behind us the flat eternity of the prairie faded into the same haze that had initially hidden these friendly intimate hills from our longing gaze.

My attire had long since consisted of no more than a pair of shorts and even Steve had shed items of his beloved cowboy outfit. In Belle Fourche our dishevelled appearance on sweating horses had raised stares and not a few questions as well they might.

Midday brought a mirage but one that stuck to its guns. It took the form of a Holiday Inn in the middle of nowhere. It couldn't be, we reasoned. But it was. A real, bricks-and-mortar hotel on the edge of Spearfish Canyon just two miles out of

Spearfish town and, though Holiday Inns don't usually send me into raptures, this one was the exception. Lunchtime business diners were thus treated to the spectacle of three horses being 'parked' among the Cadillacs and Chevrolets, and their grimy riders entering the hallowed portals. Immersed in the hotel swimming pool we happily soaked away some of our aches and pains though no doubt sorely taxing the filtering plant in the process. A slap-up meal followed to make up for the number of breakfasts we had jettisoned and in the comparative cool of late afternoon we wound a way up the mountain valley laced with running streams that we would have given an eye-tooth to behold earlier.

Our final night's encampment was within a glade of trees adjoining a gentle torrent, the gurgling water a lullaby to our ears. Mosquitoes were a bane but you can't have everything so we buried our heads in our sleeping bags and thought of tomorrow and journey's end at Deadwood.

Somewhere east of Spearfish we had passed by the last of the stage stations but its location had been lost in the mists of time and we were in no mood to go hunting for it. But who cared? Certainly not the scurrying citizens of Central City, a characterless suburb astride a lethal highway into Deadwood along which we were channelled. And certainly not those of Deadwood itself who, predictably, could raise no interest in trails or the history of them as we marched, ever so slightly triumphant, into town. The place was a well-baited tourist trap with Wild Bill Hickok and Calamity Jane bars at every turn though, at least, the beer was agreeably ice-cold.

The town was born from gold fever and raised through such Wild West characters after which the bars are named. The main street runs through Deadwood Gulch; the rest of it crawls up the steep canyon sides. At the height of the 1876 gold rush, 25,000 people swarmed over the hillsides to dig for gold and, just as suddenly, the town emptied as new strikes were found elsewhere.

We spent the night not in the best hotel as we had told ourselves we would, but, inexplicably, beneath the grandstand of the town's sport stadium. Don't ask me why; maybe, when it came, the idea of a soft bed and clean sheets frightened us. It rained like destruction throughout the night with water splashing down around us from flooded gutters but, in our dry but far from luxurious refuge, we never heard a thing.

Our ride was over. We had broken no records, notched up no great achievement, won no prizes. But, nevertheless, the glow of satisfaction that suffused our minds for reaching the end of an old stagecoach trail nobody had thought to follow offered reward in plenty.

THE CONCEPT OF the covered wagon, its day and age, is the very core of American history. Countless films and books have told the pioneering story; yet the evocative creaking of iron and wooden wheels has still not entirely ceased today.

A number of organisations continue to run wagon treks along sections of the routes of famous as well as lesser-known trails for both commercial reasons and to evoke a sense of a history of which the United States is in comparatively short supply. And none carries this out so vividly as the annual excursion arranged by the farming community of Fort Seward, Jamestown in North Dakota. Unlike some other similar outfits this was non-profit making and non-commercial; relying upon the participation in and contributions by all who possess a sense of heritage.

With Steve being the so-called honorary trail boss of the Fort Seward Wagon Train it was inevitable that I would be invited to join the current trek out of Jamestown scheduled to roll some eight days after our return from Deadwood. The week-long journey, covering well over a hundred miles, had been running annually since the end of the 1960s and though originally planned as a one-off event, its popularity and support had risen to the extent of the trek becoming a yearly exercise.

For me the ensuing ride into yesteryear was to be more of a walk than a ride since the alternative of sitting on my blister-scarred and still sore buttocks on a hard wooden seat in an unsprung wagon was not one I particularly relished.

Prior to departure from Jamestown each participant was assigned to a wagon, whatever his or her chosen method of motivation, and straight away came under the benevolent charge of a 'Big Wheel' and a 'Teamster', the whole force being commanded by the current year's 'Trail Boss' – Steve – who was to lead the long, straggling column, on a fine brown-and-white stallion. Once on the road the reliving of the 'old days' is taken seriously with no radios or modern conveniences permitted, while participants are encouraged to dress in the garb of the period, a stipulation that produced a multitude of fancy creations.

Out of the expanding suburbs of Jamestown the wagons and their retinue took to the open fields. Every year a different route is planned; the trail meticulously tracked weeks in advance. Permission to negotiate pastures and establish overnight camp sites has to be obtained in advance though landowners are sympathetic; some even participating in the journey themselves. This year the route had been titled 'The Beaver Creek Trail', which looped south through open grasslands and the wooded valleys of the James River, a region well immersed in native American and pioneer history.

The wagons on this trek were exact copies of those used on the wagon trains crossing the Dakota prairies a century earlier; some, in fact, were originals that actually had carried pioneers into North Dakota. Many of those early pioneers used oxen instead of horses or mules to pull their wagons since oxen were able to subsist better on the short and rough grasses of the plains and had no need of grain to supplement their diet as do mules and horses. Furthermore they were cheaper to buy and, later, could be utilised as food. Today only horses and mules are used with arrangements made to supply hay and feed for them at the overnight camps.

As in the old days a great amount of food has to be gathered and prepared for the trek. Wagon-train fodder was not as harsh as is often thought and it is certainly more palatable today. A chuck wagon carries food and provisions but an expert cook arrives (discreetly by car) in the evenings to preside over the production of the evening meal. The amount and variability of the food was staggering. Prepared for another week of spartan living I found myself eating better than in many a multi-star hotel. One menu included fresh strawberries and ice-cream while the breakfasts were massive three-course affairs.

Most of the time I walked directly behind my allotted wagon, chatting at intervals with its heavily-jolted passengers who, occasionally, joined me on foot when their hind-quarters could take no further punishment. I walked the bulk of the route, only clambering aboard when the convoy crossed a river. Being the only Britisher on the trek I was forgiven for wearing only my twentieth-century shorts – except by Steve, who periodically passed by importantly on his stallion to ensure all was going well with his charges.

Every evening the wagons were circled together in the form of a corral and individual tents erected. In this respect today's wagon trains remain authentic – even to a few grisly teamsters sleeping in and under their wagons like their fathers and grandfathers before them. A factor of the Fort Seward Wagon Train was togetherness, with everyone helping with building fires, cooking, meal serving and camp clean-ups. Activities such as nature walks, competitions, amateur entertainment and sing-songs around the camp fire were part of the programme. My fellow wagoners were mostly from the American Mid-West and a more engaging bunch of people would be difficult to assemble. Being the sole Britisher I was well and truly pampered by all of them.

Travelling is a little easier and faster nowadays, though the pace was a little slow for me. The old wagon trains put in an average of ten miles a day depending upon the terrain, weather and amount of Indian interference. Today 12–20 miles is the daily norm – or at least it was on my trek. This allowed an early arrival at the camp site, a swim in any available lake or river – including a leech-infested James River – and the preparation of an evening's entertainment around the fire provided by each wagon 'detachment' in turn.

The train left from the site of the old Fort Seward (which in 1872 took over duties from Fort Ransom located between Jamestown and Fargo). It returned via Jamestown's Frontier Village, a well-endowed reproduction of a nineteenth-century community. Between were days of laughter, the forging of new friendships and a host of open-air activities as original as was the whole concept. We had crossed hills and rivers, and breathed the fresh invigorating Dakota air to which I was fast becoming accustomed.

One of our wagoners was a poet, Betty La Fontaine. She sums up better than any words of mine the joy and sense of occasion inspired by the Fort Seward Wagon Train:

'What you have missed!
You there, in your paper world.
Your hot and cold tap running,
Your data-processed paper world,
Your instant reply, ten to four world.
Come along with us,
Ride up the crest of the hill,
Charge out across the prairie,
Take your fill
of the rain and sun and the sky.
Come know the chill
of a dew-soaked meadow at dawn!'

and

'We creaked and rumbled from horizon to horizon,
Reflecting on those who had gone before.
What power drove them to the farthest sky?
Perhaps we envy hopes so high,
And following their path, expect to win
New lands for the soul, to build new homes within!'

Chapter Six

TRAVELS BY ROAD

IN WHICH THE AUTHOR DODGES GRIZZLY BEARS, ARRIVES AT A TOWN CALLED DAWSON CREEK (MINUS PROFOUND-THINKING TEENAGERS), PLACES A LONELY HEARTS AD FOR AN ALASKAN CALLED JOE WHO SPENDS THE WINTER MONTHS IN TOTAL ISOLATION (SAVE HIS TWO HUSKIES) AND RIDES A BUS ALONG TREACHEROUS MOUNTAIN ROUTES THAT FORM PART OF THE ASIAN 'SILK ROAD'.

Over the years I have travelled the world's highways by car, bus, bicycle and on foot. Two of these journeys on historic arteries I have described in some detail in earlier chapters – namely the royal road of the Incas in South America and the Mores stagecoach trail in the American Dakotas. Now I turn to another historic route of more recent vintage that, today, is no more than a ghost highway, this one in the far north of Canada.

It was in spring 1981 that I was invited to northern Canada to take part in a reconnaissance of a route across the Mackenzie Mountains linking the remote oil-bearing township of Norman Wells on the great Mackenzie River to the state of Yukon. Here I was to join up with three others to traverse the lonely, rugged miles of this forgotten artery with the object of ascertaining whether any sections of it were suitable for the running of small group trekking forays on a commercial basis.

The assignment intrigued me. It had the ring of pioneering about it and my two Dakota projects had instilled in me a pioneering spirit. Perhaps the way would not be *entirely* devoid of the tracks of man, however, for once it had been a road, an old (though perhaps strictly not quite old enough to qualify as historic) highway driven through the wilderness. But now it was dead or dying and only its decaying bones would offer a banister.

The water was perceptibly rising. A bright-tinted stone clear of the stream an hour ago was now submerged. The island upon which we were standing was shrinking fast; there was no doubt about it. The previous night we had waded to the elongated neck of land with the water level no higher than our thighs. Today this backwater had become impassable. The main stream made even more of a formidable obstacle and was frightening to behold. The Twitya River is no placid stream at the best of times and now it was swollen and angry from days of rain channelled into it from the mountains.

Though midnight when we had pitched the tents on the sodden island there had been no darkness. But the June sun was lost behind heavy drapes of surly clouds vomiting cascades of rain. We slept uneasily as each of us pondered our situation. How were we going to negotiate the Twitya together with our heavy rucksacks? Previous rivers along the route had been fordable affairs even though the bitter-cold water and strong currents made the task risky and unpleasant. The Twitya, however, was in a different category. To swim it, fighting a vicious current that would all too soon sweep us helpless to the rapids below the site of the old road bridge, was out of the question, and anyway what of our baggage? No, the river would have to be crossed by raft. There were trees on the island; young saplings too fresh for raft-building and others that lay beached and waterlogged among the flotsam all around. Only some of these were suitable but here another problem had arisen. Amongst our combined stores and provisions we could locate only one small axe and a saw blade; the saw frame of which had been lost. Calculations produced the sum of 26 trees, topped and tailed, as a minimum requirement for a raft capable of carrying the four of us and our loads. On the credit side we could raise two dozen six-inch nails and plenty of cord while one of our number possessed knowledge of raft construction. The odds against us reaching safety were uncomfortably high but what was the alternative? We had arrived at the point of no return on our journey, our retreat was cut off and our refuge was reducing by the hour.

We lay nursing our thoughts, hearing the rain beating on the canvas, aware that our refuge might be submerged before we could leave it. David, our leader, was the most worried, the yoke of decision-making on his shoulders. An Englishman, residing in the Yukon town of Dawson City, this project had been his idea. A fellow-citizen but of Canadian birth was Byron, a fractious character but extremely knowledgeable when it came to survival in the outback. The youngest member of the quartet was Reinhard from Germany, grotesquely fit and never displaying the slightest sign of exhaustion following the most gruelling exercise. I was, as usual, the oldest and weakest, a walker but no backpacker, and my concern at our predicament must have been equal to David's – though I fear it was mostly concern for my own skin.

Across the Twitya the opposite bank was another world, an unattainable world flaunting our onward path, a broken banister of a ghost road leading yet another hundred miles to salvation…

The Canol Road: a thin red line on the empty map of north-west Canada that winds from Johnson's Crossing, some 35 miles north of Yukon's Teslin astride the Alaska Highway, to the Northwest Territories border. A summer-only route, north Canadians know it as a wilderness road running 300 tortuous miles into the Mackenzie Mountains to Macmillan Pass, with a lead-zinc mine and an airstrip as its terminus.

The road's history is known only by a generation of older Canadians who will remember the circumstances of its construction over 60 years ago when, during World War Two, the United States Army undertook the building of a pipeline from Norman Wells on the broad Mackenzie

River to Yukon's capital, Whitehorse. The object was to supply fuel to Alaska and the military traffic en route from the United States at a time when its far northern state and, more particularly, the Aleutian Islands, were under threat from a Japanese enemy. The project was a fiasco from the start and the price tag of $134,000,000 a fruitless waste that was eventually to undermine the credibility of the United States War Department. Additional to the pipeline was its servicing road but, with the subsequent receding of the threat, very little oil was ever to find its way into the storage tanks of Whitehorse. The pipeline and its road were quietly abandoned.

With renewed oil and gas exploration in more recent years being carried out at Norman Wells and the remoter regions of the Northwest Territories, the spectre of a further pipeline following the course of the old had arisen; the fear of energy shortage comparing ominously with the 1942 invasion threat. But though technology had changed, the savage environment of the Mackenzie Mountains remained constant and had to be taken into account. Thus the lessons learnt by American engineers had to be given serious appraisal by the new generation of, this time, Canadian pipeline builders.

All this, of course, was – and maybe still is – for the specialists and those who guide the destinies of the regions in which we live. However, for all Canadians the idea of a possible repeat of history and the recollection of a road to nowhere are surely of more than passing interest particularly to those who live north of the sixtieth parallel.

Anyone with a sturdy vehicle can drive to Mac Pass (as it is called) but the Canol Road route does not end there. It continues as the Old Canol Road Hiking Trail through the multiple barrier of the Mackenzie Mountains for another 240 desolate yet inspiring miles to Norman Wells bearing, along the way, the mouldering relics of an army's passing.

Although some maps cautiously label the route the 'Old Canol Road Hiking Trail' let me warn anyone considering following it that this is an understatement supreme. Rivers have washed away the bridges, landslides have obliterated the track, and rainstorms, cold winds and grizzly bears make the going arduous and dangerous. We thought we knew the score and guessed the path would be hard and hazardous, the elements hostile and the terrain relentless, but none of us was prepared for the physical adversities that nature was accumulating along the way.

This then was the path I had set myself to walk carrying 60 pounds of victuals and equipment upon my back, and in the company of three companions I had, again, never met.

Two weeks previously I had driven the Alaska Highway, but the walking challenge arose following the covering of the two rebuilt sections of the Canol Road. This is divided into two sections: that from the Alaska Highway to Ross River (139 miles) is referred to as the South Canol Road; the other from Ross River to the Macmillan Pass on the Northwest Territories border (160 miles) as the North Canol Road. Thereafter you are on the phantom Hiking Trail.

David's plan was to undertake the walking of it in reverse – starting at Norman Wells in the Northwest Territories and so travelling back to Macmillan Pass and Yukon border. To reach our starting point we had first to drive the 451-mile Dempster Highway to remote Inuvik and from there fly to Norman Wells out in the great void of the vast million-and-a-quarter square-mile state. That bridgeless rivers would have to be crossed was a factor we had to take into account but only one, wider, deeper and bigger than the rest, offered the slightest stirrings of concern amongst us as we unpacked our provisions and gear from the vehicle at Inuvik.

Inuvik is the second town of the Northwest Territories by virtue of the fact that, with Yellowknife the capital, it is the only other town in the state. Even so, Inuvik's population was not much over 3,000 souls. The town consisted of rows of brightly-painted buildings standing on stilts, a church shaped like a monstrous igloo, and bloated metal conduits running in and out of its houses. Yet Inuvik is one of the most scientifically-planned places in Canada; it is a government-created community designed to overcome the frightful building problems caused by an unstable ground surface and the bitter cold of a long dark winter.

The piles on which the buildings of Inuvik stand ensure stability. They are driven through the muskeg overlay into the gravel stratum 20 feet down and there frozen solidly into the gravel. The buildings sit on the piles several feet above ground level, to prevent their interior heat from melting the ground surface and turning it into a mucky sludge. And since underground pipes cannot be laid in permafrost, all utilities, including steam heat, running water, and sewage disposal, are carried through these metal tunnels.

I must admit to finding Inuvik a most depressing town. The only way in and out, besides an unreliable air service, was via the daunting miles of the tyre-lacerating, oft-blocked Dempster Highway, which was how the four of us reached it. A sensation of being entirely cut off from even the vestiges of civilisation assailed me. Here the phrase 'dead end' had literal meaning.

We spent a restless night under canvas in the town's campsite, a notorious meeting place of Inuvik's criminal fraternity, and next day thankfully flew to Norman Wells.

Here I found more a community than a township, by which I mean that everyone who lived in the expanded collection of dwellings was employed, directly or indirectly, by the oil companies who were the only reason for its existence. Though even more remote than Inuvik and not connected by road to anywhere, it gave an impression of being a cheerful spot. Again every house was brightly, even garishly, painted, as if in defiance of the staggering loneliness of its situation, but the populace was an ever-changing one; their main topic of conversation being what they were going to do when they returned home on leave or expiry of their contract. In Inuvik the people *lived* there; chained to desolation by fate. Those in Norman Wells were paid considerable sums to exist and work in the outback for a limited period, serving out their sentence based in a house that wasn't home.

I had never flown in a seaplane (or floatplane as they call them in North America) but I enjoyed the short flight, hopping across the mighty Mackenzie River, by which Norman Wells stands, to the Canol Lake, hardly more than an overgrown pond, where we landed. The banks were of soft mud which meant a damp and slimy disembarkation, as one by one with our rucksacks and accoutrements we jumped from the aircraft's float to what we fondly hoped would be terra firma. Up to our knees in clinging black slime we watched the floatplane heave itself into the air and disappear. We were alone – and rarely have I felt so excruciatingly alone.

The old road lay some miles west of the lake and, shouldering our loads, we staggered towards it across the marshy scrub – a combination of tufts of thicket grass and bog – intent upon raising our first camp astride the artery. Besides our bulging rucksacks, festooned with cooking implements, we carried coils of rope, a .303 Mk 4 rifle, fishing gear, an axe and a radio transmitter. Straightway the notion arose in me that I had, again, bitten off more than I could chew as my load turned the act of walking into a drunken slouch.

The trail, when we came to it, was plain to see: a track, not yet overgrown to extinction, etched into the landscape by tree saplings and alder growth seemingly addicted to its stony surface. As if to emphasise its presence the flattened remains of some wooden buildings lay untidily about a stream crossing. Much of the timber was rotten but made convenient fuel for a fire we soon had blazing merrily, and on this we heated up our first day's supper. Ahead, the faint outlines of the road could be discerned gently spiralling into eternity. The stream offered fresh, cold and safe drinking water, a forerunner of many such sources that precluded any concern over supply of at least *one* vital commodity. We slept, that first night, adequately but uneasily, David, Reinhard and I occupying the main tent with Byron, at his own request, in a small bivouac. 'I've been known to snore,' he told us. It was the understatement of the year.

Next morning, breakfasted on porridge, toast and marmalade with a choice of tea, coffee or cocoa, we set off down the road, a great deal more confident than we had felt the previous day when floundering through the bog. We had re-arranged our loads, adjusted rucksacks so they rode higher on our shoulders and better-distributed the loose items amongst us. And 'down' did go the road – but not for long. In the first of many 'wash-outs' – a morass of rock carried down by sometimes raging torrents that were now no more than humble streams – it disappeared, though our maps showed it to have once followed this watercourse. Thereafter the route became an uphill one, made hard going and dispiriting by the fact of its disappearance. However, the occasional leaning or broken telegraph pole and attendant coils of cable, making grim entanglement traps for unwary animals, pointed out the general direction.

Halfway up the hill we came upon traces of the road again and, at the same time, a cloud of mosquitoes to give us a sample of what these insects had in store for us. Having liberally covered all exposed skin with an evil-smelling but effective repellent we spent an energetic half-hour with arms flailing like windmills in an effort to ward them off. In spite of the mosquito menace I wore shorts as I do on most treks, since where a soaking by river, rain or sweat is to be a recurring theme I find bare legs an advantage. In this instance so did the mosquitoes.

The road re-established, it then proceeded to bifurcate though no such junction showed on the map. We chose, on principle, to follow the lower route and consumed a picnic lunch in another stony river-bed cleaved by a playful brook. As we ate, the sun sank behind a mass of grey clouds and it began to rain. If this was meant as a warning, none of us got the message. Rain, if prolonged, has an awkward habit of turning playful brooks into seething torrents as we were to learn.

The rain on this occasion was no more than a shower in company with an icy breeze and this pattern of sunshine and cold showers remained constant for the rest of the day as we toiled through the Little Keele Valley, finally raising camp close to a deep section of the Little Keele River. In an initial and misguided sense of bravado we immersed ourselves extremely briefly in its paralysing waters to be savaged, as we emerged, by mosquitoes of Stuka-like fanaticism. In future, hygiene was to go by the board with only our feet benefiting from immersion – and this on an involuntary basis when forced to wade unbridged rivers.

With each meal consumed our packs became correspondingly lighter, a condition that tempted us to make serious inroads into our food supplies. But against this had to be borne in mind the fact that we would receive no further rations for a couple of weeks when an aircraft was scheduled to deliver provisions at one of the Godlin Lakes at least a 170 miles ahead. David's resourceful Swedish wife, back in Dawson City, had packaged individually-prepared meals – main courses and puddings – to last over that period of time, and each plastic-wrapped and labelled pack was to be used strictly on the dates indicated. The fact that we carried a gun – vital for protection against unprovoked attack by grizzly bear – and fishing tackle meant that anything we might obtain for the pot could be looked upon as a bonus.

The night's slumber was interrupted when the tent collapsed, the rocky ground having defied all our efforts to insert metal tent pegs which had bent like hairpins. Thus we had to rely upon boulders as anchors for holding up the canvas and these proved unsuitable for the role.

Our continued progress in the morning was governed by the obstacles in the path rather than by the fading course of the road. The highway itself, long ravaged by a river intent upon widening its banks, was nowhere to be seen. So we walked along the centre of the wide valley still partly covered by thick platforms of dirty snow, crossing and re-crossing the Little Keel River at its shallowest points. Again fallen telegraph poles and, now, lengths of rusting four-inch pipe (incredible as it may seem the Canol oil pipeline was of no more than four inches in diameter) affirmed we were on the correct route.

Already the journey was becoming a routine march during which the highlights of each day were to be meal stops. Regular as clockwork was the solemn proclamation of our good intentions of rising with the dawn and making early starts but, alas, my companions displayed a disturbing inclination to morning lie-ins which boded ill for our schedule. Thus we usually failed to get away until after ten with a hefty portion of the day lost. On the other hand we were in a land and a season of eternal daylight so perhaps our laziness was of no consequence. Our meals too were taken at the insistence of stomachs rather than the clock.

Lunch, on the third day, was served amongst the depressing wreckage of a one-time oil-storage depot overlooking a graveyard of dead military vehicles neatly lined up as though for inspection by the keeper of some ethereal garage. Old machinery – oil pumps, generators and the like – stood directly under the skies, their once-enveloping buildings having fallen away to matchwood. Here and there a shed still stood; a Nissan hut complete with springless beds or workshop without a roof. Strangely a water-closet continued to flush but the graffiti on the wall was of a generation past. While sipping our tea bunched around an oily fire an airliner crawled across the sky. Its passing not only accentuated the loneliness but, in a limbo where time means nothing, a link with a world out of reach.

The vehicle parade marked the spot where we turned into a side valley towards the Plain of Abraham. Sunshine in a suddenly azure-blue sky beat down upon us as we slowly zigzagged our way up a minor canyon liberally sprinkled with the debris of landslides and rain-inspired flood-water. Each obstruction had to be negotiated or detoured, a fiendish test of stamina and avoidance of broken ankles; even legs, for the appalling loads on our backs continued to upset our sense of balance as we skipped from rock to rock. Hardy mountain Dall sheep grazed, uncaring, on the higher ridges and small herds of caribou stared quizzically, even moving towards us to satisfy their curiosity, as we grimly narrowed the distance to the head of the valley.

Sections of pipe with the ubiquitous telegraph poles became our constant companions as did, later, occasional traffic notices and mileposts that had survived the years and the elements. The pipes were invariably occupied by families of ground squirrels who made their homes in them to escape the attentions of bears and other predators. Their squawks had a strange hollow ring as we passed by. Otherwise a great silence pervaded the air, frightening in its intensity.

But there was beauty too. Whenever sections of the road broke to the surface, recovering from obliteration by avalanche and landslide, it showed mottled with colour by reason of a display of wild flowers seemingly addicted to its surface. Their delicate blossoms and fragrance amongst the grey dust and in defiance of a fruitless soil lightened our hearts a little. Close to the final ridge at the top of the valley the telegraph poles drew themselves erect in military fashion as if to challenge us to a race to the summit, then keeled over as if the effort was just too much.

Ahead, the scenery opened up to reveal the plain stretching away into glorious flatness to offer last-ditch encouragement to totter the last mile of a now clearly-discernible road. Only one of a number of wooden buildings of the camp at milepost 80 was habitable but it was enough. Over to our left a range of distant mountains shimmered in the haze while the crimson blooms in the road winked at us as, wiping stinging perspiration from our eyes, we made it to the night's refuge, thankful we did not have to find the additional energy to raise the tents.

The night was cold but bright as day. We lit the little cast-iron stove and were glad of its warmth though our beds were no more than the hard dirty floor. Ground squirrels and porcupines scratched beneath the rotting foundations and other noises caught our receptive ears. With the Plain of Abraham we had reached grizzly bear country. A large specimen had attempted to dislodge this very cabin occupied by a group of surveyors a month or so before, or so the story went, and the threat was not lost upon us. Thus we went to bed with the loaded rifle to hand, half-listening for sounds that were more than the scufflings of squirrels and porcupines. 'A Night on Bare Mountain' could well have been the theme of this vigil – and on two counts.

The morning remained cold but dry as we moved away along a dirt road tailing away into the distance. It continued to climb, but gently, for three miles, offering, at each bend, a false crest to be attained. The final crest rewarded us with a staggering view of another range of snow-dappled mountains though our admiration was tempered by the knowledge that our path led through them. From the viewpoint, however, it was a downhill course with the road corkscrewing into a new valley, this one designated Andy Creek. We short-circuited some of the hairpins and, risking the grizzlies prone to inhabiting such terrain, cut through a belt of spruce pines alive with mosquitoes to reach the river at the bottom.

Progress down inevitably has to be countered by subsequent progress up, but the fresh climb offered fine close-up observation of caribou herds with one handsome bull repeatedly returning to investigate us after the main herd had departed. Caribou are immensely attractive animals and how people can bring themselves to shoot them for no reason except 'prestige' is beyond me. Still-warm dung and pug-marks indicated that a sizeable grizzly was close and we proceeded with the utmost caution, the rifle loaded and cocked. Handfuls of bear-fur and porcupine quills indicated where the beast had made its last attempt at a meal, but nothing appeared. We camped close to milepost 94 in the snow-streaked Carcajou Valley with a view one could describe as alpine. Our dinner was mysteriously labelled 'Beef & Fusilli with tomato paste & parmesan cheese' which was followed by a sweet called 'Pear Brown Betty', and it went down a treat.

Footfalls in the night had us nervously peering out of tents in the small hours but the visitor was only a moose. A rain shower had turned to snow on the mountain flanks, displaying a whiter world than the one we had previously looked upon. The morning's march was marred by an erroneous decision to take a short cut across the valley for which we were punished by an excruciating one-and-a-half-mile traverse of lunar-like rock and a wet negotiation of the Carcajou River. The saving was less than a mile of easy road-walking and the crossing of a river by a bridge that still held. From then on short cuts became strictly taboo.

Whilst massaging sore feet and throbbing ankles David saw a large porcupine which we pursued with the aim of having it for supper. Difficult to catch for obvious reasons we attempted to shoot it but, with ammunition in short supply, our marksman, Byron, had to ensure he got it with the first shot. Unfortunately he failed to do so and the animal got away – to my secret relief – though they say porcupine meat is quite tasty.

A while later a brief sighting of a grizzly had us eyeing the scrub that closed in on the road with deep suspicion, but the only animals we met that afternoon were a family of wolverines and more waddling porcupines as we toiled along Bolstead Creek, with the warm sun fighting a losing battle with a bitter wind. But the grizzly menace remained. The danger with these beasts is not so much in themselves as of us getting between parents and offspring, a situation that arouses the deepest fury in the former. To fell a full-grown grizzly on the attack is no easy matter even with a high-calibre rifle. A .303 bullet will kill a man with no trouble at all but can be deflected by a bear's thick hide and immense frame. There are few spots on the animal where a single shot is likely to bring it down – and you only have time for one shot. The worry too, so far as we were concerned, was that none of us were all that sure where the weak spot was. On the assumption that prevention is better than cure we made as much noise as possible while continuing on our way, the idea being to frighten the danger away.

Our immediate destination was the long-disused military camp at the head of the valley where we hoped there would be at least one cabin suitable for an overnight stay. Long before we reached it we could see the camp buildings rotting on their timber-strewn site like discarded toys and, as we approached, we came to the skeletal remains of some mouldering Chevrolet lorries, one with its Goodrich tyres in near-perfect condition, plus Schroder valves that still held the air in them. A dirty and decaying hut makes a poor substitute for a tent but the one we found at least contained some serviceable spring beds though water for the evening meal had to be brought a considerable distance.

And so up and over Bolstead Creek and into Trout Creek to stumble through a series of 'washouts' where rivers of boulders had obliterated the road. The weather turned hostile again to unleash repeated hailstorms from a sky that made the day into as near night as I had seen. The quantity of rivers that had to be forded multiplied, the one-time bridges either no more than driftwood on the shingle or entirely vanished.

There is a technique for wading a river. First, the shallowest section within reasonable distance of one's arrival point has to be located. This is usually where the river is widest. The entry and exit point selected, one can either advance with care into the water wearing boots or these can be removed and replaced with plimsolls, but attempting the crossing in bare feet is foolhardy since the river-bed will be treacherous and very slippery. On the Canol Road Trail the rivers were running fast and exceedingly cold so that, at the halfway mark, one's legs lost their feeling and ceased to function properly. And with a heavy load – plus boots swinging round the neck – falling is all too easy, particularly as the movement of water adds an optical illusion to increase the likelihood of overbalancing.

As the trek proceeded – and the weather worsened – so the rivers became more and more of an obstacle. At first they were laughable affairs that could be bounded across with the help of a few well-placed stones but, with the Carcajou and other more formidable water-courses, the problems increased. We helped one another as best we could and the three English-speaking members of our group will not forget the agility shown and firm hand offered by the young Reinhard. It is a strange feature of life that, given a little hardship and danger, a man's character is so often enhanced. David, Byron and myself initially found it impossible to see anything likeable in the somewhat arrogant German who made up the quartet. Always he was ahead of the rest of us, marching determinedly across the countryside pausing only to express exasperation at our more leisurely progress. But the frightening negotiations of those rivers and his unstinting aid had us ashamed and humbled. I like to think that, by the time the trek ended, either Reinhard had become a very credible human being, or we had become more tolerant ones.

Byron, on the other hand, showed a fiery temperament that belied my initial judgement of his character. But his occasional unprovoked bursts of fury never did more than temporarily dent a sustained friendship. We all admired his outdoor living capacities and skill, knowing that, in the company of such a man, we had, in the last resort, little to fear when it came to survival. David, for his part, remained steadfastly calm, reassuring, kind and tolerant. When Reinhard forged ahead and had to be rebuked, when Byron blew his top and had to be pacified, or when I funked a nearly-vertical cliff of scree, it was David's action that brought encouragement, understanding and peace. He was the perfect leader, leading without appearing to do so.

We could hear the sullen roar of the major obstacle of the route long before we reached the Twitya River. Prior to plunging into a hillside canopy of trees we even glimpsed it from afar and could make out the white flecks of madness upon its surface. Everyone became unnaturally silent as we descended by a bounding outline of a road to its edge. Our future depended on the state of this river; our plans and expectations were now entirely based upon 'after we're across the Twitya'. All at once it lay before us.

The previous night's camp had been close to the Trout River, a friendly stream but one already swollen by melting snow and rain in the mountains. We had crossed it with no great difficulty on at least three occasions, aided by broken bridges, because the road kept being deflected to the opposite side by sheer towers of granite. But the road, where its route lay alongside the river, had, again, been washed away, forcing us to either make a nightmare progress along its treacherous course or to claw a way along the scree-lined buttresses of the granite walls. Rain fell incessantly adding to the misery so that when at last we had emerged upon a shelf overlooking the valley of the Twitya we evoked a false feeling that the worst was over. Even fresh grizzly dung and pug-marks in the sandy soil failed to subdue our sense of optimism.

Arrival at the northern shore of the Twitya, however, drained our hopes like water down a plug-hole. There before us lay a wide, raging torrent of uncontrolled fury, the surface a cauldron of threshing waves. The road strode straight up to this horrifying impasse and disappeared. Of the bridge or its remains that once carried the road to the other bank there was no sign. A short way downstream lay the rapids where the great surge of near-freezing water came hard up against a solid wall of rock forcing a change of direction. We gazed, aghast, at what lay before us, lit a small fire and brewed a pot of tea. It was all we could think of to do.

David's information from those who had been this way before included the advice to proceed upstream some two miles and attain an island formed between the mainstream and a backwater. From the island a raft would have a chance of making it to the opposite shore before disaster overtook it in the rapids. This intelligence was, of course, based upon *normal* river conditions and the availability of plentiful supplies of timber. For better or for worse there seemed no alternative but to make for this alleged island and then assess the situation from there.

Accordingly began a particularly unpleasant side-trek made, in plimsolls, along the river's edge: rock-infested, slippery, wet and under heavy rain. It was long past midnight when, having waded up to our thighs the wide but only gently-moving backwater, we pitched camp on the sodden soil of a fast-disappearing island.

None of us slept a wink that night as we listened to the rain beating down upon the canvas. Our sleeping bags became soaked from the water-logged ground and, for once, we rose early for there was vital work to be done. Our council of war had swiftly decided upon the only action we *could* take. With our retreat cut off by the swiftly rising waters we could but go forward – and the only method of going forward was by raft.

Under Byron's expert guidance we set to work. Felling with our ludicrously inadequate axe those growing saplings not already deep in water, and sawing, with a saw-blade alone, those not already waterlogged that formed the flotsam on the island, we heaved each trunk with brute force born of desperation to the water's edge. Four layers of logs Byron had calculated as the minimum necessary to carry the four of us and our baggage across the raging Twitya, though the only way of discovering whether, in fact, this was enough, would be when we cast off. And by then it would be too late to do anything about it.

All day we toiled in the torrential downpour meekly administering to Byron's barked instructions, and gradually the craft on which everything depended began to take shape though our island fastness reduced by the hour. By evening, soaked and shivering with cold, I experienced the initial paroxysms of hypothermia as exhaustion sapped my ability to maintain a blood-circulation while my younger companions were not in a much better condition. At one point David seriously contemplated radioing for help, though how help could be given in the present circumstances made requesting it of little use.

In all it took 15 hours to complete the craft with but one brief pause for a hot meal deemed vital if we were to retain our strength. Another hour and the weird vessel, its timbers lashed together with yellow cord, had been loaded and stood ready at the top of its 'slipway' of smoothed-down saplings. The final job was to cut ourselves long punting poles for guiding and pushing the raft to a designated landing point downstream on the opposite bank. Then we took a last look-round, sent a private prayer to the Almighty, named the craft 'Pearl' after Byron's girlfriend, clambered aboard and cut the retaining rope.

We hit the water with a great splash, sank to our midriffs, then swirled, out of control, in the scurry of water. Desperately we heaved with our clumsy poles against the river-bed, attempting to propel ourselves out of the main stream and towards the far bank, but the current held us firmly in its grip, whirling us at high speed towards those terrifying rapids.

Our designated landing point swept by and was gone. 'Make for that outcrop!' screamed Byron, indicating a small beach that protruded a little way into the water and, again, we threshed and wrestled with the poles but to no avail. The new beaching point whirled past leaving one last hope, a patch of quieter water the far side of the main stream that intimated the presence of shallower water where the river made a slight curve. Already we could hear the roar of the rapids beyond which galvanised us into further action though the cold water was fast sapping our reserves of strength, the foaming waves smashing over us, drenching the rucksacks and rocking the raft in angry little motions that threatened to loosen the

212

bindings. Gyrating madly we spun out of the main stream and, inexplicably, ground to a halt on the shallows. Leaping into the water we hastily removed the rucksacks before the tugging current could release the beached craft. Shaking uncontrollably but jubilant we never even saw *Pearl* slide away into oblivion; only triumph and a heartfelt relief registered in minds that were aware we had attained the promised land, that *other* bank of the Twitya.

But the nightmare had not quite ended. It was long after midnight and we had a considerable distance to go to reach a Canol Road encampment we knew existed that might offer the only hope of a dry refuge from the rain and the cold.

Judging the direction we plunged into the dense undergrowth, making our way through forest and bog with the deluging rain hissing against the foliage. It took our last remaining strength to fight through this morass, relocate the road and track it back to the broken-down cabin – the only one of several still habitable – a mile inshore from where the river bridge had once been.

Shakily we set about fuelling and lighting the rusty oil-drum stove and gradually our efforts were rewarded as we became enveloped in a clammy haze of steam rising from our dripping clothes and bedding spread around the dirty little room. Not even sojourns I have experienced in some of the world's finest hotels have given me greater pleasure than did that simple cabin in the wilderness.

We rose late since it was well into morning when we had climbed into steaming damp sleeping bags. The new day was a brilliant one with a sun lighting up the landscape to make the previous day but a bad dream. Snow covered the tops of the surrounding hills turning the countryside into a scene of ethereal beauty and child-like innocence. Following a substantial brunch we laid out our belongings to air and ourselves to bask anew in our deliverance.

But we had lost time and were behind schedule – we had a tryst to keep with an aeroplane at the Godlin Lakes, our subsequent re-provisioning point. In the afternoon, therefore, we reluctantly repacked the rucksacks, girded our loins and set out to put ten miles of distance between the Twitya and ourselves. The road was a gradual incline, the sun was hot, but to be warm was a pleasure. Byron expended another bullet on a spruce grouse, hitting the target this time but half blowing the wretched bird to pieces. We grilled it for supper to supplement the evening's fare and by the time we had squirmed into our bags it was raining again.

It rained all night but politely dried up before we stirred our stumps next morning. A flooded road and flooded terrain made the going tricky, involving jumping from tuft to tuft of thicket grass 'islands' marooned in a marshy sea. It was a time-consuming progress too and none of us escaped wet feet. But the reward was a luncheon of ham in sherry sauce and banana cream pudding taken by the side of a delightful stream pushing its way through a new valley. Alas, full enjoyment of the banana pud was curtailed by another downpour which, if nothing else, provided reason for hastening us on our way. With the appearance of the Godlin River, here set in picturesque Godlin gorge, movement became really tough. The road had long since ceased to exist, having been washed away by malignant flood waters, and in its place was a two-hour stumble high above the river along a near-perpendicular scree-slope of knife-sharp slate where one slip could send one, in a welter of this odious material, straight to the bottom. It would have been difficult enough to move empty-handed but with 60 pounds of dead-weight on tired shoulders it was positively hell.

We were fast approaching the prettiest section of the Canol Road and our campsite that night reflected this change of landscape. Byron missed another spruce grouse but, luckier with his rod, caught a trout to add to our rations which were showing ominous signs of extinction. A belligerent porcupine produced some light relief from the sombre task of surveying and attending to blisters, cold sores, dirty bodies and wet socks with which we were all afflicted. Abed but not asleep we became aware of sounds all too reminiscent of stalking grizzlies, but nobody felt inclined to investigate.

Any worries David may have harboured concerning food supplies were dispelled next day when, during the lunch-stop, Byron began pulling arctic thar and grayling out of the Godwin River at a ludicrous rate. We could see them in big shoals in the clear water and, getting down on hands and knees, were able to entice individual fish to a finger and, sometimes, flick them to the shore without benefit of line or hook. In a trice we had a twig fire going and were gorging ourselves silly on the most delicious grilled fish I have ever tasted.

Our route was leading us along a tranquil section of the road which ambled with no cave-ins or washouts, along a valley of sheer loveliness. White-capped peaks made the perfect setting for a river scene spliced with dark green sentinel pines and moss-covered hillocks. It was all too idyllic to last of course and very soon the river intruded rudely to cross our path, forcing another wading operation. This one however was aided and abetted by old bridge supports that stuck incongruously out of the water.

Another encampment, this one in better state of repair, became home for our twelfth night out. The reason for the higher standard of accommodation was that its buildings were in support of an air strip. We had arrived at the Godwin Lakes, and with but two hours to spare. But the aircraft was late and it was not until well into the daylight small hours that we heard the unaccustomed sound of an aero engine. We rushed out of the cabin to welcome the little floatplane as it appeared out of the subdued pre-dawn sky, circle the camp and put down with scarcely a splash on the most northerly of the small lakes past which the road had led. To reach it we had to run a mile over marshy ground, but the longing to talk to fellow-humans – besides ourselves – was strong. Until it has actually been experienced, the emotion of enforced loneliness, the results of being shut away in a vast desolation of unimagined remoteness, can barely be understood. Nor can such a visitation by strangers from the outer world arouse the new emotion of intense excitement until the first has been experienced. Like children we waved and shouted, pumped the hands of the pilot and his mate, unloaded the boxes from the aircraft's hold and, with a sickening pain, watched the machine take off, lift into the sky and vanish.

But among the packages was a bottle of whisky and two of wine. 'Why do we have to add weight to our loads?' we asked ourselves, so drank the lot and felt better. We were even able to sleep through what remained of the night. In the late morning, we redistributed the stores and, by midday, were once more on the way.

Three miles brought us to the banks of the Ekwi River to enforce the first of a selection of river crossings that had us in and out of fast-flowing icy water for days on end. The valley was steep, the choice of crossing point restricted and hardly had we fought our way across when we had to repeat the performance as the river coiled about our lame highway. Only for the first day's final crossing was luck on our side. Here the bridge was down but not out and by clinging to rusty spars and splintered timbers we managed a dry passage.

The Ekwi remained with us for three days, its tributaries catching us when the main river failed to do so. Once we became so confused we twice waded it when we didn't have to. If nothing else got washed our legs did, and the marvel is we did not end up with webbed feet. In this delta-like environment we were back in grizzly country and sightings became quite common. Whenever we espied these great beasts we gave them a wide berth – even if it involved added mileage. Our ammunition stock was down to five rounds and none of us were too sure how many would be required to drop such a hefty animal if the crunch came.

Entry into the Caribou Gorge provided dramatic scenery and a prickly detour over it by way of thorn scrub since the road through the canyon had vanished. To go with it a sun-and-showers combination of weather turned to constant shower. At mile 208 we came upon another dump of derelict military vehicles and, with the Intga Valley, we were in sight of the Selwyn Mountains standing straight-backed out of an extensive plain. Excitement swelled once more in our breasts as we pitched camp by the rock-encased narrows of the Intga River. Just behind those Selwyns lay the Mackenzie Pass and the end of the trek. While chopping wood in a surge of anticipation I cut my hand with the axe and bled like a pig.

The previous night we had camped at 5,000 feet at the head of the Caribou Pass amongst, last vestiges of snow and ice. It had rained all night and the long trudge up the muddy, waterlogged valley had almost defeated me. But on this new morning, a morning that afforded sight of the Selwyns, the sun joined us in silent thanksgiving, splashing their jagged summits an impossible hue of pink.

Plains walking had its points. The terrain was flat, the road surface composed of springy turf and the inevitable rivers were little more than trickles that could be jumped across with little inconvenience. But the Canol is an obtuse road and manages to find gradients in the most horizontal of territory, meandering mindlessly in its effort to locate and climb them. Plains, however, soon become monotonous tramping grounds; there are no surprises – cruel or kindly – to anticipate over the next crest, or the next, or the next. And this plain – the Barrens – went on forever, its little rises no more than an aggravation. But the grass verges of the road; indeed the whole endless plateau, sparkled with wild flowers though our pace did not allow for dawdling. Had I sat down I would never have got up since there was not a boulder in sight against which I could lever myself into an upright position again.

Suddenly we were in sight of Sam's place. It was like a mirage. Atop a slightly bigger hill, perversely bypassed by the road, appeared a collection of chalets that were very different from the remnants of a military camp. A handsome, even sophisticated, timber residence stood, solid and square, amongst half a dozen smaller chalets glass-fronted and fresh-

217

painted. With one accord we swung off the road and staggered up the steep incline, taking it the short way – straight up – in our eagerness to reach this outpost of civilisation.

We had arrived at Old Squaw Lodge, a naturalist's paradise built by wildlife biologist Sam Miller and his associates, an away-from-it-all guesthouse attainable by high-clearance, four-wheel drive vehicles from Mac Pass. And with Old Squaw Lodge we had indeed reached the outer fringes of civilisation.

Sam was not at home but two of his colleagues were and they invited us to spend our last night on the Canol Road beneath a solid roof. In the evening Sam arrived in his jeep-like automobile we had watched approaching from the base of a still-distant Selwyn range as radiant in the evening sun as it had been that morning. In new-found company we talked well into the night watching a sunset of an unbelievable majesty.

What a paradise for the nature-seeker is this lodge – if it is still there today – named after the melodiously talkative oldsquaw duck that breeds on the arctic coast and the barren lands of the Northwest Territories. Here among a patchwork of silver ponds, alpine meadows and mossy green tussocks is a heaven on earth. Here it would be easy to ignore the outside world – while yet not *quite* be out of touch with it – and roam for a magic week or two encountering caribou herds, listening to the soft chirp of bank swallows and langspurs, and glimpsing the flash of white from willow ptarmigan. And roaming amongst a foliage of dwarf birches turning an intense orange in the autumn, and of blue carpets of forget-me-nots and cushions of lichen curled like starched lace. Not all is cruel along the ghost road of the Canol.

The last day's march to the Mackenzie Pass was dictated by the rule of the motorcar. Vehicle tracks scarred the muddy surface of the old road and the serrated channels trapped our feet in a vice that held them in their grip the last dozen miles. There were people at the airstrip too but they took not the slightest notice of us. And why should they? For at this point the Canol becomes a highway of today; albeit a modest one. Just back down the road we had waded the sizeable Intga River, a tributary of the larger Keele, and the last obstacle. But that too was behind us and none of us were to look back. It was if the past had never been.

Few roads in the world have a more evocative image – especially to us crowded, restricted and overtaxed drivers on the traffic-snarled, bottle-necked trunk routes of Britain – than that of the Alaska Highway. I drove its full length, together with some of the other Canadian and Alaskan wilderness highways, in 1981, prior to my Old Canol Road hike across the North West Territories.

If there is an elusive pot of gold at the bottom of the rainbow then there must be reward at the end of the Alaska Highway, or so the notion came to me as I gazed at Milepost 0 in the centre of the township of Dawson Creek.

For years only a dream of far-sighted engineers of the north of North America, the highway is, today, not only a dream come true but a vital artery of communication and travel connecting Alaska with Canada's Yukon Territory and the lower 48 states of the USA and the southern provinces of Canada.

By agreement between the two governments, the highway was built by the US Army Corps of Engineers as an overland lifeline to relieve Alaska from the World War Two hazards of shipping and as a military supply route to counter a threatened Japanese invasion through the Aleutian Islands; a threat similar to that which provoked the construction of the Canol Road. The initial road was completed in eight months and then turned over to civilian contractors for widening and gravelling, replacing primitive log bridges with structures of steel, and re-routing.

Since that bitterly cold pre-dawn day in March 1942 when the vanguard of the US Army of Engineers arrived at the 'end of the steel' – the railway – at the then remote

British Colombian frontier village of Dawson Creek, the Alaska Highway has become a legend in the annals of road-building.

On 20 November 1942 in nine degrees of frost, 250 shivering soldiers, civilians and Royal Canadian Mounted police watched officials from the United States and Canada cut the ribbon stretched across the frozen road at Soldiers Summit. From this wind-swept hill opposite Milepost 1061 at the southern end of Kluane Lake, the highway was pronounced open for business. Fear is a mighty stimulus to achievement and for such a road to be hacked at such speed through a savage wilderness was nothing short of a miracle.

The Highway is like no other road in the American continent. Others are built through populated areas; they link small towns and great cities; they bear a substantial human traffic and enormous burdens of freight. The Alaska Highway is an artery running inside Canadian territory for over 1,200 miles and Alaskan territory for more than 200 more. It has a beginning and an end and almost nothing in between. It is a road without people and very little history. The Japanese threat ebbed and died; the war drew to a close. The Highway remained.

Give or take a mile the recorded length of the road is 1,520 miles or 2,446 kilometres between Dawson Creek, British Columbia in the south and Fairbanks, Alaska in the north.

In 1981, when I drove it, most of the miles through Canada were gravel surfaced while the shorter Alaskan portion was paved. Even then this highway was no longer classed as a true wilderness road in Canadian/US circles though with petrol stations and facilities sometimes hundreds of miles apart, drivers from Europe might not have agreed. Anyway, before the 'black top' or road paving spread the full length of the route I was determined, for no other reason than because it was there, to discover how it felt to drive this astounding artery in its raw state.

My vehicle was, ironically, a small Japanese Toyota, and I left from Edmonton thus adding 367 miles to my journey.

Dawson Creek was a town of some 11,000 souls perched on rolling farmland, and though it had retained an aura of the frontier it boasted all the comforts of a small city. North of Dawson the scenery changed little. Much of it reminded me of Siberia with which the land has geographical links, with trees, trees, trees – mainly spruce – marching into endless horizons. Fort St John was the subsequent urban centre of any consequence with, again, a Wild West façade hiding a highly civilised heart. Set in low rolling hills it was a rich hub of grain, cattle and sheep farming, though the original Fort St John, ten miles south of the present town site, was no more than a trading post for the Sikanni and Beaver Indians.

Beyond Fort St John the farmlands petered out. The wilderness took over, heavy forest lined both sides of the road, with here and there, through a break in the trees, glimpses of far-off hills painted a deep, impossible blue that merged into the purple of hills yet more distant.

For the driver conditioned to paved roads, the gravel highway would at first seem something of a trial. However, the surface was kept in generally excellent condition by a fleet of road-maintenance equipment so that the driving hazards resulting from those defects common to gravel roads everywhere were reduced to a minimum. Flying stones were the biggest menace and many vehicles regularly using the road had wire mesh screens over windscreens and headlights.

At Mile 296 a bridge carried the road across the Muskwa River, at 1,000 feet above sea level the lowest point of the Alaska Highway. And so into Fort Nelson, another one-time fort, this one to become a railhead in 1971 with the completion of a 253-mile extension of the British Columbia Railway from

Fort St John. The township was a focal point for exploration for natural gas and oil.

With the replacing of miles with kilometres in Canada but the retention of miles on United States territory a certain amount of confusion had arisen along the road. The new Canadian kilometre posts were being installed but some mileposts remained for the simple purpose of serving as mailing addresses for people and businesses who had utilised the mileposts for identity.

Already there were stretches of Canadian paving, particularly at the approaches to the principal townships. In between I found some extremely rough patches where ice and snow had broken up the road surface, but my chief worry was that of running out of petrol. I carried spare cans but when these were empty my eyes were more for the presence of 'gas' stations than for the scenery. Log cabins and camping sites offered sleeping accommodation at intervals along the way though these were often closed out of season.

At Fort Nelson the Alaska Highway makes a right-angled turn and heads into the Rockies. Here the foothills were no more than endless uprisings flanking deep river-threaded valleys with the real mountains lurking a long way behind. There was nothing friendly about the Rockies here. Their presence conjured a kind of sulleness; indeed all along the entire length of the highway the mountains keep their distance as if disdaining the existence of the impertinent road.

But if the mountains do not encourage overtures from man to nature they encourage them from man to man. The absence of all familiar evidences of what we call civilisation, the sheer overwhelming hugeness of the country and the increasing sense of isolation draw men together in a spirit of camaraderie rarely to be met with on more frequented highways. The number of travellers driving the Highway at any given time was absurdly small in relation to its length, the logical stopping places then being spaced about 300 miles apart. Thus sight of another human being was cause for not only hand-waving acknowledgement but, where circumstances permitted, a union of souls. Driving alone, I was particularly susceptible to the emotions of meeting fellow-travellers and was pleased to offer the occasional lift to Canadian residents en route to the next township or tourists bound for the nearest campsite. I came across disillusioned cyclists too who were pedalling the full length of the Highway and were only too pleased to stop for a chat.

At Mile 456 (Kilometre 734), about 60 miles beyond Summit Lake Pass (at 4,250 feet, the highest point on the highway), is Muncho Lake, one of the loveliest mountain lakes in Canada. Enfolded by mountains, its waters of the purest aquamarine and amazing clarity, it lay in a stillness and serenity which today are seldom found in places of great natural beauty. A single fisherman as immovable as a statue was the only human intrusion. I halted to gaze upon the scene, then crept away as if afraid of sullying it. One day, I thought, when the road is fully paved, the lake would attract commercial interest, but at least I was privileged to have listened to its as yet unbreached silence.

Beyond Muncho Lake, the Liard River – mean, treacherous, dramatic – dominated the landscape and to a marked extent dictated the route of the road. Here I found the driving more demanding than elsewhere on the route, for it followed an in-and-out up-and-down course through countryside of spectacular allure. Rejuvenation of tired cramped limbs could be effected at Liard Hot Springs – pools of water of a constant 100 degrees Fahrenheit.

The actual entry into Yukon Territory was correspondingly undramatic. The Highway crossed an unmarked boundary, bobbed back into British Columbia, then back again into the Yukon. I had also crossed a time zone at the border, the first of several that came, thick and fast, the further north I travelled.

The Yukon is more than twice the size of Great Britain and much of it is upland plateau cut by deep gorges and wide valleys and marked by mountains that are among the highest and most rugged in North America. From here onwards the land became picturesque though tinged with sombre loneliness. Other motorists sounded their horns and waved as they went by and, at the rare eating houses and snack bars, the staff as well as the transitory clients were, as everywhere else, addicted to much bonhomie and an intimacy that was surprising even for a North American. My gargantuan breakfasts, usually taken at the first 'eating joint' I came to of a morning, invariably turned into social events with a bunch of travellers avidly comparing road conditions and locals interrogating new arrivals.

Yukon's first non-native visitors were Russian who arrived after Vitus Bering, a Dane serving in the Russian navy, explored the coast in 1741, and within a few decades American whalers were coming to the area. By the mid-1800s the Hudson Bay Company had established a number of trading posts in the interior and on the Pacific coastline of what is now Alaska. Russia sold Alaska to the United States in 1867 and on August 17 1896 George Washington Carmak discovered a rich streak of gold in what was renamed Bonzana Creek which runs into the Klondike River and, today, the Yukon means only one thing to most people – if it means anything at all. The Yukon means the Klondike, and the Klondike means gold. To the more mature of us – and perhaps the more romantic – it may also invoke the poets and authors such as Robert Service and Jack London. The year 1898 saw the famed procession of would-be prospectors over the infamous Chilcoot Pass from Alaska into Canada. The Klondike gold rush was henceforth on with a vengeance and history has recorded its passing, much in the form of historic legends including those of the doings of Sam McGee and Klondike Kate.

Six miles inside Yukon lies Watson Lake. For hundreds of miles and kilometres I had been subconsciously counting them to this name on the destination signs and my mind had built up an impression of a great metropolis. But Watson Lake turned out to be hardly a ball of fire. In fact I was out of it before I realised I was in. Its population was given as 1,167 so you see what I mean. The place had two attractions. One was the famous sign forest started by a home-sick American serviceman working on the construction of the road in the 1940s, with travellers still adding signs to the collection – mostly town or village nameboards – from all over the world. The other attraction was the chain of lakes that turns Watson Lake into a centre for fishermen.

The 285-mile run from Watson Lake to Whitehorse I found agreeably restful by comparison with that of the previous day. Here there were long stretches of road with few steep gradients while, for much of the distance, the route was along pleasantly wooded valleys reminiscent of the Scottish Highlands.

Spanning an arm of the Teslin Lake was the Nisutlin Bridge, the longest water span on the Highway, with awe-inspiring views of distant mountains, and across it was Teslin township situated at the confluence of Nisutlin Bay and Teslin Lake. No more than a sprinkling of log cabin homes, it held the distinction of having the largest native population in Yukon, many inhabitants being descendants of the Tlingit tribe. Alas, as elsewhere in Canada, there was a problem with regard to the Indian minorities, many of whose members lived on social security and were more often drunk than sober; I was to see many of them in the few bars I visited.

Between Teslin and Whitehorse the Highway was continuously in sight of water with, nearing the Yukon capital, a horizon full of the great Alaska range amongst which can be seen the snow-capped bulk of 20,230-foot Mount McKinley, North America's highest peak. But perhaps the most exciting moment for me was the first glimpse of the river – at this point narrow, tranquil, giving no hint of its turbulence a few miles downstream – which more than any other in the north country bears in its name connotations of romance, of suffering and heroic deeds.

The Yukon is one of the great rivers of the world. It flows for a distance of 2,300 miles from the remote Mackenzie Mountains to pour its muddy waters out of an equally desolate mouth on the Bering Sea.

With that first glimpse of the Yukon one is in touch with history, folklore and legend. Here is the land of gold-hungry miners where great and strange and terrible things occurred and mighty deeds were done. For this is the river down which men once swarmed by boat, raft and canoe in the age-old search for El Dorado.

Whitehorse, Yukon's capital, came as a pleasant surprise. It could, for these parts, be classed as a mini-city which, when I first arrived there, held a population of around 16,000. I found it to be an attractive urban centre with log cabins side by side with comfortable hotels, supermarkets and a modern shopping mall; not at all the one-horse town I had envisaged. Yet even in town the wilderness reaches out to touch the urban-hungry visitor as if to remind him or her of the void beyond.

Whitehorse came into being as the northern terminus of the White Pass and Yukon Railway, running from Alaska's Skagway, and it was here that the famed river steamers connected the railhead to Dawson City by way of the Yukon River which runs sedately through the town. The gold rush and the Klondike stampeders have left their mark and have twice turned Whitehorse into a boom town. The stampeders landed here to dry out and repack their supplies after running the infamous Whitehorse Rapids, while the gold-diggers came to town to either celebrate their luck or, more likely, to drown their sorrows. But the town does not rely solely upon its boisterous past. More respectable now, it boasted one of the most modern hospitals I had ever seen and a Civic Centre second to none. The old SS *Klondike* paddle steamer and the Log Skyscraper – relics of a bygone age – looked out of place in a town fast ridding itself of its Klondike image.

On to Haines Junction over some rough sections of road needing careful driving to the first of two natural features which, even in a land as rich in scenic grandeur as the Yukon, must rate as spectacular in the extreme. The first was Kluane Lake, a blue-green strip of water extending 40 miles or more between mountains that were the colour of rusty iron. There were several minor gold rushes in the Kluane Lake country, notably around Burwash Landing near the north end of the lake. Destruction Bay, a settlement a few miles south, memorialises in its name the many miners who are alleged to have lost their lives in the shallow but often storm-hit waters.

The second landscape feature is the St Elias mountain range which includes Mount Logan, Canada's highest peak of just under 20,000 feet. They, together with the Kluane Mountains, paralleled the highway, presenting an almost unbroken chain of lofty summits interrupted only by a few wide valleys cut by glacier-fed rives and streams. Amongst all this jumble of granite is the Kluane National Park, a paradise for trekkers and wilderness-seekers since its many acres were virtually undeveloped and encompassed extensive ice fields.

Haines Junction itself was no more than a grandiose main street with no town and the northern terminus of the Haines Highway to the Alaskan township of Haines situated at the head of the Lynn Canal which, in turn, links it to the coast.

Perhaps the dullest section of the Alaska Highway was that where the road nears the Alaskan border. Having cleared Destruction Bay and the Kluane Park the countryside, exhausted after its exciting display of drama and beauty, fell flat on its back. The road snaked over the terrain in an aimless fashion as though it were following the wanderings of a drunken moose. For no obvious reason it developed a rash of 'S' bends, the explanation being that, back in 1942, the road builders were in such a hurry they simply followed the gravel ridges to avoid the marshy ground and swamp which is a feature of the region. To halt at the border was a relief.

Canadian Customs and Immigration Authorities were based at Beaver Creek but the actual border with Alaska was a further 19 miles ahead and this fact was made startlingly clear by the refreshing sound of tyres swishing smoothly along on a paved surface. But all was not quite perfect. Permafrost had caused horrific potholes in places which could have broken the axles of vehicles of unwary motorists who celebrated the occasion with bursts of long-denied acceleration.

The scenery of the road changed not at all with the new territory, but with the vanishing of the winter snows the Alaskan woods and meadows produce many varieties of wild flowers, including iris, blue lupin, marigold, larkspur, sweet pea and the tiny forget-me-not, the state's national flower. Along the Highway the ever-present fireweed of late summer added bold strokes of mauve and magenta to the colour of the landscape, contrasting agreeably with the sombre greens of the spruce. The wildlife of these northern climes comprises black and grizzly bears, caribou, moose, red fox, wild buffalo, Dall sheep and mountain goat while the many lakes and river deltas are nesting grounds for a huge assortment of water-fowl. Dall sheep are shy creatures and are rarely seen, I was told; though I was forced to stop on more than one occasion when a herd blocked the road. Buffaloes, too, roamed the verges and I was to see innumerable moose and caribou.

Tok at Mile 1,314.2 – we were now back to miles – was a place of which I myself had no preconceived ideas about because I had been there already. The well-stocked village was on a junction of both the Alaska and Glenn Highways which made it an important communication centre. Based on Tok I had journeyed north along the Klondike Loop Road to join a character by the name of Joe O'Bailie prospecting for gold under the South Forks River near a hamlet rejoicing in the name of Chicken. Together we had searched and sifted but neither of us were to make our fortunes on that occasion. Joe, however, had been there for years, and was making a reasonable living from the resisting soil – though I could think of easier ways of earning a buck.

For a time after I left he kept in touch and the following extract from one of his letters offers a graphic idea of conditions to be found in rural Alaska:

'...It's been down to minus 60 and 70 degrees for about two months with warming spells of up to minus 30 degrees from time to time so I was able to walk out of my cabin down to the post office to get my mail. I've not seen anyone for four months so it was quite an event. I got two husky pups just before the road closed for the winter and I'll use them next year to haul my provisions back to the cabin so that I won't have to backpack them up the hill anymore. What a chore that is. I did get stuck out once when it [the temperature] went from minus 40 degrees to minus 78 in two hours and I spent the night in a drift keeping a small fire going until about noon the next day when I got hungry enough to make a break for the cabin a mile away. I froze part of my face and nearly froze both hands doing it. This kind of cold can freeze your lungs in seconds to kill you if you're not careful. The worst of the cold I hope is over now that it's the end of January but it [the temperature] could still drop again before March. The days have started getting longer too; for a while I only saw three hours of daylight so had to walk back and forth from the digs [work site] in the dark. The trouble is I'm nearly out of provisions so I'll have to get serious about bagging a couple of caribou since, except for an occasional rabbit which are tough as a boot, I'm out of meat. The caribou should be migrating through here any day now but I've spotted some fresh moose tracks so I'm going to try to nail the critter next week. Rice and beans are fine but sure can get monotonous after a while... The northern lights are still out, all blue and green; they remind me of a woman's eyes. Sure gets lonely around here and I've even broke my mirror so can't even talk to myself. The pups are good company but they're not much on conversation.'

In a subsequent letter Joe asked me to place a lonely-gold-digger-bachelor-in-outback-Alaska-wants-to-meet-suitable-girl type of advert in a magazine. This I did and the response was overwhelming. His last letter to me read: *'Wow! I was in agony being alone and now I'm in pain because I'm having a heck of a time making up my mind which one to choose! Dave McCall down at the store took a few pictures of me and I've been sending them to as many girls as I can. I feel like a kid in a candy shop.'* I've heard nothing from him since.

Not everyone realises that the search for gold continues and strikes are still made, if not on the scale of a century or more ago. Along Taylor Highway and the Klondike Loop were not only the rotting remains of nineteenth-century mines with their unsightly 'tail' – the debris of gold-bearing rock – and rusting dredges, but new sites occupied by dedicated men with one eye on the big chance and the other watching out for the income-tax man. Some, like Joe, were doing quite nicely; others found it as good a way as any to occupy themselves while playing truant from the mainstream of life.

The penultimate community south of Fairbanks, the road's northern terminus, is Delta Junction and it is *officially* the end of the Alaska Highway since the remaining distance to Fairbanks is covered by the Richardson Highway. Milepost 1,422, an elaborate affair with the United States and Alaskan flags flying above it, proclaimed this fact and, if one was required, the nearby visitor's centre provided a gratis certificate confirming one's feat of driving. Beyond the silt-laden Delta River the Alaska Mountains spread over the skyline in snowy grandeur while cool winds from their flanks tempered the warmth of an abruptly sunny day.

North Pole, yes North Pole (population 500), was the home of many a Fairbanks commuter, being just 14 miles from that city. The main business of North Pole was the promotion of Christmas – all through the year. Its post office enthusiastically franked letters and cards especially brought in for its exclusive postmark by travellers worldwide. Santa Claus House, built like a doll's house, was a unique if pricey gift shop, and for laundering there was Santa's Suds.

Hardly on a par with Anchorage, Fairbanks gave a fair imitation of a city nevertheless. Situated in the heart of the Tanana Valley, with gold-bearing hills rising in the north, it was still, in spirit, a frontier town. Only too happy to get out of the car I walked the streets side by side with twentieth-century miners, Indians, Innuit and pioneers, if not tobacco-chewing cowboys with or without snow-shoes. To use a well-worn cliché, it was a city of contrasts with old (by American standards) timber buildings mixed with modern façades of department stores and office buildings. Fairbanks was born in 1902, when an Italian miner, Felix Pedro, discovered gold 'in them thar hills'. The resulting rush brought the prospectors who, in turn, brought their families, and so the town blossomed.

The address of my hotel into which I had pre-booked was given as 'Fairbanks', and my enquiries as to its whereabouts elicited the fact that it was 'just up the road'. The Alaskan perception of distance is well illustrated when I tell you it was actually 65 miles 'up the road', though still within the borough boundary of Fairbanks.

My reward at the end of the Alaska Highway? The real pot of gold for me will always be the remote land of Alaska itself, vibrant with the promise of adventure amongst its silent backwoods. Yet there it lies, just a spin up the road...

THE FIRST PART of this chapter covered just two of my journeys, on foot and by car, following a one-time road and an existing highway of considerable but recent historical significance that came into being, in the north of North America, as a result of the Second World War. Now I widen both the geographical and historical scope as well as category of road upon which I have travelled by bus, taxi, bicycle, lorry and, again, on foot.

I will start with a journey by taxi made in the Indian sub-continent in 1986.

I sometimes wonder what thoughts pass through the heads of Japanese tourists when they perceive a like party of their

European counterparts. Do we too all look the same? Do we mouth the equivalent of 'Ach, so'? The coachload I saw outside one of the better – though hardly ostentatious – hotels in Kargil looked more out of place than ever in such a wilderness. I asked them whither they were bound. 'The load to Reh,' they said.

I too was on the road to Leh, deep in the fastness of the Himalayan Ladakh Mountains. I had come from Kashmir where I had spent a lazy ten days on a Lake Dal houseboat. Being something of an active type of person, I find relaxing to be hard work but, ensconced in such a flat-bottomed vessel of Victorian elegance where one reclines on stiff velvet cushions surrounded by lace doilies with a servant to serve every need, undertaking anything other than relaxing is difficult. Even on the occasions when I left the boat it was only to glide across the mirror-smooth lake, lying on cushions under a silken canopy, in a gondola-like craft called a *shikaras*, propelled by a boatman. Alas, Kashmir is currently in the grip of political strife and such indulgences are no longer attainable.

Now, however, I had embarked on a project of less refined ornateness. And Kargil proved it. The second town of Ladakh is the halfway point on the road to Leh; the place where the coaches, buses and lorries take refuge from a storm of rock. A solitary street, wooden box-like houses and cheap hotels, it was a blend between sleazy decadence and the vigorous though monotonous precision of the army which, even then, was very much in evidence. The military's red-and-white brick walls and gravelled drives of its barracks had barely dented the confusion and clangour of the town. Chaos thrived. Slim fine-boned Baltis with hennaed beards and skullcaps walked pensively along the earthen street as the Muezzin's call honed the chill morning. A clutch of dark, squatly-built Dards, Sikhs, Kashmiris and Ladakhis completed the improbable ethnic medley. A century earlier Kargil, doubtless equally distasteful, straddled three trade routes linking the Indian empire to Russia and China – the legendary Silk Route. Now it had become a shrunken town diminished in stature, straining to regain its historic importance as a junction on both the road to Leh and an artery arching southwards to the remote vastness of the Zanskar valley.

Srinagar, from whence I had set out, to Leh is something of the order of 460 kilometres. I had reached Kargil by bus but, for the final 200-odd kilometres, my vehicle was to be one of India's ubiquitous Hillman Ambassador taxis, and to make things more interesting, I had chosen to make the trip literally hours after the road's re-opening following its winter closure, the way still made formidable by deep snow at the Zoji-la Pass of 11,578 feet. It was alleged to be a maelstrom of melting ice walls, floods, landslides, crumbling snowfields and fissured rock so my forthcoming ride promised to be eventful.

Seven thirty a.m. A late start. Since four a.m. the civil trucks, their cabs gaily painted and decorated, had been grinding their way out of town. My driver was a cheerful Indian of have-a-go disposition. 'We'll get through, just you see,' he had affirmed as his frail little vehicle snarled into life. Barely out of town the hills rose sharply above the muddy Suru River swirling by like liquid chocolate and all too soon we attained the Zoji-La and my driver's boast was put to the test.

Great walls of wet ice and snow hemmed us in. The road, ice-covered, was a skating rink made the more slippery by streams of water flowing over its surface. In places deep slush took the place of the wet ice and it was here we experienced the greatest difficulties. The game little Ambassador did well on the ice, skidding from side to side of the restricted track but making erratic progress all the same. The slush defeated it, however; there was no alternative but to get out and push. With me up to my calves in freezing slush pushing behind and Amrit both pushing and steering on the driver's side we won through. With the thaw more advanced, coming back would, we hoped, be easier.

The second pass of the three that barred the way to Leh caused fewer problems. The air was astonishingly clear. The absence of dust played tricks upon the senses and remote mountains appeared to be within a hand's reach. Gigantic streaks of purple, rust, maroon and deep blue criss-crossed the ranges in spectacular serrations like the handiwork of some surrealist artist. The sun climbed into an azure sky as its warmth built up while the landscape turned increasingly barren save for slivers of cultivation alongside the riverbanks.

Away from the snow the dust returned, enveloping the car like a smokescreen as the worn tyres bit into sand, sending pebbles ricocheting off the hillside like angry missiles. With each passing vehicle a fresh coating of dust settled on our skins as the sun burnt with vicious intensity, sending rivulets of sweat coursing down our faces.

Once a day, the army sent through a convoy of upward of 100 trucks carrying provisions for their garrison at Leh guarding a belligerent border with Pakistan and China. They moved in great serpents of brown smoke, grinding along the single-track road. The military had priority over all other traffic so that civil vehicles were held up for hours at special laagers to await their passing. Those civil vehicles following in the same direction then had the daunting task of attempting to pass each slow-moving, unyielding truck on what is little more than a country lane edging through hostile shale. And we were one of those civil vehicles.

The mountains here were stark and jagged, almost Tolkienesque – lurching in fantastic shapes and forms, the valleys sweeping bowls of grey rubble, magnificent in their desolation. The temperature had dropped sharply with the climb to 12,200 foot Namila-La Pass but it was a 'dry' crossing as it was with Fatu-La at 13,430 feet, seared by a fiend of a wind. Each successive village displayed its *chortens* and walls of inscribed stones, often bedecked with flags and bunting. The road twisted and turned and dropped into a valley below, sheer and precipitous. Signs common all over India exhorted drivers to proceed with caution, though few took heed. The chief danger on the eastbound route, when the drop is on one's own side of the road, was from oncoming vehicles sweeping round corners at speed. There were also impenetrable herds of goats, sheep and horses that had to be negotiated; mixed among the herds were women and children and great St Bernard-like dogs. These people were mainly Gujars – nomads – who came over the passes from Pakistan to feed their flocks and herds. Villages, with their smoke-blackened *chai* houses, offered unsavoury but welcome refuge from the desolation – the hot, milky tea a balm to dry throats. Drass, proud of its reputation as the coldest township on earth, was sweltering in a heat wave. Mulbekh displayed its rock-carved Buddha. Lamayaru pulled us off the road to stare at its gompa as did Spitk, Finag and other monastery communities along the way.

We approached Leh, even in a twentieth-century taxi, with something of an ancient traveller's ardour not dimmed even by the rows of military hutments that made up its suburbs. Beneath the dominating semi-ruin of the castle-palace, designed along the lines of Lhasa's Potala, the old city's narrow lanes were reminiscent of any medieval town; nondescript yet enchanting. Inscrutable yaks meditated in the market place and gorgeously attired women wearing triangular *peraks* brought back some of the fading charm. Perched high above the palace on Namgyal Peak was the windowless Avalokitesvara Temple, reached by a centuries-old path that becomes a real test of one's ability to walk uphill at the 12,000-feet level.

The road along the Indus River from Leh to the Hemis Gompa was remarkable for being straight; a typewriter ribbon rolled across a sandy waste of foolscap. Prayer flags fluttered in villages and large copper prayer-wheels, driven by wind and water, creaked mournfully. Shey Gompa was a stark outline against the still, blue sky and the township below agog with brightly caparisoned *chortens* and genial old men swilling *chang* or rice beer.

At Hemis, the largest and most famous of Ladakhi gompas, I was privileged, and lucky to be present at the right time, to witness the annual *mela* or Festival of the Lamas; its participants grotesquely masked in mass procession. Their strange dances to sounds emitting from long, straight horns continued into the next day and to see this bizarre, colourful spectacle, which never takes place on any specific date, was alone worth every tortured mile of the journey.

I TURN NOW to another historic road, this one arising from tracks of aeons past. Again it runs through the giant mountains of the Indian sub-continent, in this case those of Pakistan. My vehicle for this artery was a bus and it was to carry me, in 1983, on perhaps the most lethal of all the world's operational highways.

The Karakorams are the north-west extension of the Himalayas. Wedged between Afghanistan to the west, Russia to the north and the People's Republic of China to the east, these mountains bridge the gap between the Hindu Kush and the Kun Lun range. In this remote location the two giant landmasses of India and Asia meet, throwing up rugged peaks to the sky. Among them are 12 of the world's highest summits and some of the longest glaciers to be found outside the polar regions. The collision between these landmasses results in the confusion of geography for which the Karakorams are noted; deep river gorges, impenetrable passes and intense earthquake activity. These extremes of landscape form, in effect, a glaciated desert – a mass of bare tortured rocks and unstable scree slopes into which run massive tongues of debris-strewn ice. The annual rainfall averages only four to five inches though flash floods can result in devastating land and mud slides.

Throughout the centuries men have dreamed of a road between China and the fertile plains of the Indus River. Throughout the centuries, too, the harsh and inhospitable mountains of the Karakorams have thwarted them in their purpose. When the Chinese pilgrims, such as Fa-Hsien, came to Buddhist Swat and from there to Taxila in the fourth, fifth and sixth centuries AD they wrote of the primitive people with goatskins on their feet crossing swirling torrents over bridges made of ropes of willow. In their Imperial Archives they record the use of wooden ladders and wedges employed along these trackless mountain walls. Later, the silk, tea and jade-laden caravans from Central Asia toiled, for centuries, over these routes, many perishing along the way.

It was these 'Silk Road' routes that formed the basis of the Karakoram Highway (or KKH as it is locally known), construction of which was to commence the second half of the twentieth century. In spite of the most gigantic obstacles with which any landscape could harass a road the project went ahead, first on a piecemeal basis and modest scale, but developing into an engineering feat of unprecedented magnitude. It was in 1959 that a single Pakistan army engineer battalion constructed a 155-mile dirt road between Swat and Chilas, following the Indus River, and then extended this to Gilgit, another 90 miles. The 1965 war with India halted operations for a while but, with hostilities at an end, it was decided to not only extend the road to the Chinese border but to also raise the specification generally to that of two-lane heavy traffic proportions.

The Chinese then came into the picture by agreeing to construct a similar highway on their side, joining up with the KKH at the Khunjrab Pass and linking it to Tashkurgan, Kashgar and Urumchi, capital of Sinkiang province and a railhead. A second war further delayed operations for Pakistan but, when it was over, the Chinese government offered help in the form of a skilled labour force to work side by side with Pakistani workers on Pakistan territory. Thus, during the 1970s, the total number of men and women working on the project was around 25,000.

With the KKH finally completed at a frightful cost in lives, a road, at last, linked Peking (now Beijing) with the Indian Ocean, a distance of about 4,750 miles. The mileage from Islamabad, Pakistan's capital, from whence I commenced my KKH journey, to the Chinese border is 545, though the highway, as such, does not start until beyond Thakor where the ponderous grey Indus sweeps in from the west. A memorial to the dead – Chinese and Pakistani – marks the official starting point, and to gaze upon the bland stone tablet offers a sombre start to what was to become a hair-raising drive that few Pakistanis living in the plains will undertake. No figure for the dead has ever been given but it is supposed that the human price of the highway is no less than one man per kilometre.

There were a dozen of us, of various nationalities, on the brightly-painted and decorated bus. The seats were padded but covered with plastic so that, in the heat and wearing a pair of shorts, my thighs and the back of the knees were in a permanent state of adhesive sweat.

The first village astride the KKH was Besham Qala where Alexander the Great crossed the Indus in 327 BC on his way to conquer India. It was a typical bazaar with tea shops and diseased dogs snuffling through the garbage in the road. From the flat fertile lands of the Punjab, the road wound past tiers of paddy fields and into the mountains, twisting a tortuous route parallel to the swirling, silt-laden river. The first portion of the road north had lain in an alpine environment as it slowly climbed up and over the foothills. This section was not unlike any other high mountain roadway in the world and it created the normal nervousness one would expect from a combination of Indian driving and bad surfacing. But it had no relevance to the degree of hazard we were to face beyond Besham Qala. With the real mountains came the change when the full horror of the road was revealed. In essence it was a ledge that had been chiselled out of the cliffs hanging precariously above the Indus that, after Patan and Kamila – dirty towns with streets awash with filth – ran all the way to Gilgit, the terrain surreptitiously changing from small cultivated squares between widely-spaced pine trees to sheer rock desert.

The driver plainly knew his vehicle but, with the beginning of the KKH, he visibly began to concentrate more fully on his driving, staring fixedly ahead through a windscreen half obscured by plastic foliage and psychedelic patterns. He drove fast, the horn constantly blaring even when there appeared to be no reason. I noticed that his eyes were not just for the highway and its obvious perils but also for what lay poised *above* it. My eyes rose likewise to fasten upon the many dangerous overhangs of rock, cracked and fissured. More often than not at these points the pot-holed tarmac had long disappeared beneath successive tons of rubble from previous rockfalls, landslides, mud flashes and cliff collapses, leaving a narrow way across the debris which had to be negotiated in bottom gear. On huge scree slopes I saw boulders perched with no visible means of support or reason for not thudding down onto the carriageway. The driver invariably hesitated momentarily at such places prior to a burst of acceleration to take us under and past each threatening slide, an action not lost upon my fellow travellers. Being struck by such a boulder would sweep a vehicle either into the turgid waters hundreds of feet below or, equally likely, onto the morass of dragons-teeth rock that formed the river's banks. In the 65-mile gorge beyond Kamila, there was no escape from this hideous danger, the enormous granite walls rising perpendicular from the road, even leaning ominously forward over it. Below, the Indus, flecked white, hurled itself through the narrowing channel as if both river and mountain were combining to crowd out the impertinent highway.

Apart from the rock we were to meet troublesome stretches of glacial moraine and highly unstable scree and colluvium deposits which can collapse without even a hint of disturbance. The infamous Patan earthquake of December 1975 released a large number of landslides and blocked the road for weeks, as well as levelling entire villages. Further north are 12 glaciers close to the road which are a constant threat. In 1971 the snout of the Batura glacier came down the valley to knock over a large concrete bridge. In 1975 the Momhil glacier activated a massive mudflow which blocked the Hunza River – there accompanying the road – forming a lake ten miles long burying the bridge at Shishkot which still lies under 60 feet of silt. All this fatalistic information was imparted to us by our driver and as we bowled into the next nightmare of rock I pondered the likely disaster 1983 might have in store.

The highway crossed the Indus on a massive bridge and gained high ground again. Far below was the river, deep within the earth's crust, and, bordering it, the desiccated landscape, its colour burnt to soft tones by the fierce heat of summer. It was a bitter scene, seemingly lifeless except for an occasional tuft of coarse grass, and, overhead, a lingering flock of choughs. My gaze swung in an arc to embrace the mountains behind and upwards to a brilliant peak of ice that illuminated the sky. It was not just a mountain but a focal point of the universe. *Nanga parvata,* 'The Naked Mountain', as the ancients called it, rises in one immense sweep to a height of 26,660 feet. A Sanskrit proverb states: 'A hundred divine epochs would not suffice to describe all the marvels of the Himalayas'. *Nanga parvata* alone transcends description.

It was some ten miles into the gorge that we witnessed our first accident – or at least someone else's accident and a horrifying one at that. An open lorry came hurtling down one of the rare straight stretches of road towards us but failed to take the corner at the bottom of the incline. Riding in the buck were a number of passengers and as the vehicle hurtled over the edge of the unguarded lip of the escarpment, brakes screaming, it floated momentarily in mid-air, then turned slowly over and over with rag-doll figures, arms flailing, flung from the stricken vehicle and everything falling, falling like autumn leaves, to smash all of a heap on the cruel rocks bordering the river. My companions, ashen, spoke not a word and I made towards the driver to suggest we do something to help. He shrugged forlornly, intimating that there was nothing anybody could do and pointed to a group of military engineers by the roadside who had also assuredly witnessed the calamity. We drove on relentlessly. Life is cheap in this part of the world.

The highway had its 'black spots' but these were solely where landslides and avalanches were a reoccurring theme and we were not to escape the consequences. Army engineer units had heavy-duty equipment and troops were standing by at every such known high-risk area. Near Chilas the road had been blocked that afternoon by a landslide and lines of vehicles waited on either side of the obstruction. Troops were already at work and we were ordered by an officer to take cover behind an outcrop while a series of charges was detonated to fragment the rubble. The explosions echoed and re-echoed across the chasms and slithers of dust and pebbles descended upon us from the towering walls above. That the explosions could set off another avalanche was all too possible but Allah was with us that day and to show our gratitude – and to hasten our getaway – we lent the soldiers a hand shovelling the rubble from the carriageway.

Against the tremendous background of one of the world's most titanic convulsions of nature such occurrences take on the ambience of minor incidents. Everywhere were soaring peaks like giant white swords, or colossal squared battlements, filling the sky in every direction. Our whole visible world was a mad jumble of crags, cliffs, rocks, boulders, stones, pebbles and sand. In the river-bed detritus of all shapes and sizes had been flung down by landslides to mix with enormous accumulations of alluvial deposits. leaving vivid scars on the awesome slopes beyond the river. All the time, the fractured façades of cliffs promised further disintegration to come, while below lay boulders as big as cathedrals, smooth and shiny, and, beside them, huge sharp-edged chunks of rock, newly-riven from their parent crags.

For much of the way to Gilgit the road hugged the swift mud-carrying Indus before transferring allegiance to the Hunza. It was only as it neared the one Pakistani town along

241

the way that nature relented enough to allow the mountains to stand back and green cultivation to take a tenuous hold in the widening valley. Abruptly the terrain softened but, even here, geography and the elements co-operated to battle against the encroachment of man. The winters are bitterly cold and windy, and because of the scarcity of rain the valleys below Gilgit were burnt black in the intense summer heat which can rise to temperatures in excess of 120 degrees. As we entered Gilgit a scorching sun had warmed up the saucer of rock in which the town stands to send the temperature soaring into the 100s, turning our bus into a mobile oven. Not even the breeze blowing up the valley could bring relief, for it had picked up this heat to playfully blow dust-filled gusts of hot air.

Gilgit spreads itself thinly about two rivers, the Hunza and the Gilgit which meet nearby. Shaded by a double row of trees, the main street was lined with shops and one-storey government buildings with the bazaar the centre of activity and from which the aroma of smoke from unseasoned wood mixed with that of *karva,* a green tea flavoured with cardamom and almonds. I found it not a particularly attractive place though better than some of the unsavoury villages we had seen earlier. An aura of British lineage permeated the streets.

In the heyday of the Silk Route it was an important staging post but with the decline of the Tibetan Empire it slipped into oblivion surrounded by hostile tribes. But the nineteenth-century British Raj brought a new *raison d'être* and a new prosperity. In 1877 the British established an agency at Gilgit which subsequently became a garrison and the most isolated outpost of the British Empire. Occupied with suppressing the local tribesmen, watching for Russian incursions from their own expanding empire, and involved in devious political manipulations, the town's new occupiers brought prosperity back to Gilgit. Now, under Pakistani jurisdiction, trade was once again the order of the day. From the lively bazaars, heavily-laden trucks set out for China to deposit apricots, peanuts and almonds in return for rich cargoes of silk from Kashgar. Engaged in this healthy enterprise were a colourful assortment of peoples of many races – Pathans, Kirghiz, Chitralis, Kashgaris, Tshins, Hunzakuts and the pale-skinned Gilgitis themselves, reputed to be descended from the armies of Alexander the Great.

Though their dress was the drab uniform of today the faces of the men spoke from the pages of history. As I looked at them the present receded and once again Gilgit was a famous trade centre on the Silk Route. Agents of the Han emperor Wu-Ti first opened the Silk Road in about 120 BC and then patrolled it, protecting it from bandits, as caravans carried silk and other luxuries to the West. For 2,000 years the caravans struggled over the rugged Mintaka Pass on their way to and from Sinkiang. Then in 1949 Communist China closed its borders to end an era.

Beyond Gilgit the KKH battled its way northward through a new storm of mountains, its patchy tarmac interrupted for long stretches where landslides had swept away the original surface. Here and there, side roads, mere dust tracks signposted as 'jeepable road', led into the granite fastness. And it was one of these tracks that guided me, together with a new driver and suitable vehicle, to the unbelievable oases of Chalt, Nomal, Dianter, Nilt and – most astounding of all – Hunza, that border the highway.

With my heart in my mouth I was driven wildly along tracks that, in comparison, gave to the KKH the semblance of a motorway. In this manner I came to Chalt and Nomal, tiny stone villages wearing lush collars of apricot, apple, cherry and peach orchards, grapevines, stately poplars and carefully-tended meadows of yellow corn bisected by irrigation canals fed by mountain torrents. The change of environment had happened so suddenly I was taken aback; one moment all was solid inhospitable granite; the next a soft land of plenty.

At the community of Naltar, where the Pakistani army had a mountain training camp, I was to witness a spirited polo match; the army versus the locals, which offered me an insight into the expertise of the riders on their tough little horses. The basic difference between 'Karakoram Polo' and the more genteel version played at Cowdray Park appeared to be that only six players constituted a team and the side to score nine goals won. Other than that there seemed to be no further rules; it was all a question of nerve and degree of aggression.

To reach the communities of Gujjar nomads who occupy the summer-only villages of the smaller valleys it was necessary to proceed on foot. The walking was hard in the rarefied atmosphere but the welcome I received from the delightfully unspoilt villagers was ample reward. At minuscule Shani, its hutments hardly distinguishable from the glacial refuse of stone, I was invited to attend a wedding party where the lengthy intoning of passages from the Koran was interwoven with dancing and the serving of choice portions of goatmeat. Not a woman – including the bride – was in sight but surely no wedding reception could boast of such a stupendous venue as that of the snow-capped peaks and sparkling glaciers of the surrounding Karakorams. In place of the Wedding March there was the incessant rumble of snow avalanches.

The way out of the Naltar valley led over the 15,000-foot Diantar Pass, an exhausting climb that had me on all fours in snow and ice at the summit. On the other side lay the Diantar valley, a replica of the Naltar, and a botanist's joy of exotic wild flowers. The gorge of the Diantar too had to be negotiated, the path overlooking a 1,000-foot sheer drop as it zigzagged down to the warmth and the vivid green of another oasis.

My interlude away from the KKH at an end it was back to the bus and the highway, but, following the Hunza River northwards for very few miles, I once more found myself in Valhalla. On one side of the river lay the territory of Naga, a small state in its own right, within the Hunza valley dotted with a few trees and the occasional cultivated plot. Included in its boundaries was not only the icy spire of 25,550-foot Rakaposhi, but also Dumani peak of 23,600 feet and the 38-mile Hispar Glacier, all dwarfing the valley with their magnificence. The one-time kingdom and bread-basket of Naga is celebrated for its happy, healthy people who, it is claimed, never suffer from disease, especially not from tuberculosis and rheumatism.

Experts differ about the causes of this alleged phenomenon. Some see the Hunzakuts as a superior Aryan strain isolated from contact with the germ-laden outside world. Others point to their food which has influenced 'natural' diets in the West. Whatever the reasons, it has to be said that the Hunza people seem to be of an intelligence and integrity far higher than other Karakoram denizens. It shows in their husbandry and thrift. Nothing is left to chance and each minute portion of land is carefully sprayed and seeded every year. The slightest wastage of land or time could be fatal in their eyes. When supplies are running low, the head of the family ordains that it is better to fast than dip into stocks reserved for planting. These facts I learnt from Qudratullah Beg, a former Hunza State minister of education who, with his charming family, had lived all his life in Karimabad, the capital.

Karimabad offered an awe-inspiring view of Rakaposhi at the further end of the valley, a valley overlooked at the opposite end by Ultar Nala which is both a ravine and a multiple peak. Directly beneath it stood the fairy-tale castle of Baltit, for 600 years the home of the *Mirs* – or rulers – of Hunza. Slowly rotting on massive timber pillars, the castle's wooden bay windows, ingeniously carved, added a touch of history to the magic of this secret world.

I walked again and again through the big village among the laden apricot trees. *Was* this really a Valhalla? To the south the shining mass of Rakaposhi pervaded the valley. Behind me, high above, was the whitewashed fort looking down at the huddle of drab houses and chequerboard of fields. It was a typical Tibetan fort, vaguely ominous with its high walls and slit windows with wild dark crags towering above it. Rows of poplars along irrigation canals added a touch of gentle elegance to the starkness. I found it easy to appreciate why Western visitors imbue this valley with a romantic aura, infusing a scenically lovely spot with their dream of a Shangri-La where everyone possesses the secret of health and tranquillity and lives to a ripe old age.

On the move again, motivated by the impatient demands of the KKH, I journeyed another 60 miles to the small community of Passu and the great Batura Glacier. To the north of the Passu plain a ridge comprising a score of pinnacles dominated the horizon. Behind them runs the Shimshal River, entering a valley that is the epitome of remote but inhabited areas in the Karakoram where the snow lasts all through the year and avalanches thunder down its slopes well into spring. But here in Passu village, its own glacier scarring the mountain flanks on which it lies and the sun-burnt walls of the continuing Hunza valley showing the way forward for both river and highway, I was forced to a halt. In a sheen of sweat I walked a mile down the road to the military-guarded bridge. I could go no further, since the border with China was closed. Today it is open and travellers with the correct documentation can carry on into China's Sinkiang where I had already been. For me, on this journey, a point had been reached where politics provided a more effective barrier than had nature in all her fury.

I NOW TURN to climes nearer home; to Europe, and to some journeys where my mode of transportation has been no more than Shanks's Pony and a bicycle.

I have always proclaimed that walking – using one's legs as their maker presumably intended – is the best method of getting acquainted with a country and the countryside; but the next best thing is cycling since, again, one's feet do the work and the same health-promoting advantages apply. And whereas a walker is unlikely to exceed 20 miles a day, a cyclist of even my limited ability and age can cover 50 or more with still time to dally in places of interest.

Environments for the perfect cycling tour are legion. Across the Channel the Netherlands leap to mind as the cycle touring paradise, a country geared to the whims of its 11,000,000 cycling citizens and providing a comprehensive network of cross-country cycle paths across helpfully flat polders. In 1988 my son Paul and I made a ten-day circuit of the Ijsselmeer – better known to us as the Zuider Zee – on cycle paths and by-roads, staying at small guest houses along the way.

But Britain and Ireland, though not yet in the Dutch league for cyclist's facilities, hold a rich variety of landscape – and seascape – for rewarding pedalling. In 1981 I was requested by the English Tourist Board to promote the so-called Heritage Trail between Norwich and Durham so I covered it by bicycle, staying, as a guest of Best Western, at plush hotels en route. And, this accomplished, I continued to the Lake District to make a circuit of the newly-opened Cumbria Cycle Way that nearly ended in disaster when I struck an out-of-season blizzard which had me pushing my bike over snow-blocked roads and spurning the rescue efforts of a military helicopter much to its crew's chagrin.

IT IS, HOWEVER, the coastal routes of Ireland, Wales and Scotland that particularly attracted me during the early 90s.

One of my most memorable journeys was that around the rugged coast of County Donegal from Sligo to Ulster's Derry. The very fact that in the Republic alone there are 11,000 pubs, many no more than musty Victorian retreats where Guinness is the oil for the serious business of conversation, offered an extremely valid reason for setting out on a voyage of discovery. Staying in homely B & Bs whose owners cosseted my son and I unmercifully and refreshing ourselves on the 'Black Stuff' at nearly every pub we came to made for a delightful ride.

Pembrokeshire's coastline in South Wales was another joy of pedalling. Leaving from Swansea I followed the coast by way of Tenby, Pembroke, Milford Haven and Fishguard to Cardigan across smooth green hills, purple moorland, deep wooded valleys, wide estuaries, tall cliffs and huge swathes of golden sand. And back again to Swansea via the Preseli Hills littered with Druid temples and burial chambers. In Scotland Paul and I chose the lesser-known east coast for a journey commencing from Perth and taking in Dundee, Aberdeen, Peterhead, Fraserburgh and along the coast of the Moray Firth to Nairn and Inverness, passing through and pausing in evocative John Buchan territory where the ghost of Richard Hannay haunts the land, and, of course, the emotive battlefield of Culloden, a place of still more ghosts and the most poignant place in all Scotland.

IN 1993 CAME my seventieth year and I had two choices of celebrating – if that's the word – the event: a family reunion party or a 2,000-mile cycle ride through a still semi-bankrupt Eastern Europe. I chose the 2,000-mile cycle ride.

Accompanied by Paul, my serious bout of pedalling was to begin at Tallinn, Estonia's capital on the Baltic Sea, and end, all being well, at Constanta, Romania's port on the Black Sea. Our baggage, carried in pannier bags, included a small bivouac and the very minimum of camping and cooking equipment. Though we envisaged spending most nights under canvas we had pre-arranged a trio of hotels and a few private home sojourns in Estonia, Latvia, Lithuania, Poland, Slovakia and Romania, to obtain an insight into the lives of people who had, until very recently, suffered for 40 years or more under the yoke of Communism.

Today Communism in Europe seems just a terrible memory. Was it only a decade ago that stone-faced men still presided over 'workers' paradises' in the name of 'the people', while millions endured grinding poverty and mind-controlling servitude? Or that the world seemed under threat from nuclear annihilation? The world has moved on since then with other threats to worry about.

We arrived in Tallinn following a ferry voyage to Gothenburg, a train journey across Sweden to Stockholm, a bike ride through the city and embarkation on the subsequently ill-fated Baltic ferry *Estonia*.

The project hardly started encouragingly. Just three days before departure I was propelled over the handlebars of my bicycle onto the tarmac in a near-collision with a car just yards from my home. This resulted in a sprained wrist and elbow of the right arm which was to plague me throughout the coming journey.

In Tallinn docks we were met by our host family and taken for a night in their Russian-built apartment block in the suburbs before being given a tour of the city. And a wonderfully preserved old Hanseatic League city it is; with atmospheric, cobbled streets lined by a jumble of medieval walls, turrets and spires all dominated by a hill called Toompea over which it has tumbled since the Middle Ages. All three Baltic states have an unfortunate history of being dominated by other nations, the last two being Nazi Germany and the Soviet Union under which they suffered for 51 years.

Our kind hosts saw us off the next afternoon and, with a strange reluctance, we headed south along a dead straight, flat but soulless road. As a cycling highway it had advantages and on some days we were to clock up between 100 and 150 kilometres helped by the fact that, when camping, we were on our way soon after dawn.

On our first night 'in the field' we thought we were being clever by utilising a perfectly smart-looking but derelict cabin equipped with two bunks. We cleared the accumulated rubbish, wondering why the hut had been discarded and discovered the reason when it rained. The roof leaked like a sieve. Thereafter we stuck to our restrictive but trusty bivouac.

Inevitably our days became ruled by a routine, the purchasing of basic provisions in near-empty shops at the top of the agenda. In every township larger than a village we would search for a rare restaurant that could produce a hot meal to placate rumbling stomachs while raging thirsts sent us into countless bars of varying degrees of respectability. At eventide the raising of the tent, having pushed the bikes through undergrowth or deep into fields to locate an unobserved site, became a drill, as did the striking of camp with the dawn. Our morning cuppa, usually made without sugar or milk, was enough to wash down our often unappetising pieces of cheese, salami or sardines. Between bouts of primitive camping, our hosted sojourns were oases of both anticipation and memory.

After Tallinn came the pleasant and unpretentious coastal resort of Parnu where a young family had offered us their home and a day's exploration of their town. And so out of Estonia with its flat but evocative expanse of forest – useful for camping – and limitless horizon, and into Latvia with more of the same. Riga was our second Baltic capital and we battled our way to its throbbing heart along uneven cobbled streets into the cratered gutters where we were pushed by uncaring trolley buses and lorries.

The Laine Hotel provided our next island of comparative comfort. Our bikes had to be up-ended and carried by lift to the fourth floor there to be deposited with us in our bedroom – a chore repeated in subsequent hotels, though some did not even have lifts.

We found Riga to be less picturesque than Tallinn but it nevertheless holds some fine architectural gems. Lying at the mouth of the Daugara River, its historic German connections are clear to see in the face of fine old Teutonic buildings. Founded in 1158 as a river-mouth storehouse for Bremen merchants, it was, like Tallinn, seriously damaged in the Second World War.

Refreshed by a night between clean white sheets our sights were set upon Lithuania and, in particular, the country's second city of Kaunas. So far the weather had been mixed with some warm sunny spells interwoven with long bouts of rain. Now things changed; the warm bright spells evaporated and relentless rain took over. Under a grey wet sky we pedalled on, our spirits at a low ebb; our feet soggy.

We were enticed into spending two whole days with our new hosts who resided in a suburb of Kaunas and so got to know the city quite well. Less well-endowed architecturally than the capital, Vilnius, it still could display a fine old quarter of restored merchant's houses as well as a substantial castle situated at the confluence of the rivers Neurunae and Neris.

Again it was a wrench to leave generous hosts. Seldom do cities and their populace evoke such affection within me. And seldom too have I looked upon a happier people, still amazed at the sudden turn of events that delivered them their freedom; though I also noticed slight concern at what a capitalist future might hold. We had not far to go to our next host family: just 70 kilometres to the town of Alytus.

Battling against a head wind we made it by mid-afternoon and our arrival coincided with the worst the weather could fling at us. That night the sky belched forth a never-ending torrent, holing us up for three days and nights in the family's sizeable home. But at least it gave us a chance to look briefly upon the third Baltic capital, though we saw little enough of Vilnius through a sheen of water. The good family took us there on the third day and on the 70-kilometre drive back to Alytus the non-stop downpour slackened a little. Rain or shine we determined to leave next morning.

In the event it was raining again as we left and we got another soaking while pedalling miserably towards the Polish border. It so happened that a border dispute was in progress at this time and the four-mile queue of cars waiting to leave Lithuania dispirited us still further. But assuming that bicycles were immune to queues we pushed to the head of it and sailed serenely through the four control points only coming to grief at the fifth. At each checkpoint we had been handed a stamped slip of paper but at the last hurdle found we could produce only three. So the whole rigmarole of checkpoints had to be gone through again. It was akin to a game of snakes and ladders with the dice repeatedly falling on the head of the snakes.

Damp, but triumphant, we stepped onto Polish soil and the threshold of a series of countries I knew in far less genial circumstances. Henceforth, for me, progress would become something of a journey down memory lane; a pilgrimage, if you like; for the route ahead would take me through lands in which I had been in the dark days of the Second World War as well as the dismal post-war Communist era.

Poland has long intrigued me, an intrigue that never ceases with every visit I make. The country has always been the underdog; a lost cause throughout history. Her record of gallant victories in defeat, of uprisings and frightful calamities, has aroused world-wide admiration and sympathy. The bestial savagery that befell Poland in the Second World War was perhaps the most terrible episode in her long and painful history. And I was 'privileged' to have witnessed something of the country's agony in 1944 as both Red Army and German Wehrmacht took their revenge on the stoically-resisting populace.

The prisoner-of-war slave camp to which I had eventually been assigned following my capture in Normandy was a Silesian coal mine. Not approving of coal mining as an occupation, particularly when it benefited the Nazi cause, I took 'French leave' and made my way eastwards towards the advancing Allied Russians since the British and American armies were even further away on the wrong side of Germany. This first of three escape attempts was effected with the unwitting co-operation of RAF Bomber Command and a stolen pair of wire-cutters one dark night when the camp lights were temporarily extinguished while the bomber fleet was overhead. Initial eastward progress was made on foot, robbing isolated German farmhouses of food, clothing and, when available, cash en route but such was my physical condition that some form of transportation became the only way forward. Thus I turned to the railway and that's when my troubles really began.

We spent our first night in eastern Poland camping deep in the forest of Augustow sprinkled with lonely lakes. The rain had desisted for a while but came down again soon after we had struck camp. Our subsequent destination was the industrial city of Bialystok but first we intended making a 50-kilometre detour to the small town of Tykocin which had been recommended to us. Only too pleased to leave Highway 19, the main north-south conduit, we camped damply in a wood near the township of Knyszyn to reach Tykocin the following early morning. Situated astride the River Narew, the town's chief interest lies in the solidly-built Jewish Synagogue, now a museum containing relics of Jews murdered in the forests. A Jewish cemetery lay at the edge of the little town; rows of broken tombstones lying neglected at drunken angles; a forgotten corner seldom visited.

Our detour had the advantage of allowing us to attain Bialystok by small traffic-free roads and we found the first of our trio of pre-arranged Polish hotels at the edge of the city. Bialystok was virtually annihilated by both Germans and Russians during the war, but the unremarkable town contains an interesting mix of Catholic and Russian Orthodox churches including the Orthodox cathedral, the double-barred cross of which shone bright against a rare blue sky. Before the war a sizeable Jewish population lived here in the old Jewish quarter prior to the Nazis setting fire to the great Synagogue burning to death some 3,000 souls. We explored the city from end to end, enjoying meeting some of its citizens unused to seeing Western visitors in their workaday streets.

Having washed our dirty linen together with ourselves in the same hotel bath for which, unfortunately, there was only cold water available, we found our way out of Bialystok on another small road that deteriorated into cobbles for miles, making for difficult cycling and hell for my injured wrist. A snarling, slobbering dog with bared fangs lunged at me in one village but my own snarl coupled with a good kick on its snout sent the animal whimpering away.

Back on Highway 19 we made good progress towards Lublin, accomplishing 150 kilometres on one day, a feat that had me in the final stages of exhaustion with only wayside wild raspberries to sustain me the last miles. Provisions in the shops were slightly more available than had been the case in the Baltic States but still very basic and all too often our evening campsite cooking expertise was hardly tested to its full potential when all we could muster was a tin or two of beans. With Paul not the slimmest of figures our nights in the bivouac were extremely compacted which at least kept us warm when the weather turned cool.

Our hotel in Lublin turned out to be the most luxurious to date and we made the most of it. With unlimited hot water we immersed ourselves in baths using the shampoos and bath foam provided with wild abandon. Again our bikes had to be accommodated with us in the bedroom and this provided opportunity for something that I have always had a secret yearning to do – namely *cycle* down long hotel corridors!

The location of this chief city of central-eastern Poland protects it from Western influences and gives visitors a peek at the old Poland – less prosperous and more traditional. Historically Lublin lay in the heart of the country when its frontiers ran further eastward, serving as a crossroads for East and West before finding itself sitting near the Soviet border when the map of Poland was arbitrarily re-drawn.

At the top end of the Krakowskie the quaint cobbled streets of the old town were amassed with rubble and debris from crumbling façades when we were there. But a start was being made on a much-needed restoration. Out in the southern suburbs stands a gigantic stone memorial that dominates the site of Majdanek Extermination Camp, perhaps the most notorious after Auschwitz, where thousands of doomed wretches met their hideous deaths.

We toured the sparsely-visited site and its sickening apparatus of extermination and my mind slipped back again to personal memories of 1944:

That first escape attempt of mine had ended in the transit cage of Auschwitz-Birkenau when a three-man Wehrmacht patrol found me wandering the streets of Cracow after curfew and had been obliged to hand me over to the Gestapo. Earlier, things had gone from bad to worse. It was with the greatest difficulty that I managed to board the high-sided steel coal-wagon of a moving east-bound freight train and, once aboard, the damn thing stopped ten kilometres up the line then reversed 80 kilometres in the opposite direction to that I wanted to go. Leaving the train when it halted at a small goods yard close to a station I bought a first class ticket with some of the money I had stolen and found myself ensconced on a Cracow-bound first-class compartment of a passenger train. In the compartment too were a couple of German officers who took me for a Hungarian and fed me with grapes!

Not wishing to show myself in a Gestapo and military police-ridden main station I jumped off the train in the suburbs of the city to make my way towards the centre, completely forgetting the night-time curfews that were strictly imposed on occupied towns. Caught breaking into a bakery my days of a precarious freedom ended dismally.

After days of painful Gestapo interrogation I was subsequently incarcerated in Birkenau where I was to witness sights so unspeakable they remain with me to this day.

Our Highway 19 sped, straight as an arrow, towards its terminus in the far south-east, but we had been recommended an alternative route that, though adding 100 kilometres, included the historic town of Zamosc. The new road bucked gently across undulating countryside close to the Ukrainian border and via the Chelm region wherein lies another obscenity of war: the site of Sobitor Concentration Camp where a desperate breakout was staged by the inmates. Like Warsaw – the saddest city I know – Poland is awash with such mementoes of a cruel past; of brave and obstinate gestures to show her enemies that she will never be destroyed.

Short of Krasnystaw, on a section of road that narrowed and zigzagged to negotiate a steep cleft, I came as near death as I ever want to be before my time is up. Paul, behind me, saw the two heavy lorries with their respective drivers racing neck and neck on the straight portion of road immediately prior to the narrows. I heard the squeal of brakes over my shoulder and sensed the danger hurtling towards me. But fate was kind to us that cloudy afternoon. The bank was too steep to climb with a bicycle away from the threat, but by squeezing against it our demise was avoided, though the vehicles grazed our arms as they sped by.

Zamosc is a precious relic of early architecture and town planning. Founded by the Grand Chancellor of the Crown of Jan Zamoyski in 1580 and surrounded by fortifications, the square of arcaded house façades is world-renowned. We spent some hours exploring and provisioning ourselves from shops holding a better choice of food than we had found elsewhere.

We were living reasonably well by now and had learnt how the Poles liked to conceal their sources of hot meals under the pseudonym of 'bar' or 'buffet'. One hot meal a day in such an establishment had become the order of the day and our evening campsite cook-ups, though no more than soup or tinned stew, were reinforced with bread, jam, cake and biscuits. In open countryside we often had problems in locating a site away from prying eyes and, once abed in our sleeping bags, the confined space produced disadvantages. The further south we travelled the warmer it became but clouds of mosquitoes forced us to batten down the hatches so leaving us to sweat it out in airless purgatory until long after midnight.

Our way out of Zamosc led through the Puszcza Solska – Solska Forest – to tongue-twisting Szczebrzeszyn – an endless industrial town. We found a plentiful supply of raspberries again in the forest to supplement our rations and at the small village of Sieniawa we managed a visit to the recently restored palace of the Czartoryski family, now a sensational hotel. Escorted through palatial chamber after chamber and boudoir after boudoir, the prospect of our forthcoming night in the humble bivouac became distinctly anticlimactic. With Przemysl, on the Ukrainian border, we were close to the last town of any consequence in eastern Poland – Rzeszow – just 35 kilometres down the road. The third Polish hotel was the magnet that drew us there the faster and we got into its portals just as the heavens opened once more.

There was not much to see in this nondescript town but the rain held us there for a further day. A signpost indicated Cracow to be barely a day's pedal distant but that fair city was not on our route. My previous visit to it had been before the country had emerged from Communist rule when I had located the building that had once been Gestapo Headquarters. It had become a supermarket but I was taken down to the cellars to find my cell among rows of others. And there on the wall, scribbled across a maze of graffiti, was my own observation as to what the Gestapo could do to itself. I was unable to remain in that awful place for more than a few seconds. Nausea overcame me; the smell of sweat, urine and blood once more assailed my nostrils to render me physically sick.

Two days later a small road took us in hand to lead us towards Poland's south-eastern border; the terrain abruptly turning from vague undulations to low but very definite alpine hills; its villages donning the guise of what might be described as a poor man's Switzerland. By-passing Krosno we spent our last night in the country deep in a pine forest at the northern end of the Dukla Pass. It rained as we pedalled across the border and down the other side of a valley famed as the point where the Red Army and Czech and Slovak partisans broke through the German lines to free Czechoslovakia from Nazi domination – only to enslave it under Communism. It was still raining as we freewheeled into the newly-independent Slovakia.

My previous sojourn in Slovakia had been made shortly before the country's cessation from the Czech and Slovak Federation and I had obtained the distinct impression then that few of the populace approved of the impending split. Now, in the eastern cities of Presov and Kosice; the cessation a *fait accompli*, my impressions were confirmed. Everywhere I heard rumbles of discontent.

In my mind, however, I continued to look upon Slovakia as the eastern half of Czechoslovakia, a country that has shaped my life and destiny.

In 1945, I was herded, with untold millions of others, onto the notorious 'Death March' and it was while the surviving columns were passing through the territory of Czechoslovakia that I was to make my second escape, this time with the aim of joining the partisans. Winter had relaxed its grip; a touch of spring was in the air and we were in a land intensely sympathetic towards us. Making my way to Prague I was directed out of the city to an industrial town to the north alleged to be a hotbed of resistance but, on the way, was offered shelter, at the risk of their lives, by a Czech family. I refused their invitation to remain in their house but suggested that maybe they could find me a place of concealment nearby. Thus I spent some ten days in a quarry with the daughter of the family daily bringing me food on her bicycle while I spent the days effecting fruitless acts of sabotage on the adjoining railway and telephone lines to pass the time.

Recaptured and returned to the marching columns I was to carry the image of the girl with me and when, following a third and successful escape in Bavaria, I reached the American Third Army front line to eventually return home, I realised that this girl had captured my heart.

The war over, it took years to make contact with her in a shattered Europe since I knew neither her name nor that of her hometown, but once this was accomplished we began to correspond regularly. And then, in 1948, just at the point when the girl – Anna – and I had mutually decided that we might make our future lives together, the Communist-inspired Iron Curtain descended cutting a recovering Europe in two and barring any hope of reunion. A barrier of watchtowers, triple electric fences and a minefield now lay between us.

However, love and determination are potent forces and one dark night in 1951, with a pair of insulated wire-cutters, I breached the barrier, lying on my back clipping through the wire strands with minutes to spare before a patrol came by, and got 12 kilometres into Czech territory. But on a railway bridge I was ambushed by border guards. Awarded 104 years hard labour by the regime for 'spying' I was released after four months following pressure from the British government. Pronounced persona non grata *by the Czech authorities it was to make my further attempts to be with the girl I wanted for my wife to be very much more difficult.*

At the Ruthenian village of Vys Komarnik we paused to investigate one of the many wooden churches of the region and, still in the Dukla area, observe and speculate upon the many T34 tanks, aircraft and artillery pieces that rusted away among the cornflowers and poppies; a reminder, again, of a war that had scarred Slovakia too.

We approved of Presov, our next objective, partly perhaps because a pre-booked hotel lay in its heart. A modest town, it sprawls around an attractive central street with its oldest church on an island in the middle.

A hotel also awaited us at the much larger Kosice, just two hours cycling away. Here we found a modern metropolis that, over the centuries, had been knocked around like a Ping-Pong ball between Hungary and the former Czechoslovakia, changing nationality four times in the process.

The Hungarian border lay but 23 kilometres beyond, the road leading straight and flat towards Miskolc. The relaxed border reflected the tranquil countryside through which we were passing and bright sunshine illuminated a rural Hungarian landscape of wheat, corn, potatoes and sunflower fields. Over two days and nights we crossed this narrow neck of Hungary under, for once, idyllic weather. All around combine harvesters purred, apples, plums and raspberries lined the smooth tarmac and romantic-looking castles topped distant hills. We felt utterly at peace with the world as we headed for Tokaj.

The Tisza River joins the scenic Bodrog at one of Hungary's most famous towns. But Tokaj we found a disappointing little place, though the hinterland rejoices in acres of vineyards the grapes of which produce the 'Wine of Kings and King of Wines'. We spent a night under canvas amongst the tall vines and, next day, presented ourselves at the Romanian border.

There was no love lost between the two nations, Romania insidiously repressing the considerable Hungarian minority on what is now her territory. For much of the month it took crossing Transylvania we were to be in close contact with a Hungarian people who steadfastly refused to style themselves Romanian and so suffered accordingly.

A long queue of cars heralded the frontier but our policy of cycling straight past such inconveniences again paid dividends and we found ourselves without undue complications in the seventh country of our itinerary. Its visible border defences, all too reminiscent of the Iron Curtain, made ominous viewing, however, and that we had entered a country in the throes of economic crisis was obvious the instant we set out on a diabolical road surface the ten kilometres to Satu Mare. But, contrary to expectation, we were to find Romanian drivers a lot more tolerant of cyclists than elsewhere since their roads, being booby traps of potholes and slow-moving ox-carts, horse-drawn 'haystacks' and other such hazards, forced mechanical vehicles to take extra care.

Satu Mare's rutted streets and broken curbs occupied our attention as we pedalled through a town of much architectural merit, including a beautifully restored former edifice of the Shoemakers Guild, now a hotel. The legacy of Communism showed more strongly here than in all the countries through which we had passed and though we managed to obtain a meal of watery soup, veg and unidentifiable meat, we were not to know that this was to be the last hot meal for many days.

The English-speaking world knows little about Transylvania beyond its wholly undeserved reputation inflicted upon it by Bram Stoker's *Dracula,* and only then the recent tragic events of 1989-1990 – the violent overthrow of the dictator Ceausescu which freed the country from Communism but plunged it into economic chaos – are remembered.

We were soon to discover the insatiable curiosity Transylvanians had for foreigners that was coupled with a remarkable capacity for hospitality and kindness towards them. And their sense of optimism too; few Transylvanians we met admitted they were destitute or that their future looked bleak. An early example of this impulsive hospitality was encountered as we bumped through the village of Ladara on a dirt track of a road. A car drew up beside us, the driver inviting us to his home for, by Romanian standards, a hefty cold meal following which the family forced upon us a supply of bread, peppers, tomatoes, a bottle of home-brewed *tuice* firewater and a hunk of smoked pork fat, or *slanina,* which was to last us a week. In other villages we were regaled with plums brought out by little old ladies upon learning we were '*Ongel*' (English).

It was such acts of spontaneous kindness that saved us from serious hunger. Village shops were bare of edibles except tins of sardines and bottled plums (both of which became our regular camping diet) and even bread was hard to come by. In one such village we ran to earth a rare loaf and searched the supermarket shelves for a spread other than sardines. Spying a tin of a red substance we bought it and, later, applied it liberally to our slices of bread – only to discover it was floor polish! Actually the taste wasn't bad!

In the larger urban centres the shops held a better selection of foodstuffs but even here the choice was severely limited to such as inferior biscuits, jam and stale cake. Wayside apple and plum trees and occasional wild raspberries and strawberries helped a little but the finding of food continued to dominate our daily routine; we often climbed into our sleeping bags with rumbling empty stomachs.

Baia Mare, Dej and Jibou were our urban landmarks that showed us the way to the city of Cluj, camping in forests or deep in fields of wheat en route under continuing fine weather.

In the former capital of Transylvania, Cluj, we were spontaneously hosted by a Hungarian doctor and a youth who insisted upon taking us under his wing. Both showed us the sights of the city, an important centre ever since the time of Emperor Hadrian. In all we spent three days here, sleeping in the youth's apartment; one of thousands in rows of jerry-built Ceausescu-inspired blocks.

This interlude over we continued across central Transylvania via industrial and polluted Turda, camping nightly under an increasingly warm sun that had us all of a sweat by day and by night. But better 'hot sweat' than 'cold wet' we maintained, and in this manner we attained the town of Turgu Mures along a main road that had dissolved into what the French describe as *route déforme*.

Our first task in this sizeable town was to locate the address of the Virag family with whom we had been in contact before leaving England. And with them we remained another three days so insistent were they to show us the locality. Those days were like a holiday, with the family not only making us completely at home but taking us swimming in the Mures River and driving us to Sovata spa with its unique saltwater lake. Their great kindness and generosity made me feel immensely humble and though they had so little to offer they gave us all they had, their delicious home-cooked apricot dumplings making a particularly welcome culinary treat.

Turgu Mures contains much of baroque magnificence headed by a cathedral-like Roman Catholic church, an imposing Palace of Culture and the Teleki Reference Library of early books produced by printers whose names, like William Caxton, are world-renowned. The town was another we left with sorrow.

Sighisoara made amends with its faded beauty. The town's most celebrated citizen is the son of Vlad II, or Vlad Dracul, as he is better known, who signed himself 'Dracula', and his birthplace has become the most perfectly preserved medieval town in Romania. The citadel sat atop a hill, ringed by walls which climbed steeply around it. Within these walls rose the points of Gothic spires, the knotted tower of the main gate, and, on the very summit, the brooding bulk of the Bergkirche. The Pied Piper was once credited with bringing the Saxons to Transylvania and it was easy to picture the Piper jigging through the ancient streets luring the children of Hamelin into the mountains.

We partook of our midday repast in the square, giving the passers-by a treat, then, mounting our cycles, we made tracks towards Odorheiu Secuiesc, an obscure, unpronounceable town we came to rename 'Social Security'. To escape the worst of the daytime heat we were striking camp even earlier in the morning – the countryside at such an hour presenting surrealistic views of misty hills and far horizons – and laying up at midday for an hour or two in the shade of any available tree.

Two days later a thunderstorm struck at midnight giving us a soaking as we lay in a flooded tent; a soaking that was to be repeated next day as the rain persisted. On wet roads clogged even thicker than usual with broken-down Trabants and lorries we came to Sfintu Gheorghe – translated more simply as St George – to find a restaurant that doled out hot beans, cheese and potato, pasta and tomato soup in individually weighed portions, so we purchased them all and scoffed the lot.

A certain Albert Levente, a journalist, was our last contact and we ran him to earth with some difficulty. He was good enough to loan us his flat for a couple of nights, he himself spending them in his girlfriend's apartment. Albert showed us round his newspaper publishing and printing works as well as the rather dull town but the highlight of the sojourn was the first hot bath for weeks. We slept on the floor on a couple of mattresses listening to the rain outside thanking our lucky stars it wasn't beating on our porous fly-sheet.

The route now led across the Carpathians proper involving some exhausting pedalling and, more often than not, uphill walking, which I found to be a relief for a sore bum. Since Turgu Mures the terrain had risen into low hills but, after the town of Buzau, it transformed further to modest mountains hiding deep valleys, gorges and cols. Atop the Buzau range we looked down upon the flat Romanian plain that would be with us virtually until the Black Sea.

For a day and a half it was mostly downhill; a joyous freewheeling through pastoral alpine-like country that flattened out with every mile. A hoped-for campsite away from prying eyes at a spot where the highlands ended proved a disappointment when it was overrun by herds of cows and their inquisitive young minders. The following day was Friday the thirteenth and to mark it our bikes developed a rash of punctures.

Coinciding with the flat plainlands came the heat; a hot sticky heat that fried us as we ate up the kilometres. At Slobozia a lack of direction signs had us pedalling towards Bucharest instead of Constanta and, so eager were we to reach our destination, that we ignored our midday rests and forged on through a new province, that of Wallachia.

A week later, on a beast of a traffic-snarled highway, we arrived at the pot of gold at the end of the 2,000-mile rainbow. But Constanta, an industrial port, could offer no comforting reward for our efforts; not even a secluded night-time camping place for our weary bodies. Furthermore all the coastal camping sites and hotels were bursting with ex-Eastern Bloc tourists enjoying their Black Sea summer holidays. Additionally, we were within an ace of being arrested by undercover police with one-time *Securitate* (secret police) mentalities who tried to catch us out buying black market dollars. And worst of all came the revelation that Romanian Railways, upon which we pinned our intentions of returning homeward, were to go on indefinite strike that very midnight. But we did achieve one longed-for prize; that of prolonged immersion in a tepid Black Sea that must have turned the blacker by virtue of the grime it washed off us.

Our race to Constanta railway station to see how far we could get before the trains ceased running produced mixed fortunes. The first service to Bucharest was packed solid, whilst the next was inexplicably half-empty and we gained the Romanian capital, together with our bikes, an hour before the strike deadline. Here we managed by dint of luck and brute force – using the bicycles as alternate ramrods and shields – to board a Timisoara-bound express, that city being but 70 kilometres from the Hungarian border.

Never – even in the Indian sub-continent – have I ridden such a packed train. The nine-hour journey was a nightmare; our bikes and baggage smothered in compressed bodies including our own. From Timisoara we not only pedalled across the rest of Romania to the border town of Arad but, because of Hungarian reluctance to carry bicycles on their trains, right across the whole of Hungary too, adding a further 500-odd kilometres to the journey. And even that wasn't the end of it.

Hungary is an agreeably flat country for a cyclist and its negotiation on abruptly smooth tarmac was no great trial. With pauses in towns such as Mako, Szeged and a town I'm unable to spell or pronounce, plus a campsite amongst ranks of sunflowers, we made Budapest in two days, camping a further night on its outskirts.

Choosing to pedal through the Hungarian capital in the morning rush hour was not a good idea but it attained us the further end from whence we aimed for Komaron on the higher reaches of the Danube. And it was here, against the background of the steel-lattice railway bridge which spans the river upstream of the town, that more memories flooded back.

Although banned from Czechoslovak territory I nevertheless made repeated efforts to reach it. From such diverse northern countries as Finland, Norway, Sweden and Denmark as well as southerly Austria and Yugoslavia I launched clandestine and semi-legal attempts to gain admittance to the forbidden land. Some of these were failures; others were successful, winning me seven and nine minute trysts with Anna at Czech border stations, 48 hours with her in Prague when granted a 'business' visa by a Czech consul in Scandinavia who forgot to check the 'Black Book of Undesirables' and, once, a whole fortnight with her when I entered as a pseudo-'Communist sympathiser' on an unchecked group visa.

It was in 1955 that I got myself onto the first British tourist group permitted into Communist Hungary and, although heavily controlled, I managed to break away in Budapest to reach Komaron by train. I had noticed the bridge to be under repair on the way to the capital and resolved to test its possibilities for reaching Czechoslovakia on the further bank.

The scaffolding around the bridge's pier enabled me to climb into the lattice girders that formed the span. It was dusk and I hoped nobody had spotted me. Planks made a narrow passage along the inside of the lattice framework which workmen had lain to facilitate the painting of the bridge's underside. I crawled cautiously along this, the dark water below and the rail tracks above, taking care to conceal myself from border guards stationed at each end of the structure. A train, its wheels inches from my head, sent showers of rust down my neck and the noise was horrendous. Halfway across I perceived a wide gap in the passageway that brought me to a halt and it was while I pondered as to what action to take next that I was spotted by the captain of a barge passing below who raised the alarm. The sound of running feet and rattle of weaponry sent me into full retreat. I beat the soldiers to it by a short head and melted into the darkness to return to the station and, eventually, to Budapest. The group minders never learnt of my illicit absence.

It was such episodes as this that occurred for four years before, tiring of the bad publicity it was provoking from the British press, the Czech government, divesting her of nationality and property, expelled Anna from the country. We finally married on a spring day in 1957.

Now, after nearly 40 years, I reached the other side of the river.

On Slovak soil we continued westwards to Bratislava, the weather deteriorating again into cold wind and rain to make camping unpleasant. And from the Slovak capital it was a case of returning to Hungarian territory before finally entering Austria, our last night being spent in the shell of an abandoned van.

The Vienna Hilton, to which we had been invited, surely never received a more scruffy but appreciative pair of guests. My bed was so comfortable I barely slept a wink.

YOU MIGHT NOT credit it but, just four years later, I made a parallel journey across central Europe but, this time, on foot. I suppose it was a natural transition from my seventieth birthday bicycling journey across Eastern Europe while, being more walker than cyclist, such a journey seemed appropriate in recognition of my approaching seventy-fifth year.

The original plan had been to go all the way from the Baltic to the Adriatic thus adhering to the oceanic nature of the start and end points but time dictated otherwise. So I decided to stop short at the Danube which at least retained a nautical theme, with Vienna as the terminus. The 1993 jaunt covered a basic route of some 2,500 miles; the current walking route involved a slog of something in excess of 800 miles with our start point of Gdansk further south than Tallinn. Thus the route would be considerably shorter than before – but there's no freewheeling with walking.

Again Paul was to accompany me and, since all our baggage would have to be carried on our backs, this necessitated an even lesser amount than had been the case on the bicycle journey. This had to include a bivouac and bivi-bags in lieu of sleeping bags which were deemed too bulky. As before, our cooking gear was laughably inadequate.

We left Gdansk, the former Danzig, a historic city reborn after total destruction during the Second World War, in a heatwave with temperatures pushing into the high eighties. Initially we set ourselves a daily kilometreage of 25 but, as the weather cooled, this was to increase to between 36 and 42. As before we aimed to partake of one hot meal a day plus the acquisition of provisions locally, while, for our overnight layovers, concealed sites would have to be found on which to raise the bivouac. What I hadn't taken into account was the fact that the summer of 1997 would turn out to be one of the wettest on record, triggering catastrophic flooding of the countryside bordering the Oder River over which our route lay. Our chosen route across Poland we designated as Grudziadz–Torun–Konin–Kalisz–Kepno–Brzeg and then across Moravia, the Czech Republic's eastern province, and into northern Austria.

After only a few dozen kilometres we discovered the folly of long-distance road-walking. Many roads, marked as minor arteries on my out-of-date maps, turned out to be virtual interstate highways which were racetracks for speed-crazy drivers who had been deprived of vehicles for 40 years of Communist prohibition. So for 'road walking' read 'verge-walking', for this is what our progress, more often than not, became, as vehicles from speeding Trabants to giant trailer-hauling juggernauts forced us to take refuge in verges.

The heatwave lasted about a week as we sweatily trudged south, camping nightly in mosquito-infested woods. At first the terrain was bland and unremarkable but improved visually as we traversed the lake district around Osiek where we thankfully immersed ourselves in cool water. People with whom we came into contact were wholeheartedly friendly and generous, not to say amazed when they learnt of our final destination. 'You must be mad' was a frequent intimation and, you know, they were dead right! In a Skorez *pivnice* (pub) we were pressed to a succession of beers as well as lunch by the incredulous clientele to the extent of us having to sleep off our excesses under a tree when outside the village. And on the banks of a lake at Krzewiny a picnicking group shared their cold chicken lunch with us, even donating a basket of strawberries before they left. In the stifling heat of midday the buffeting slipstream of lorries became our only source of a cooling breeze – albeit one laced with diesel fumes.

The first rain struck while we were camping on the outskirts of Warlube and, from then on, the weather deteriorated steadily though not appreciably until Torun, birthplace of the astronomer Copernicus, where we were scheduled to spend two days and nights; one night with a family and another in an hotel – the Kosmos – offered us by Orbis, the Polish state hotel agency.

I had been to Torun before but there was still plenty to see and learn about from our host family who lived in an apartment at the end of a suburban tram line. They led us enthusiastically around their city to cover everything from the tiny Church of the Holy Cross to the austere St Mary's off the old town square. In between came a leaning tower, the monastery gate and, of course, the Copernicus Museum. On our way out of the city on the third morning a flooded road beneath a railway bridge had to be waded, our boots round our necks like water-wings, giving us a taste of what was to come.

By-passing the connurbation of Poznan – but, alas, not its horrendous commercial traffic-congested approach highways – we came to Radziejow where a continuous downpour found us hungry, thirsty, wet and exhausted, unable to find succour in a Sunday-afflicted township with virtually every restaurant, bar, store and means of shelter firmly closed. For a while we took refuge in the draughty bus station before a false let-up in the downpour had us back on the road again. Beyond Sompolno the storm clouds to the south east turned as black, dense and widespread as I have rarely seen to belch forth their liquid loads while we were in open country devoid of any cover whatsoever. Eventually, soaked, we came upon a broken-down bus shelter in which we stood, dripping and shivering, for the worse onslaught to pass. Sodden fields and woods precluded camping for the night so at the village of Kramsk we asked permission to sleep in a barn which provided warm, soft hay for our weary bodies. What's more we were offered breakfast next morning by the jovial wife of the village priest, to a background of religious music from the adjoining church. The following day another farm barn became our overnight pad, the owner of which, this time, pressed us to supper in company with his substantial family. Paul being able to speak Russian and some Czech together with my own very limited German provided a tenuous means of communication with such generous folk.

The city of Kalisz – oldest in Poland – was reached via a musical chairs progress with bus shelters in lieu of chairs as we attempted to dodge the worst of the deluges. Here we were blessed with the second Orbis offering – the pleasant Prosna Hotel for a dry night in a real bed. To add to the delight the editor of a local newspaper took us to his home for dinner and to obtain the story of the walk to date.

Razed to the ground by the invading Germans in the First World War, Kalisz is no architectural gem, but we rated it an exceptionally agreeable city with the Old Town pleasantly situated in the angle between the Prosna and Bernardynka rivers.

A dose of the runs afflicted me on the subsequent days' march and this, plus a flooded tent, made unhappy milestones along the way to the small town of Kepno where another generous family had requested our presence. However, the road to it was mostly a rural one and, for the last few miles on a main highway, we joined a religious procession led by a brace of priests and marshalled by orange-jacketed police which had a marked sobering effect on the crazed traffic. There was much chanting and waving of ecclesiastical banners so, squaring our rucksacks and mouthing the only line we knew of 'Onward Christian Soldiers', we entered the outskirts of Kepno. Earlier a passing car being driven much too fast had grazed us on a corner while, later, an old man on a bicycle wobbling uncertainly in the middle of the road had waffled on about a murder that had taken place in the vicinity – though whether this was yesterday or years ago we couldn't make out. But it caused us to keep a sharper than usual lookout when we bedded down in a forest that night.

The Kaluzny family turned out trumps. They took us under their wing the moment we knocked on their door and, next day, not only took us swimming in a lake near Ostrzeszow but also to the Radziwill family hunting lodge at Antonin to which Frederick Chopin had been a frequent visitor. Set in an arboretum the unique octagonal timber palace was once the summer residence of Poland's richest and best-known aristocratic clan.

It was while we were relaxing in our host's apartment that we first became aware of the disastrous events that were taking place in Wroclaw, not so many miles away and where the family's two sons were studying at the city's famous university.

Scenes of devastation on both sides of the Oder River, which flows through Wroclaw, filled the television screen together with reports of thousands being made homeless by horrendous flooding. And not just in that city either. Many bridges to the east had been destroyed or made impassable by the raging water; the whole region declared a major disaster zone.

Our onward journey continued under bright sunshine that made a mockery of what was occurring ahead. The bridge at Brzeg was the point we hoped to cross the Oder. A night under canvas in a damp mosquito-fraught forest beyond the town of Namyslow and we trudged on, hoping that, by some miracle, the road would remain clear. But the miracle was not to be. Fifteen kilometres short of Brzeg a posse of police barred the way. The town and its bridge were under water, they told us; we would have to divert 60 kilometres eastwards to Opole; maybe the bridge there would be open. Maybe.

With the help of a lift given by the driver of a BMW and a ride by public bus we reached Opole, but that city too was half-flooded, its bridge overwhelmed. The flat countryside all around was like a huge lake with the upper floors and roofs of villages and farmhouses protruding through the waters. And all the while the sun blazed merrily from an azure sky.

The town of Krapkowice, 25 kilometres on, held the next possible crossing point, and to thence we proceeded on a further bus swishing along flooded roads. Our maps showed a subsequent bridge to be at Raciborz on the southern edge of the Silesian industrial region where I had been a slave-miner in 1944. Raciborz. A wartime memory again jogged my mind. Here I had witnessed the hideous spectacle of a mass-execution of dozens of concentration-camp victims that ghastly winter of 1945. No, I had no desire to look upon Raciborz again.

In the event, following a long trudge from the flooded town of Krapkowice, we came upon a viaduct carrying the Wroclaw-Cracow motorway high over the Oder which lay, swollen but confined, in a deep valley. A gigantic traffic-jam of vehicles stood, motionless, on the elevated carriageway, the drivers standing by their sides resigned to an interminable wait. Only those on foot could make any progress so we had an advantage. And once on the western bank of the accursed river a 60-kilometre slog had us back on the alignment of our original route.

At Glucholazy we crossed into the Czech Republic and into its eastern province of Moravia. Political borders rarely have much effect on geography but one did here. Barely had we set foot in Moravia when the countryside bucked itself into engaging tree-clothed hills; a scenic feast but, as we progressed deeper into the province, one sadly devastated by the titanic forces of water hurtling debris along angry streams to scythe down trees, smash bridges, wash away roads and twist railway track into spirals of scrap-iron. Police were everywhere diverting vehicles – but not walkers – from near-impassable highways while, in that innocent sky, helicopters clattered incessantly.

Our onward traffic-barred road took us through Bruntal and Sternberk. And thereafter the sky turned from blue to black and down came the rain in a deluge that intimated prolonged intent. A campsite by a stream that was fast turning into a river was the last occasion we were able to erect the tent for many days so sodden had the ground become. Thereafter our nights were to be spent in half-built houses, under road bridges; anywhere, however uncomfortable, that could deflect the never-ending deluge. Flood-battered Olomouc was a sad sight, its muddied streets lined with water-ruined furniture ejected from saturated houses. And still the rain fell.

In varying degrees of discomfort, everything in our rucksacks soaked, we attained the townships of Tovacov and Kojetin – this last a low-point in our fortunes until, at a police-station where we begged to borrow a warm dry cell for the night, we were directed to a hostel a kilometre out of town. A pretty basic sort of place it was but, to us, that night in a proper bed out of the rain was heaven. On again, via a series of villages that could have made highly picturesque viewing had they not been obscured by the driving rain, to the battlefield of Austerlitz, its blood-soaked acres more sombre than ever in the day-long downpour, as we squelched miserably across it. Shelter was nowhere to be found; not even a tree. Then suddenly – could it be a mirage? – there appeared before us on the dead-straight road a McDonald's! It stood in the middle of nowhere, a building of familiar design. Never have I been so thankful for such an establishment as we sat dripping on the floor in its fuggy, beefburger-tainted interior.

Two days later the Moravian capital, Brno, clear of floods, provided us with the balm of two morale-boosting nights at Best Western's International Hotel in the centre of the city. Our reluctant departure was blessed by continued fine warm weather, the only jarring note being the dull international Highway 52 we had to follow. Dull it may have been, but the smooth tarmac white-line bordered verge clear of traffic gave us the impetus to break all our previous daily walking records by covering 44 kilometres and so gaining a smaller artery which was to bring us, camping again as we went, to Hevlin and the Austrian border.

Alas, the Highway 52 marathon had cost me dear. A sprained tendon in my left leg resulted in me limping painfully along playful little roads switchbacking through the alluring countryside of rolling hills and *Sound of Music* townships of the likes of Staatz and Mistalbach. Our campsites became golden wheatfields and bushy hedgerows under star-studded skies.

All at once, far away, a silvery ribbon glittered in the sunshine. Water. But this time not the sort that had fallen so long from the sky, but an unswollen river. The Danube. The town of Korneuburg lay on its banks and the last dozen kilometres were pain and grief as I limped into its trim streets. Vienna lay within our grasp.

A night on a slug-infested site on the very outskirts of the Austrian capital formed our last camp and, next morning, we followed the Danube into the city, me hobbling and hopping to our final goal – the Vienna Hilton again. It was like coming home.

NOW TO LONG-DISTANCE coach travel in Europe, a mode of transportation, and indeed holiday touring, that has a growing following in Britain. However, for reasons I don't really understand, there remains a vestige of stigma to this mode of travel.

In Britain our main national road-passenger carrier is National Express, for whom I have the highest regard.

Coach travel constitutes a far more comprehensive network than that of both railway and airlines within Britain and to this can be added the facet of general interest and sheer beauty of some of the National Express routes. Many of the Scottish services score best here. Those that take in the lonely, wild terrain of Sutherland between Inverness and Thurso, or that between Glasgow and Fort William, leap to mind as ones that traverse some of the country's most magnificent countryside. And lowland England is not without some picturesque routes too; the 315 service follows the south coast between Eastbourne and Plymouth offering fine sweeping views of the Dorset hills as well as passing through evocative towns like Portsmouth, Southampton, Weymouth, Dorchester and Exeter.

In 1989 National Express formed an associate company called Eurolines, which has become the country's leading operator of international coach services to continental Europe, offering a huge selection of destinations in 20 countries, plus Morocco in North Africa. Its success can be attributed to the strong links the company built up with many of Europe's leading express coach service operators, including those of the former East Bloc countries.

I have ridden a number of such Euroline services including those between London and Cannes, Amsterdam, Brussels, Prague, Gdansk, Vienna and Moscow. Indeed Paul, residing in Prague, uses the London-Prague service regularly which, for a scheduled service, is far less expensive than similar services by scheduled air or rail operators.

In 1919, Elliot Brothers, whose coaches made up the erstwhile 'Royal Blue' fleet and who had actually run one of the earlier horse-drawn services, introduced a limited form of express coach service operating between Bournemouth and London. However, Greyhound Motors of Bristol are acknowledged as introducing the first daily all-year-round motorised express coach service in Britain. Their service, introduced in 1925, linked Bristol with London and expanded rapidly. Thereafter other operators, aware of the commercial benefit of long-distance travel, introduced similar services, and the race was on.

But it wasn't until 1930 that a system of licensing, covering drivers, conductors and routes operated, came into being. This brought about order to a chaotic, rapidly-growing and somewhat haphazard industry wherein 'predatory' operations – i.e. trying to reach passengers waiting at a bus stop before one's competitor – were becoming not only unacceptable but downright dangerous.

Thankfully, public road-transportation has advanced a long way since the charabanc and the 'Royal Blues'.

Britain's largest coaching company is National Express, operating as a parent company to several allied companies serving 1,500 destinations throughout Britain; the longest route being that between Dundee and Penzance – 685 miles – believed to be the longest daily scheduled coach service in Europe.

The London-Moscow run I undertook quite a number of years ago when Russia was the Soviet Union and, though little to do with the subject of road travel I can't resist briefly mentioning a couple of the 'quaint' hotel idiosyncrasies in that city and elsewhere that were prevalent at that time.

The old Bucharest, for instance, where registration and the process of so doing dragged on for hours while massive ledgers were laboriously filled in with one's most intimate personal details. And though the Soviet Union was, allegedly, lavishly equipped with IBMs, this abundance didn't seem to stretch to carbon paper. My room, when I found it among a tangle of corridors and plumbing, smelt of disinfectant and mothballs. The windows were unopenable; there was a telephone and a radio and a washbasin with, traditionally, no plug. At four in the morning it was like having a Red Army band in the same room, so loud was the Soviet National Anthem booming from a left-on radio. And at 4.30 a.m. came the first of a series of early calls I'd never requested.

On several occasions, in Irkutsk, I was forced to eat my meals with 'packaged' groups of Romanians, Czechs or Bulgarians because of the collective-mindedness and security-consciousness of the management who could not conceive of an individual eating alone. This was fine by me since, invariably, these groups were nice people but, more to the point, when it came to paying for my meal I was briskly informed that it had been paid in advance by the relevant state tour-agency! And in a Khabarovsk hotel I once found myself imprisoned in my room through some fault in the lock mechanism. So I dialled 100 which, in Britain, obtains the operator. In Khabarovsk it obtained the fire brigade. I heard the clanging in the streets outside and, 15 minutes later I was free; a concerned hotel manager and a chap wearing a steel helmet and holding an axe ruefully examining the remains of the door.

Coach touring within Britain and the Continent likewise has a strong following though it's not to everyone's liking. The largest such tour company, with a fleet of many hundred vehicles, is, assuredly, Shearings, and their blue-and-white coaches are to be seen everywhere. It has to be said that there are great advantages with this mode of holidaymaking. It is relatively inexpensive, comprehensive and free of travel hassles, while, for those of us who are community-minded, the security and fun of being among like-minded companions is not to be denied. Though motorway scenery is seldom of great allure, road travel offers the opportunity to observe the passing countryside, especially on lesser highways. The downside is long hours of driving, particularly those getting to and from the destination, but this is mitigated by frequent halts for refreshment and leg-stretching while in-coach entertainment usually includes videos and films. There are, of course, two types of coach tours. These comprise the multi-centre tour involving brief sojourns at specific cities or resorts, moving from one to the next, and the single centre tour of just one main destination. Both invariably run local excursions.

BEING SOMETHING OF an individualist I hesitated when Shearings Holidays invited me to sample one of their long-distance services. Nevertheless I accepted and chose a single-centre tour to one of the most distant European destinations – the Tatra Mountain resort of Zakopane in Southwest Poland – to put the company to the test.

Included in the tour were two excursions with further ones offered on an optional basis. Our drivers were full of bonhomie and very helpful while light refreshments were always on tap additional to the restaurant halts, on the longer legs of the journey. And my fellow-travellers were a great bunch of people.

OTHER COUNTRIES TOO have their scheduled coach services and I shall end this sub-chapter with a short narration of a four-day trans-Norway ride I took a number of years ago. The company was the Nord Norge Bussen (North Norwegian Bus Company) and the route was that between Bodo on the Atlantic coast and Kirkenes on the Russian (then Soviet) border taking in Narvik, Sorkjosen and Lakselv and passing through Lapland and Finnmark.

For much of the way, additional to my daughter Alice who is not into world travel in the same way as is her brother and father, my companions were Lapps, a somewhat gaunt people with slit eyes and dressed, as if to contradict their dour features, in colourful costumes of which dark red predominated. Opposite us in the bus a slit-eyed baby gazed fixedly at us for hours and we felt something akin to triumph when, at the end of this period, our attempts to break the severe little face into a smile was successful. Its mother, who 'wore' the baby on her chest in a kind of cradle, perceiving our breakthrough, smiled too, spoke words we could not understand and gave us a sweet. Expecting a plug of bladder I was nonplussed to discover it was a well-known brand of peppermint.

The bus moved slowly along the road, the only road, halting at lonely villages to allow passengers to alight, pick up others and stow on board sacks of mail, groceries, newspapers and old Johan Hansen's prescription. Everybody seemed to know everybody but our efforts to learn the tittle-tattle of the Norwegian North was confounded by ignorance of the language. Occasionally men swollen in thick pullovers spoke to us in broken English and their womenfolk conveyed their friendliness and acknowledgement of our Britishness by copious smiles and nods.

Both Sorkjosen and Lakselv were points of substance on the map but tiny beleaguered outposts in fact. Immured by weather and a frightening loneliness, Lakselv stood at the head of the Porsangerfiord encircled by low, unenticing mountains, scarred by scree and lacking the beauty of those further west.

Lakselv's existence stemmed from the presence of a military airport and junction of the single road. From the heart of the wooden township the new highway snaked out across barren countryside of rock and stunted silver birch towards Karasjok and the Finnish border. The town itself had that scrubbed and solid quality so common in the Scandinavian countries, and its houses, though mainly of timber, were carefully built, well-proportioned and colourful. A white church, grey-slate roofed with a black wooden spire, made a stouter landmark than did the steel lattice-work of the airport radio masts.

The bus and its passengers did not travel at night. Those passengers with no local homes to go to stayed in a hotel; in most cases the *only* hotel in the main centres and their offerings and facilities were of the simplest. Prices were high for they had you over a barrel.

The narrow traffic-free road onwards to Kirkenes was so devoid of landmarks that even road signs drew the eye. One, at a tight hug of houses called Russenes, indicated the road leading provocatively towards the northern extremity of Europe, locally known as 'Nord Cap'. Everyone on the bus made sure we knew where it led for the famous cliffs are a source of pride in a land of nothing

Small herds of reindeer scampered daintily across the road ahead and it was always possible to tell who were the strangers on the bus by the way they excitedly pointed them out; the local regulars remaining smugly indifferent. Approaching Kirkenes an insignificant river flowed merrily between rocks and we were told that it offered probably the best salmon fishing in the world.

But for all its natural beauty, take away the giant iron-ore smelting plant from the town and you'd have no Kirkenes. Or that is what I concluded at the time. It is a place at the end of the road like Vladivostok is at the end of the Trans-Siberian

Railway and, to me, it felt the same. Next stop would be Soviet Russia and nobody seemed to want to go there. I didn't have to wonder why.

Chapter Seven

TRAVELS ON TRAINS

IN WHICH THE AUTHOR TRAVELS THE LONGEST PASSENGER RAIL ROUTE IN THE WORLD AND THE HIGHEST (THIS LAST JOURNEY INCLUDING MEDICAL STAFF ARMED WITH OXYGEN EQUIPMENT), AS WELL AS EARNING HIS KEEP AS A STOKER AND RELAXING IN THE LATE MRS INDIRA GHANDI'S STATE COACH IN INDIA AND ENDING UP 6,000 MILES OFF COURSE WITHOUT A VALID VISA IN SOVIET RUSSIA.

I suppose a natural transition from road travel would be rail travel, after all, our American cousins call their railways 'railroads', though that has nothing to do with it. Call me Indiana Jones if you will, but second only to that offered by my two feet, my favourite mode of conveyance is that of the train and this vehicle, in many shapes and sizes, has carried me in varying modes of comfort and discomfort, over much of the world.

There really is no better way to view the world than from the window of a moving train; a traveller has the pick of an extensive assortment of worthwhile railway journeys across the earth.

IT WAS CURIOSITY, pure and simple, that sent me on my most recent European rail journey to the Russian enclave of Kaliningrad now cut off from the Motherland by Lithuania.

That and a sneaking desire to complete a hat trick and traverse the whole of Poland by train since I had already bicycled and walked across it. Years before I had looked into this enclave, then highly sensitive: territory forbidden to the likes of you and me, which made it all the more imperative that I visited it in due course. What I found when I succeeded was a mite depressing. Entering the enclave via Lithuania – until quite recently an integral part of the Soviet Union – I found a land years behind its Baltic States and Polish neighbours in quality of life and state of the economy. And this included its rail system. Such was the neighbourly hate in this part of the world it took me almost as long getting in and getting out as did the whole train ride across Europe, due to the excruciating border formalities.

BUT POLITICAL CONSIDERATIONS seldom dictate my long-distance rail journeys. On trains of varying degrees of efficiency and luxury I have traversed much of the world, riding the tracks of east and west Europe, the Balkans, the Middle East, Asia, north, south and east Africa, North and South America and the Far East. From this pot-pourri of rail travel extravaganza, allow me to select and detail a few of the more memorable journeys.

Let's start with an adventurous one in the Indian Sub-Continent.

It is not, perhaps, universally realised that you can pick up a train at Calais and jog amusingly nearly all the way to the Taj Mahal and beyond by rail. Unfortunately the spotlight must be turned upon the little word 'nearly'. The dream of a through train from Dover to Delhi has receded, though, in point of fact, the mechanics of such a service have become simpler by virtue of certain track extensions undertaken by Iran. There are actually two routes to India where the railway can offer a vehicle for a considerable portion of the way. The more northerly of these is via Afghanistan, a trainless nation that sits stubbornly athwart the lines of Iran and Pakistan. To the south the gaps are, however, narrowing. Some 30 miles of sand-embedded date palms and a considerable river are not insurmountable geographical barriers to a linkup between Iraq and Iran while, further east, Iranian State Railways are already closing the gap between Yazd and the terminus of the Quetta line at Zahedan.

In 1973 I girded my loins with the requisites for a rough ride and set out to test both routes. At that time Afghanistan was not engulfed in war but between Iran and Iraq there existed a hate that was about to ignite into one. Also then there had been no rail extension southwards towards Pakistan beyond the southern Iranian town of Kerman. Given these conditions my journey promised some eventful travelling – and I was not to be disappointed.

I reached eastern Afghanistan by way of an assortment of consumptive trains and, in this particular country, by splendidly-painted buses in which, to beat the intense heat, I travelled atop the vehicle amongst the goats and the odd amorous tribesmen. I arrived, more or less in one piece, at Landikotal at the head of the Khyber Pass.

Landikotal is a den of thieves if there ever was one, but for me the township held one priceless attraction: a railway station. And luck was with me since the no-charge weekly train to Peshawar, at the bottom of the pass, was due to leave the very morning of my arrival. The train is run by the Pakistan government simply as a demonstration to the local gun-toting tribesmen that *they* run the region; not the tribesmen.

There was, however, not an inch of space to spare on the three-coach train that waited at the platform, so I took up residence on the left-hand front buffer of the Sheffield-built Vulcan Foundry-made 1923 steam locomotive, the same age as myself. Already there was a necklace of humanity strung around the boiler as well as a couple of jovial Pakistanis on the opposite buffer. With me on mine was a third who gave me pride of place in front of him though I wasn't sure if this was a good idea.

My 40-mile ride that followed was a high spot of my many years of train travel as we wound down the famous pass. Empty forts made a walnut topping to every hill and jutting rocks proclaimed the names of regiments – British, Pathan and

Indian – carved in stone where years and blood lay eaten by the sun. The Khyber is the steepest non-rack-and-pinion stretch of track in the world and, even with two engines (there was a 1936 German oil-burner at the rear) progress was heavy-going. Initially I felt extremely insecure on my metal perch with only the flanged buffer head, acting like the pummel of a saddle, as a handhold. But my companion wrapped his arms around my waist, which was some comfort.

The route took the form of a letter Z, the train changing direction at each apex, the locomotives taking it in turns to lead. On the steepest sections, safety track had been installed so that runaway trains whose brakes had failed could be diverted up into the hills. I was acutely aware that, were we to hit something, we front buffer-riders would become no more than strawberry jam.

Via Peshawar, I attained Delhi on a frontier-mail 'express' in the close proximity, in my (then) third-class coach, of some 36 fellow-travellers compressed into a compartment designed for a maximum of eight. And in the Indian capital I varied my sojourn – perhaps 'recuperation' would be a better word – between a cockroach-prone hostel in Connaught Place and the luxurious apartment of a prosperous acquaintance in a well-to-do suburb. In their different ways both were to prepare me for the long and incident-full haul to come.

I left New Delhi Station, then went on through Multan and Sukkur, crossing the Indus River on the huge Landsdowne Bridge. The Punjabis in my compartment became swarthy-faced Balochs flaunting fierce bushy eyebrows and beards. They stared at me with a prolonged and disconcerting intensity and when they spoke their questions were sharp and to the point. Why had I come to Baluchistan, they asked as if my invasion of their ancient and terrible land was a grotesque anachronism. Up until then I hadn't realised that we *were* in Baluchistan.

Sibi sits on a junction of the line. Its scattering of houses, cowering beneath a merciless heat, served a railway that was as grotesque an anachronism in this land as myself. At intervals along the track were white-painted markers carefully framed in painted stones that showed a devotion to duty inherited from a past generation of railway staff.

Onwards still we rolled, through the historic Bolan Pass where General Roberts bade farewell to his troops after the epic march from Kabul to Kandahar, and on again to the Dozan Gorge through a storm of rock to enter the calm venues of Chinar trees that grace the former capital of Baluchistan, Quetta.

The next leg of the journey was that to Zahedan in south-eastern Iran. My purchase of a second-class ticket included advice on how to dodge the ticket inspector and travel first class. The train was a mobile oven headed by a museum piece, an ancient steam engine, circa 1930 of uncertain parentage. On leaving Quetta, in which city I had spent a hardly restful night with a cheerful lovemaking American hippie couple in a tin shack, we moved a few miles before stopping ostensibly to allow another train to pass on the single track, though the chief reason seemed to be for the playing of a football match; passengers versus a local team. I was convinced the signal system was geared to the football schedules.

This lonely line was once known as the Nushki Extension and was built during the First World War as a strategic expediency. It runs hundreds of miles past Nushki, 50 miles into Iranian territory and commences with the bifurcation from the Quetta line at Spezand, home ground of the football match, to run parallel with the Afghan frontier.

Between Dalbandin and Nok Kundi, a distance of 104 miles, the landscape is wholly without habitation, virtually devoid of vegetation and can only be described as a hell on earth. The track crosses stretches of ground covered with sharp black stones broken only by patches of coarse sand. For eight months of the year the heat is fierce and the so-called '120-day wind' lashes the sand so that it lacerates the skin like a sandblast. The whole desert is coated with sulphur dust, and water, when it is obtainable, is a concentrated mixture of common and Epsom salts. When there is any rain the year's fall may occur within an hour. The river-beds, bone dry for 99 out of a 100 days, then hurl a mixture of water and stones at the exposed railway. To overcome this disconcerting obstacle the engineers constructed Irish bridges or 'dips', and the steam-engine drivers using them were expected to rely on their discretion as to whether or not they could get through without the water putting their fires out.

Another surprise on this bloodcurdling route is the *do reg*, or marching sand hills, which, driven by the wind, are constantly on the move. Time and time again new track is laid to avoid this fresh obstacle and the duplicated rails left in position so that there is a chance of a line clear of sand at a particular time.

These then were the potential vicissitudes of my trans-Baluchistan Desert journey. Another was to come. Caught by the ticket inspector while dozing in a first-class compartment having barely left Spezand, I was banished back to second, i.e. bottom, class. With every seat occupied I took refuge, during an unexplained halt, in the cab of the locomotive, where I was welcomed like a long-lost brother. However, the transfer was akin to jumping out of a frying pan into a fire, the heat of the roaring boiler matching that of the sun. By sticking my head out of the cab I caught the remnants of a breeze while mugs of oily, sweet tea went the rounds of the crew to lubricate parched throats. I felt it expedient to earn my keep so, as well as taking over the duties of look-out, I periodically acted as stoker.

The scenery, shimmering in the savage heat, was austere desert backed by a long low range of lifeless mountains on the distant Afghan border. I stripped down to my underpants and suffered an endless day in a lather of sweat, oil and dirt. Evening brought a delicious coolness; the horizon joining forces with the dying sun in a great suffusion of vermilion and gold. Then darkness.

It was early next morning, while on look-out duty (i.e. catching the breeze), that I spotted the bent rail. I shouted and we slammed on the brakes. Together with most of the male complement of the train we walked over to examine the damage. The blistering heat had caused excessive expansion and it was obvious that the rail would have to be replaced. With spare rail alongside the track and a potential workforce to hand the problem of rectification was minimal.

Having done my stint I wandered off into the desert intent upon investigating a tiny mud-walled village in the near distance. I was to pay for my nosiness. Just short of the first dwelling I was intercepted by a gun-toting warrior of bearded magnificence who stuck his musket into my ribs and demanded money. And he wasn't joking. I hunted about for loose change and flung a handful of rupees onto the ground with the idea of belting him when he bent down to pick them up. Perhaps fortunately for both of us a commotion in the village sent him into retreat, while I prudently returned to the train to help with the track-replacement.

We limped into Mirjaveh, the Iranian border village, many hours behind schedule; hardly, it transpired, a rare event. The faint outlines of a live volcano, the sometimes smoking Koh-i-Taftan, stood out in an otherwise empty landscape and in the grey shrouds of another dawn, we drew into Zahedan.

FROM THE RIDICULOUS to the sublime. As readers may have discerned I am not one for luxurious travelling though, in the realm of the railway, I have sampled the not unappreciated delights of South Africa's *Blue Train* and the *Pride of Africa* run by Rovos Rail, this last taking me in exalted comfort on a three-day foray from Durban through Swaziland to Pretoria.

But I now relate in some detail the inauguration journey I made on the celebrated *Palace on Wheels* luxury tourist train in 1982, covering much of the fairy-tale state of Rajasthan, this wholly within India. My seven-day royal progress aboard the *Palace on Wheels* was a highlight of my more grandiose rail journeying.

On my viceroy of a train I was accorded royal treatment, given a golden coach that was once the mobile home of the late Mrs Indira Gandhi as well as that of the Maharaja of Bikaner, and the freedom of a region that is the stamping ground of princes.

The long line of dun-coloured coaches that awaited my evening arrival at Delhi's Cantonment Station hardly gave the impression of a palace, wheeled or otherwise. But what I found inside them was a different matter. In awe I gazed upon my spacious sleeping compartment replete with wardrobe and double bed, plus refinements such as table lamps, fans, and a telephone. The lounge contained a sofa and armchairs of quality brocade; the walls lined with heavy polished mahogany. A well-fitted-out bathroom and toilet and a further two small bedrooms completed the suite of rooms, beyond which lay the servants quarters, the domain of two most gracious Rajasthanis attired in crimson and gold tunics and turbans to match, their sole object being to wait upon me hand and foot. Heading the train a giant steam locomotive wheezed in stentorian fashion, its pistons, boiler and smoke stack reflecting a surfeit of elbow grease and pride of maintenance.

There was a ring of pride too in the voice of the manager of the *Palace* as he told me that it was Indian Railways who had carried out its major refurbishing in their own workshops. The rolling stock had been rescued, item by item, from railway sheds and disused sidings at remote locations all over India. Saved from the grave but rusted from the monsoons and bleached by the burning sun the coaches were assembled and painstakingly restored to their former glory or rebuilt from a basic framework.

As the evening wore on and the European clientele of the train dribbled into the station to be led, wide-eyed, to their respective quarters I fought to come to terms with this latest grade and quality of transportation on which I found myself. At intervals during the evening I sallied forth from my exalted eyrie to survey and mingle with my fellow mini-maharajas prior to the call to dinner.

No corridor linked the coaches since the princes and maharajas who rode them had no need of such frivolities; indeed visitations were positively discouraged. Thus progress to and from the dining saloon had to be fitted into the not infrequent stopping schedule though I had been notified that, in my case, I could halt the train at the press of a bell or a word with my coach captain, as the senior of my two flunkies was titled.

The dinner, like all the meals to come, was, of course, a banquet, and the coffee and liqueurs concluded, we bade one another goodnight and scurried to our respective bedchambers to await the maharajan movement.

The jerk nearly shot me out of bed – but we were away. I lay listening to the sound of wheel on track and the clickety-click which is now lost in Britain. But though my first night's sleep was elusive I gained enormous enjoyment since, for me, going to bed on a train heralds the beginning of a potential adventure.

Rajasthan at sunrise was a promise of this gentle adventure with its sounds and sighs wrapped in a cool mist. But the relentless blast of the sun was soon to tear the mist asunder. Not until the unhurried consumption of breakfast in bed or in our private lounges were we invited to leave the train and cast our eyes upon the sights available outside the train.

To be pitched suddenly into India is an awesome experience. We had only been on the train for 12 hours but its tranquillity and unreality made the transfer back to the world outside the more bewildering. All at once we were enveloped in noise, smells, incomprehensible chatter and colour. Especially colour. For in Rajasthan it is, more than everywhere else, colour that transcends everything in that first initial curious glance. Together with gaiety it abounds everywhere. Their picturesque costumes reflect the joy by which the people of Rajasthan seek to enliven their existence. The smells are India.

At Jaipur, the 'pink city' built of local rose-pink coloured stone in the 'tone of autumn sunset', as the historical writings put it, we were greeted by a cavalcade of elephants, not pink but vivid nevertheless in glittering headdress, a band of folk musicians warbling boisterously and the first of half a dozen marigold-garland welcomes from smiling girls of exotic allure. In the station square a luxury coach awaited to turn us seven-day maharajas into mere up-market leathernecks for a tour of the city.

Encircled on all sides – except the south – by rugged hills surmounted by forts, Jaipur is enclosed in battlemented walls. Within them is medieval bedlam. The Hawa Mahal – Palace of the Winds – is the landmark of the city though its elaborate, fanciful and pink façade stands amidst the high street chaos of clogged roads and rude houses. In the centre of Jaipur is the City Palace – now a museum – more dramatically perched on high. A few miles away, at Amber, came the scheduled elephant ride on which we progressed regally up the hill, musically-escorted, to the deserted Mogul edifice reminding me a little of Dartmoor Prison except for the environment. A lesson on sundials at the Jantar Mantar Observatory, tea on a maharajan terrace of a British-designed garden watching a very un-British sunset, and dinner among the floodlit remains of the ruined fort of Nahargarh overlooking the sprawling city, brought us wearily back to the peace of our train.

Following a more successful night's sleep, my mind and body now attuned to the new motion and environment, I transferred, almost thankfully, from the luxurious splendour of the abode of the Maharaja of Bikaner to the sooty glamour of the cab of the train's locomotive, the *Desert Queen*. Here, with my eyes full of smut and a tummy full of oily sweet tea, I rediscovered a joy of travel that was in danger of eclipse under the welter of high living. Thus, in the grimy confines between tender and boiler, amongst a cab-full of dials and levers, I was back in a corner of real India and in the company of real Indians, these ones plainly appreciative of my interest in things railway. Here too, the shudder and shake was not only doubly pronounced but accompanied by the glorious whiff of steam, the searing blast of heat from a roaring flame, the high-pitched scream of the whistle and the sheer exhilaration of riding a mechanical animal vibrating with unleashed power.

It was from the engine crews that I learnt of the importance attached to the *Palace on Wheels* in Indian railway circles. At the time of my journey the train had become the most prestigious one in the country. It took priority over every other on the tracks of Indian Railways, was the only one double-crewed and its drivers were the most experienced in the business. All along the route crowds turned out to gape at the long winding serpent as well as the un-maharajan incumbents who emerged to daily greet the cities of Rajasthan.

All morning I remained with the *Desert Queen*, returning only to my abode simply for the purpose of removing the coal dust from my frame in time to join my compatriots for the grand emergence into Udaipur. So, running the gauntlet of the reception committee, we struggled into another sprawling city, this one given a romantic air by the steel-blue waters of a lake. Moated Udaipur, ethereal, unreal, holds island palaces galore that sparkle with pinnacles of coloured glass, of amber and pale jade created by Maharaja Udai Singh in the sixteenth century. His palace fort, massively bastioned and gated, erupts from the crest of a ridge and is the largest such pile in Rajasthan. A less sombre palace takes up the whole of an island in the artificial lake where it serves as a high-class restaurant in which we very adequately lunched on asparagus and venison.

There is something curiously theatrical about an empty train and returning to one in the middle of the night makes for added piquancy. In the waiting silence the presence of long past occupants hovers; the maharajas who travelled in the coaches to state occasions, on hunting parties or to polo matches; the maharanees who made their bridal voyages; the Queen and the Duke of Edinburgh who travelled on one when they stayed with the Maharaja of Jaipur. As the light seeped out of the sky and we climbed aboard our respective coaches the slumbering train came to life again, though its new occupants were unable to raise the aura of grandeur, the royal grace or proud disdain that surrounded their predecessors.

That night was, I remember, an idyllic one. We remained stationary and there was ample time next morning for shopping and bargaining in Udaipur's warren of bazaars. Here again was a moment, a fragment of the real India intruding into our pseudo-royal progress; the India that is contradictory, confusing, elusive, inexplicable. Streets full of people selling; selling anything – even the unsellable. The town centre of garish signs and toppling buildings was bulging at the seams with the movement of people all intent upon some purposeful errand that held commercial enterprise, or so it seemed. Women squatted silently in doorways and children played and laughed in rancid gutters. And pervading everything that smell of India that cannot be described or analysed.

Then we were off again leaving the confusion behind as we puffed importantly over the flat semi-desert where the tiniest of hills drew the eye. I spent the remainder of the day again in the locomotive, this one the *Fort of Jodhpur* emblazoned, like its fellow, with a large shiny coat of arms in front of its boiler, where I was once more regaled with coaldust and plentiful libations of tea from proud, but kindly, engine crews who, surely, are the salt of the Indian earth. It was quite a horrendous ride for, as we ground across the steppe, whistling mournfully, we mowed down one water buffalo and two goats that refused to move away quickly enough from 300 tons of train. And at one station we very nearly ran over a mentally sick woman when her attempted suicide brought the train to a juddering, screeching halt.

Long before the end of the week all the reserve only thinly breached the first evening had broken down and our contingent of guests intermingled, chatted and visited their companions in their respective coaches to compare furnishings, experiences and reactions to the trip. The few train buffs were euphoric; they had supped full on steam and all that goes with it. The nostalgic and romantics were gushing happy. Me? I was content enough, having found my luxury legs.

'Island in the Sand' describes Jaiselmer and, for most of us, it was the most fascinating city of all. A delightfully remote little town, it conjures the image of the *Thousand and One Nights* with its temples, fortresses and, of course, palaces – all constructed of the local yellow stone; a yellow city in a yellow ocean. Our welcome was the sincerest of all prior to our day's excursion to see its labyrinth of strangely-carved houses, handsome façades and elaborate balconies amidst a colourful fairytale population. On all sides the desert sweeps away into eternity and it was to a distant range of sand dunes at Sam, more Saharan than the Sahara, that we were taken for our scheduled camel ride and to listen to a performance of Jaiselmer musical talents. Dinner was held at a hotel back in the outskirts of town followed by a cultural presentation that included rhythmic offerings from an Indian ex-jailbird sporting what was the allegedly longest moustache in India.

No palace was to be seen at Bharatpur, our last city in Rajasthan. Instead a bird sanctuary – the Keoladeo Ghana Bird Sanctuary, an ornithologist's paradise. During winter, birds flock here from as far away as Siberia making a remarkable concentration of every feathered creature imaginable that flies and floats. We breakfasted at the lodge and were punted around the reed and island-impregnated lake before moving on by coach into the neighbouring state of Uttar Pradesh. After the magic of Rajasthan, the ghost city of Fatehpur Siki and the forts of Agra were something of an anti-climax. Fatehpur Siki is an imperial city deep frozen in time. Built at the command of Akbar to become the capital of the Mogul Empire it surpassed even London in size and grandeur before it died for reason of a simple lack of water. Our guide put it more quaintly: 'The water was not very delicious,' he explained, referring to the failed reservoir. Akbar was also instrumental in the rise of Agra, the rusty-red sandstone of its forbidding walls surrounding white marble palaces another memorial to that empire. Faded they are now but the glory of the Taj Mahal never diminishes however many times it is seen.

I had looked upon it the first time at the end of another Indian rail journey years before. Then I had set myself the task of seeing the country the hard way, of experiencing it from the level of the ordinary Indian, utilising third-class train carriages and equally over-crowded local buses. With ordinary Indians I slept on station platforms and in hotels that were no more than doss houses, living on local curries supplied for a few pence at wayside stalls. The exercise had taught me much about India and lost me the best part of two stone in weight; a tough education which had added to my appreciation of the modest comforts offered me on my subsequent visits.

The memory certainly added spice to my present journey now nearing its end. I had become inured to the insulation from the grit and grime of the 'real' India, the pretence that kept us from making contact with 'real' Indians, the illusion of grandeur that we had not earned or inherited. We had observed rather than become part of the country but then this is the very essence of a journey on the *Palace on Wheels;* a dream with no real substance.

A last night in the golden coaches and we were rolling towards Delhi from whence we had come. The countryside was agricultural, full of buffalo and sugar cane and it had ceased to interest us. Dinner was in the restaurant car; a choice of Indian or vaguely European dishes. I spent the last morning hours in the cab of the *Desert Queen* re-learning the rules of an old-fashioned semaphore signalling procedure from the crew. We were an hour late but it didn't matter. Back at Delhi Cantonment there were no garlands. We were maharajas no more.

TO SOUTH AMERICA and, in particular, the Andean countries of Peru and Ecuador. It was a walking project; a 1,400-mile trudge – told in some detail in Chapter Three – that took me to that part of the world in 1977, but I found time beforehand to sample the rail networks of the two countries.

The most evocative railways in South America are, surely, those of the trans-Andean lines, especially those in Peru. Crossing the Andes meant constructing the highest railway in the world, and the highest of all is the Peruvian Central Railway. Railway construction in such circumstances presented civil engineers with major problems for they had to, in a confined space and short distance, build lines over passes which exceeded Mont Blanc in altitude. The solution they adopted were tight curves, zigzags and rack sections. Operating the lines created further difficulties; steep gradients, lack of local sources of fuel, heavy wear and tear on locomotives and rolling stock, and frequent landslides and washouts. Changing from steam to diesel was, initially, a step backwards because diesel units were prone to losing power in the rare air and there were many cases of trains being unable to take the gradients.

My first experience of riding a trans-Andean train was on the Southern Railway of the country. Three lines serve the *altiplano,* a grassy windswept plain 12,800 feet above sea level, and one of them is the Southern. Of standard gauge, it runs from Mollendo on the Peruvian coast through the country's second city, Arequipa, to the town of Juliaca on the *altiplano.* Here it divides. A short section continues to Lake Titicaca and around its shores to the port of Puno while a 211-mile line from Juliaca runs north to Cuzco, the ancient Inca capital, crossing a summit of 14,154 feet at La Raya. I was to ride both.

The Puno train was supposed to leave at 08.15 and, in the event, left at 09.15 which is not bad at all in a land where *mañana* doesn't just mean 'tomorrow' but can also mean 'never'. The early morning scene as the train wound up the valley towards Juliaca was enchanting. All around were fields of alfalfa and corn and, behind Arequipa, the volcanic peaks of Misti and Chachani. After Crucero Alto, the highest point on the line, the first mountain lakes appeared: Lagunillas and Saroco, each on either side of the train.

I travelled second – lowest – class and though the seats were hard my journey was not uncomfortable. The coaches were

British-made, sturdy and ancient, their windows either jammed shut or jammed open. The train was full, but not overcrowded, with cheerful people. I was soon to learn that there is no need to go short of food on an Andean train for there are vendors both on the train itself and at every stop. And Andean trains do a lot of stopping. All sorts of edible oddities were thrust under my nose by large peasant women wearing bowler hats and voluminous skirts of many colours inflated by layers of petticoats. There was no restaurant car on my train, but that a kitchen existed was plain from the huge roast-chicken dishes that none-too-clean waiters brought round to those that ordered them. With the chicken went generous measures of *Pisco* brandy which kept everyone in high spirits.

Virtually all my fellow travellers were of Indian extraction. The older womenfolk in their absurd hats and skirts wore their hair in standard greasy black plaits joined at the nape of the neck. For most of the day-long journey everyone gorged themselves silly on huge chunks of semi-raw meat cut from an obscure joint of an equally obscure animal which was hawked by vendors from bundles of filthy rags. I stuck to the *Pisco*. The train was diesel-hauled but so much black smoke issued from the locomotive it could have been a steam engine at its head.

Puno, where I stayed awhile, boasts a fine square, a coldly austere cathedral and a lively market full of local colour. But around the small port there was ugly poverty that could not be hidden by the description 'quaint', an adjective which my guidebook was fond of using for everything that differed from the British middle-class way of life.

Thereafter the northbound line climbed gradually, reaching its climax at La Raya. The countryside became pure magic with astonishing panoramas of snow-capped peaks, tall mountains, green pastures and woods. With La Raya behind, the train picked up speed and pounded down the straight to Sicuani, near which the ruins of the Inca temple of Viracocha, grandiose and lonely, stand. North of Sicuani the fields were vivid with Californian poppies and wild lupins before they gave way to the River Vilcanota which the line accompanies. More stops with strange alien names, and we came to Cusipata, Rumicola and Huambutio. Dusk saw us in the rugged sierra surrounded by mountain rocks of purple and red, cacti with long fingers, and grey moss hanging like a tattered veil from cliffs and shrubs. Scotch broom trees added a more cheerful note of yellow as we emerged out into the valley head with its gnarled pepper trees. And all this to music, thanks to the guitar and mouth organ talents of a blind family and their sweet rendering of a well-known Quechua love song. A golden sunset was to climax our entry into Cuzco.

During my stay in Cuzco I caught the early morning train to Chaullay which dropped me (and a thousand others) at the legendary Machupicchu – the 'Lost City of the Incas' – which Hiram Bingham stumbled upon in 1911. There are no roads to Machupicchu so the train is the only vehicle for reaching this edifice of supreme drama that is upstaged only by the utter magnificence of its surroundings.

I was tempted back to the trains at Huancavelica. A glance at the rail-system map of Peru will show you the route of the Central Railway as a lop-sided T with Lima at its base, running up to La Oroya at the junction of the crosspiece. The main line runs from Lima through La Oroya to Huancavelica, its terminal on the right. A privately-owned line runs from La Oroya to Cerro de Pasco on the left. My first journey on the former was to Lima, the Peruvian capital.

The Central Railway is regarded as one of the wonders of the Americas and the engineering of the route involved immense problems. The deep Rimac valley between Lima and La Oroya, the only feasible route to the central region of the country, narrows to a maximum width of about 656 feet. Within its limits the engineers had to find a way of climbing nearly 13,000 feet within a distance of less than 47 miles which is the length of the road along the bottom of the valley. The twists and turns which the railway needs to gain height have made the railway considerably longer at 73 miles. To keep the gradient down to the necessary 1 in 23, the single track railway has to utilise the whole width of the valley, crossing frequently from one side to the other. Even this would be impossible without the use of the famous zigzags to gain height. Between Chosica and Ticlio, the highest point of the line at 15,693 feet, there are six double zigzags, one single zigzag, 66 tunnels and 59 bridges to negotiate.

Construction of the line, which began in 1870, presented problems in addition to the geographical ones. A mysterious disease killed off thousands of workers in 1877, then Peru went bankrupt, which effectively held up completion until 1929. The chief interest of the Central Railway has always been freight, particularly since 1897 when the La Oroya copper mines opened. However, the incredible journey still remains attainable to the traveller. Except for those unfortunates who suffer from altitude sickness and have to be given oxygen by the attendants on the train, all will marvel as I did at the ingenuity of the men who built this railway amidst some of the most rugged landscapes on earth.

Between Huancavelica and Huancayo, midway to La Oroya, the line is metre gauge. I travelled in a crowded railcar that whizzed along merrily before it broke down. A normally three hour journey turned disconcertingly to one of ten hours. At least I was lucky to get a seat, though I paid dearly for it by having a perpetually howling baby next to me dribbling all over my trousers.

The delay resulted in a night on the tiles at Huancayo, an old market town that I could have found quite pleasant at any time but two in the morning. The night was bitterly cold and I blessed a kindly bunch of vendors for allowing me to warm myself around their brazier. The nightlife of Huancayo is not without incident to judge from some of the prostitutes and shady characters who likewise came to warm themselves by the fire.

The 07.00 to Lima was the *tren de sierra* and of much more substance than the previous day's railcar. En route towards La Oroya the hilly scenery reminded me of North Wales and the industrial town into which we drew carried overtones of Port Talbot. La Oroya station was the usual jumble of humanity with everybody selling everything to everybody else. While I was sampling a fruit that I think was chirimoya and spitting out the pips like a consumptive machine gun, the engine driver came over, tapped me on the shoulder and said, 'El Inglish, we go.' It was one of the few times in Peru I was given a title other than 'Gringo'.

All the way from Huancayo we had been climbing steadily though the gradients were not noticeable. Now the name of a station – Ticlio – came into view with its altitude (4,782 metres) prominently displayed on a board. Nobody in my compartment appeared to be affected by the height though oxygen-bearing officials haunted the corridors to help those that were. The line reaches its highest point in the tunnel between Ticlio and Galera and, thereafter, the train is off the leash and on the downhill leg of the journey. On the seat opposite me a German breathed heavily, as I suppose I did too. In addition to their pale faces foreigners on this train are distinguishable by their heavy breathing.

The Andes are great humblers of men. They stretch the length of South America, forming a crenellated wall 4,500 miles long, draped at the northern end with vegetation and at the southern end with ice and snow. And down the length of the range, and on its slopes, lie untamed regions of snow, ice and fire, of dripping jungle and seared desert, of cloud cover and merciless sun, of intense heat and killing cold. This is the barrier that railway builders had to contend with when they planned and constructed the lateral lines that wind inland from the tropical coastline. As the pace of the *tren de sierra* slackened with the application of the brakes, a feeling of awe descended upon the whole train almost tangible in its intensity.

The Rimac valley is not beautiful; it is savage, bleak and remorseless. The great walls and escarpments hem in the fragile track forcing it to curve, wind and dodge in a kind of desperate progress that is more like an escape. Where granite buttresses bar the way the line doubles back on itself, forcing the limping train to grind to a halt up against the canyon wall and reverse downwards the moment the hand-operated points have been switched by the guard. Forwards, backwards, forwards, backwards, slowly we spiralled down the valley. We all chatted inanely as the coaches traversed delicate lattice bridges over bottomless chasms and crept along the edges of sheer precipices on narrow ledges hacked from enormous cliffs of granite.

Nine hours after leaving Huancayo the valley flattened out and entered upon a warm, tropical expanse of green countryside that had pushed aside the mountains to substitute terraced cultivation and urban development. Ahead lay the sea with Lima shimmering in the heat haze.

A few days later I returned by the same route just for the hell of it and also to sample the local line that branches off the main one at La Oroya to see what Cerro de Pasco had to offer besides copper mines. The local train there was packed so I shared a seat with a substantial bowler-hatted lady, each of us supporting one buttock on the wooden slats. The three-hour journey along the crest of the range cost me the equivalent of 15 pence – but I'm not sure if this was a bargain.

Many hundreds of miles of daunting, spectacular territory separate the Peruvian Central Railway from the Ecuadorian seaport of Guayaquil, the southern terminal of the Ecuadorian State Railway of which the chief component is the Guayaquil and Quito Line. Misleadingly nicknamed 'the Good and the Quick', it connects the two main cities of the country, the former on the coast and the latter 9,000 feet up in the mountains.

Construction began in 1871 but it was not until 1908 that the contractors completed the rare 3' 6" gauge line. To traverse the 288 miles and 11,840-foot altitude, tight curves and zigzags were incorporated. It has never been a commercial success and its resulting near-bankruptcy has given it a dreadful reputation for chaotic administration, breakdowns and derailments. Its rolling stock is antique and the fact that the railway continues to operate is probably more amazing than the fact that it was ever built. 'The world's mightiest roller-coaster' it has also sometimes been called.

Guayaquil itself – Ecuador's second city, though larger in terms of population than Quito – is something of a garden metropolis though its prosperity derives from the industry it encompasses. The odd thing is that the railway fails to enter the city; the terminus being at Duran on the east bank of the Guayas River.

For my ride to Quito, the Ecuadorian capital, I made the mistake of catching the more expensive *autoferro* – a clapped out railcar – which, surprisingly, was the luxury vehicle of the line and the only sort to go right through to Quito. I ought to have boarded the cheaper and unreliable *tren mixto* which went no further than Riobamba and then caught the *autoferro*. As it was, my train was full of tourists and a few Ecuadorian businessmen.

Leaving Duran we whizzed across the broad, fertile Guayas Valley, passing fields of sugar cane, rice and split cane houses built high on stilts overlooking waterways speckled with thousands of water birds and big dugouts piled high with produce. After Huigra and the River Chanchan the line began its zigzagging course within a narrow gorge and, past Sibambe, climbed the famous Nariz del Diablo (Devil's Nose), a perpendicular ridge rising in the gorge to a height of 10,600 feet. Another engineering challenge, this almost insurmountable obstacle was finally conquered by the building of a series of switchbacks on a five and a half per cent grade.

First one way and then the other the train zigzagged higher and higher to gain an altitude of 11,840 feet at Urbina. Coming down the valley of the volcanoes to Quito the views from the train windows were probably the most spectacular to be seen from a railway anywhere in the world. One by one the towering volcanic summits of Chimborazo, Carihuairazo, Altar, Tungurahua, the burning head of Sangay and Caropaxi appeared in the clear atmosphere.

I had made a detour from Sibambe where I rode the branch line to Cuenca, a gracious town that has preserved its colonial air with cobblestone streets and picturesque old buildings. Then I returned to the so-called mainline.

Few cities have a setting to match Quito. Although nearly three kilometres high – it is the second highest capital, after Bolivia's La Paz, in Latin America – the mountains which circle it are higher still. Modern Quito extends northwards into a luxuriant plain but the city's attraction lies in the old south-western section where cobbled streets are steep and winding, and the houses are mostly Indian-made adobe brick with low red roof tiles, or whitened stone. Quito's heart is the Plaza Independencia, dominated by the usual grim-looking cathedral.

It was in the modern part of town – and in the posh embassy sector – that I fell victim to a pickpocket gang on a crowded city bus. I managed to retain my passport and a few remaining travel cheques but lost my air ticket, credit cards and all my money. I made myself extremely unpopular by yelling to the driver to stop, denying exit to all those wishing to alight and dragging aboard a reluctant policeman on point duty who felt impelled to line everyone up against the bus exterior to be searched with their hands above their heads. Meanwhile the villains, who had escaped before the hullabaloo, simply melted into the horrifying traffic pandemonium that resulted from the now uncontrolled intersection.

Fortunately this incident occurred towards the end of my sojourn in South America, but thereafter my onward journey to Bogota, the Colombian capital from whence my flight home was scheduled, was to be accomplished with the minimum of funds, enough only for very basic feeding and none at all for hotel accommodation. And I had a whole fortnight to spend in such circumstances before departure.

The first move obviously was to get out of Quito. Capitals are expensive luxuries and hotels – even the strictly basic variety – were emphatically out. The northward route towards Colombia offered Ibarra as the subsequent destination and, with a gratis railway ticket prized out of the Ecuadorian railway authorities that gave me free travel from Quito to Ibarra to San Lorenzo and back if I wanted, I decided to take advantage of part of it. I would go as far as San Lorenzo but return to Ibarra ready for the final leg of the journey to Bogota. At least my dallying on the trains would offer me a kind of refuge.

Ibarra I found to be a friendly town neatly ringed by a mountain range, a volcano and a lake. Here I spent the first of two nights on the floor of the stationmaster's office with strident bells and telephones ringing unanswered all around me. In the morning the staff arrived, stepped over my prostrate form wrapped in a sleeping bag and commenced their duties as if stray English sleepers on their floor were the most natural thing in the world. For breakfast I consumed half a pint of rum donated by the staff and half a loaf of bread contributed by a local grocer in the town.

My train to San Lorenzo, when it condescended to put in an appearance, promptly quashed any notions I might have entertained about sleeping cars and plush first-class compartments. On offer was a little monster called an *autocarril*. Basically this was a vehicle that was born as a common o'garden British Leyland lorry ending a long hard life on flanged wheels and a fixed course.

The initial portion of the journey was very definitely second class. My ticket (first class) stipulated a reserved seat, but there were no seats to reserve. The cope bulged with people standing or squatting amongst bags of flour, trussed chickens and a nanny goat. We were classed a *tren mixto* and the definition was accurate. In a tunnel we ran out of petrol and the nanny goat deficated over my sandals.

A few miles on the train ran out of track at the edge of the River Mira. The river had cut the line in two – literally – by having swept away the bridge. We all had to disembark and cross (no more than four passengers at a time) using a temporary rope structure that swayed alarmingly above a seething brown torrent, to the second train that waited the other side. I asked when the flood had brought down the bridge and was told four years ago.

The second train was an old British Leyland bus and so was a step up in the comfort scale since it held seats. At least it did for some but not for me. We moved like the proverbial bat out of hell along the badly laid and worn track, swaying from side to side in hair-raising fashion, while the driver talked animatedly to a girl by his side and I wished he'd watch where he was going. Several hours later we came to the stock joke of the run; a waterfall that descends directly upon the track. All those in the know had quietly closed their windows but of course I hadn't and so received a powerful deluge of cold water to huge guffaws of mirth. With the Mira Gorge behind us we hurtled through a steamy jungle and swept into San Lorenzo.

If I expected the cool clear waters of the Pacific and soft beaches upon which to recline I was doomed to disappointment. What I got was a fetid mangrove swamp and a tropical downpour. I spent the night on the concrete floor of the tin-roofed ticket office of the station being eaten alive by mosquitoes. Seldom have I come across so awful a place as San Lorenzo, a township of wooden shacks and a bazaar rotting in its own sweat. Not even my guidebook dared call it 'quaint'.

My morning alarm clock was the arrival of the first potential passengers queuing for tickets over my sleeping bag (with me in it) and I was delighted to return to the train, even obtaining a whole seat to myself. Again the driver was a speed maniac. Not once did he slacken the pace even for the most excruciating bend. Around one of them, with his foot down hard, we ran over a yellow triangle placed on the track – the one piece of signalling apparatus on the entire line – and ploughed straight into a sea of mud obliterating the metals. As with the Baluchistan line in Pakistan a little passenger participation is expected on such occasions.

In the pouring rain we emerged from our bus, were issued with shovels stored in the cab and put to work clearing the track from the sticky soil and boulders that had slid down from the hillside. Nobody except me appeared the slightest put out by being made to help and by the time we ran into the second landslide an hour later I was an old hand at the job.

Back across the Mira River obstacle and aboard the old lorry waiting patiently for the 'connection' in the tunnel mouth, I returned thankfully to Ibarra. Except for a short ride in a goods train in Colombia it was my last railway ride in South America.

In that country the northbound tracks, for me, started again at Cali, but since they didn't link with Bogota, I had to complete my travels using thumb power. In this my efforts were not completely unsuccessful since I managed to make the Colombian capital without quite starving to death.

AND SO, FINALLY, to the longest continuous rail link in the world, that of the Trans-Siberian Railway, a link that I have, during the Soviet era, ridden three times. The first was in 1970.

I boarded the Trans-Siberian Express – in my case a train titled the *Russia* – for the sole purpose of reaching the end of the line at, then strictly out-of-bounds-to-foreigners, Vladivostok. I reached it with the help of a little bribery and corruption of a Russian fellow-traveller, a sucker for my duty-free cigarettes and who obtained my onward ticket for me. From Khabarovsk, the furthest a Westerner was permitted to go and still 500 miles short of Vladivostok, I joined the same train next day utilising the lowest – hard – class where a coachful of amused peasants took enormous pleasure in concealing me in their bed rolls whenever authority hove into view. Leaving the station within the ranks of a company of Red Army soldiers I attained the city centre, had a good look round and returned to the station for my return journey to Khabarovsk only to learn that my ticket was for a one-way trip. To obtain a further one required a permit which not only did I have but, added to my deficiencies, was a lame passport containing a visa valid for Moscow only – and I was nearly 6,000 miles off course. Thus I was unable to book into a hotel for the night. However, an office back in town, to which I was directed, finally produced the permit allowing me to buy a ticket at the station. This largesse came about following production of a series of my membership cards – Royal Automobile Club, Regimental Association, driving licence and, last but not least, my Barclays Bank Visa credit card which, inexplicably, did the trick! Back in Khabarovsk I found myself in dire disgrace since a lady guide of Intourist had spent 36 hours searching for an expected but lost British tourist. I was accused of having spent a night with a woman of ill-repute (in spite of the fact that Intourist had invariably insisted that in the enlightened Soviet Union there was no prostitution) and, though it hurt my pride, I let her believe this since I felt my incursion into a forbidden city was a greater crime.

MY SECOND CROSSING of the mighty USSR was in 1985 when I made the longest rail journey of my life – London to Hong Kong.

Those, like myself, who find bliss in trundling 10,000 miles by train across Europe and Asia from London, might spare a thought for their point of departure. The railway-lore-impregnated Great Eastern Hotel and its adjoining cast-iron and brick Liverpool Street Station have been built upon the site of the Hospital of St Mary of Bethlem, known as Bedlam for short, and for centuries London's chief hospital for lunatics. For me at any rate, it put things into perspective a little as my train slid through the begrimed bottleneck of Bishopsgate at the start of one of the longest train rides in the world.

The portion of it to Harwich and the sea voyage to the Dutch coast were civilised enough, shaming the subsequent offerings of the then East-West Express on its 48-hour stop-start progress to Moscow. Perhaps in keeping with a route following that taken by bloodied invasion armies of history, its vicissitudes included not only lack of a restaurant car but the ferocious border controls between two Berlins, two Germanies, Poland and the European USSR.

At the Russian capital's Jaroslav Station commences – or ends – the gleaming tracks of the Trans-Siberian Railway, a stupendous 5,778-mile iron road to Vladivostok which I had ridden earlier on that train called *Russia*. Now I was to board a vehicle titled the *Baikal,* which was going to carry me just 3,221 miles to Irkutsk in a scheduled four and a half days.

In the summer Siberia can be a very pleasant spot. The train halted long enough at stations for a leg-stretch and purchase of fruit from free-enterprise stalls on the platform, while sprawling cities like Kirov, Sverdlovsk, Omsk, Novosibirsk and Krasnoyarsk broke the monotony of a mainly flat countryside of endless birch trees. Our four and a half days lengthened into more than five by reason of a serious freight train collision the fourth day out. The accident occurred ahead of the *Baikal,* totally blocking the line for 12 hours. The following Peking Express drew up beside us, adding its complement of passengers to our own and spewing two trainloads of them into a flower-strewn meadowland and village assuredly not on any tourist itinerary. The incident gave opportunity for me to gain access to our huge locomotive and I was there when the signal flashed green and the train had to move off, carrying a Western capitalist in its cab until I could be unloaded at the next station.

Reduced to a restaurant car diet of macaroni, caviar and Russian champagne, we crawled into the capital of Siberia more than 14 hours late, and the eight left that my schedule gave me in Irkutsk was, to my mind, plenty. Having stayed there before, I was aware that there is little for a visitor to see in the city beyond the mighty River Angara and some fast-disappearing timber houses of the Chekov era.

It was here I bade farewell to the *Baikal* and transferred to the optimistically titled Ulan Bator Express, its hard-backed seats, dirty blankets and even dirtier windows boding ill. In this plainly lesser train we continued along the Trans-Siberian line as far as Ulan-Ude, there to be connected to a rust-pink – more rust than pink – diesel unit of Mongolian Railways to deflect southwards on a non-electrified single track snaking into low hills of downs-like gentleness.

Why the Soviet Union had to insist upon the full paraphernalia of electrified fences swept at night by the blue-tinged beams of searchlights on the border of her subservient Mongolian satellite I failed to understand. Honour among thieves I supposed. But with the surly five-hour attentions of Soviet authority at an end, the train, off the leash at last, pranced merrily across lovely rolling plains, the habitat of the wild camel, horse and Gobi bear.

Ulan Bator, capital of the Mongolian People's Republic, lay swathed in a dawn mist. The station was a handsome building smaller than a London suburban one, while the city itself is not unattractive, though a rash of construction work was producing rows of cheap-jack standardised apartments to house its citizens still residing in the traditional but despised *gers* or *yurts* that, in fenced ghettos, made up a lot of Ulan Bator's suburbs.

Ulan Bator means 'Red Hero' and the city took over the capitalship from Karakoram, further to the west, in 1924, before which it was a disease-ridden feudal township called Urga. Now a small city of tree-lined avenues, apartment blocks, schools, colleges and factories, it contained, even on that first visit of mine, a still-functioning Buddhist monastery.

There were two trains a week onwards to Beijing (then known to the West as Peking) and no air service, so the railway was the sole link with China. Both trains were labelled 'express', but one was more express than the other. I caught the slower of the two and straightway came under the influence of Mongolia's southern neighbour, with Chinese rolling stock of considerably more quality than the Russian. Abruptly my tea issue became jasmin-flavoured and the furnishings included elegantly shaded table lamps, soft seat-backs, dainty coverlets and chintzy curtains.

The terrain outside flattened out but my image of the Gobi Desert, evoked by the chronicles of Marco Polo, of sandy wastes and evocative desolation was shattered by an abundance of flora and fauna. Central Mongolia is dominated by the Hangai range which holds some of the country's richest grazing land, and only on the southern border do the wind-eroded tops of the Gobi-Altai undulate into desert tracts of gravel.

For some of the new 36-hour journey I was invited into a neighbouring coach full of Chinese refugees expelled from Mongolia with only the belongings they could carry with them. Their hospitality was genuine in spite of their unfortunate circumstances, but there was a motive behind it. With a Westerner in the compartment, the Mongolian customs officials at the border were likely to be a lot less ruthless with them than they would have been had I not been present. And so it was, though the authorities must have wondered why I was carrying so much baggage that was hardly of Western origin.

From Erhlien, the border town, to Datong, the train was headed by a giant black QI class steam locomotive, a product of that Chinese city which held the last remaining steam locomotive factory on earth. And it was here that I spent an unforgettable day touring the factory complex of workshops, steel forgings and pressings, boilers, fireboxes, couplings and connecting rods, smoke stacks and endless pairs of magnificent red driving wheels. And when the factory tour was over I was taken out into the yards and into the cab of one of the great new black monsters to accompany the crew on a ten-mile test drive.

The line from Datong to Beijing was electrified, and a new dawn saw the train among the first mountains of the entire journey, these ones made the more evocative by having portions of the Great Wall perambulating about their flanks. Beijing Central Station is something of a railway cathedral, its twin clock towers giving an air of nobility. In the early morning its cavernous interior was well nigh deserted, but I was to see it later when it had become a seething mass; fast flowing rivers of humanity into which one is propelled remorselessly.

The last long haul – again of 36 hours – was that from Beijing to Canton (now reverted to its Chinese name of Guangzhou) which I began four days later. The 1,500-mile route is a pleasant one via Wuhan and Changsha, through a countryside I thought existed only in the fanciful minds of Chinese painters: fields of lotus flowers backed by impossible sharp-pointed hills. We rumbled across massive bridges spanning gigantic waterways of the calibre of the Yangtse and Yellow River, the former structure having taken ten years to build after the Soviet Union had withdrawn her labour and destroyed the blueprints.

I remained in Canton but a day and a night; the night spent in a run-down hostel in which resided the biggest cockroaches I have ever beheld. My Chinese companions in the dormitory inveigled me into a farcical game of cockroach racing on the floor, each insect having a number inscribed on its brittle back.

But, all of a sudden, I was eager for Hong Kong and a dose of its flamboyant capitalism. The two and a half hour journey there was the smoothest of them all; the train never even stopping at the border, surely the one iron-cum-bamboo curtain at which I would have expected to be delayed and checked.

And there was nothing like a month on Communist Asian trains to give added lustre to this fabulous capitalistic city sitting on the edge of the Communist world.

AFTERWORD

Travel, they say, broadens the mind. It is also addictive and, according to Robert Louis Stevenson, a better thing than to arrive.

My dictionary, as I stated earlier, defines the word 'travel' as '...to move along a course, to go with impetus'; this impetus today being, I suppose, business, exploration or pleasure, though for some maybe a bit of all three.

Travel for the sake of tourism occupies by far the largest segment of the travelling public as it migrates, annually, to the beaches of Continental Europe, the Caribbean or even the seaside resorts of Britain. I suppose this migration stemmed originally from what used to be known as 'The Grand Tour' when certain cities on the Continent were considered by the well-to-do to be socially essential to visit – Paris, Florence, Venice, Rome and Naples. Yet, as another author-colleague of mine, Patrick Delaforce, points out in his book, *The Grand Tour*, these early tourist/travellers had to contend, in centuries past, with the hazards and discomforts encountered en route to and from these fabled destinations. There were *banditti* in most of the countries. There were encounters with wild dogs, sometimes wolves. There was often vermin in the wayside inns. Customs officials needed bribing. Police officers, moneychangers, postmasters, tollkeepers and local officials exacted what they could get away with. The innkeepers vied with the postilions in insolence towards their temporary clientele, as well as constantly overcharging them. Indifferent food and wine, the dangers of illness and pestilence, even plague, were further inevitable hazards. Indeed some travellers died on the Grand Tour. A cynic might be of the opinion that not much has changed today! But since it was only the moneyed classes who went on the Grand Tour it is surprising what they were willing to put up with to attain their goals. Almost it puts them into the impetus category of exploration.

There is an almost legendary affinity between the British and the great deserts and jungles of Africa. 'Doctor Livingstone, I presume' are words that epitomise the British love of inflicting discomfort upon themselves in the interests of exploration, discovery, experience and conquest. We accept the occasional Frenchman or Scandinavian upon the scene, for even other countries have their eccentrics. But Peter Fleming spoke for the majority when he said that the trouble about such journeys nowadays is that they are easy to make but difficult to justify. Only a few places on this earth remain untrampled.

With the spread of the package tour and ever-faster, ever-larger aircraft, the days of the explorer could be said to be numbered. And with most of the challenges of geography overcome by intrepid pioneers, there is a certain amount of frustration creeping into the deliberations of the would-be explorer as he or she glowers perplexedly at the globe now singularly devoid of all that red which Doctor Livingstone and his kith went to such pains to daub. Thus it is becoming a case not so much of being first up or over a feature of this earth, but of finding a way to negotiate it in an original and sometimes gimmicky manner. There's always some bright spark waiting in the wings who can dream up a new way to suffer in the interests of conquest or experience.

Though these interests may have diminished, the same need not be said about those of investigation. Here the choice widens dramatically. There are many regions of the world today that have been traversed by intrepid footsteps, but there's always something new to learn.

THE WORLD COMMUTER
GREAT JOURNEYS BY TRAIN

CHRISTOPHER PORTWAY

summersdale *travel*

The World Commuter
Great Journeys By Train
Christopher Portway

'Commuters catching the 07:55 five days a week can hardly be expected to go into raptures about train travel . . .' but this type of travel is far removed from the stories that Christopher Portway has to tell. *The World Commuter* embraces half a lifetime of travelling around the world by train. Attempting an escape as a POW in Nazi-occupied Europe; ducking under the Iron Curtain to reach the 'closed' city of Vladivostok; steaming down the Khyber Pass on the train's front buffers; plush and hard travel to Pyongyang, Kaliningrad, Bogota, Baghdad and all stops in between.

Portway's fellow travellers are as much of a feature as his journey, the eccentric Englishman is entertained by Jordanian royalty, Red Army soldiers and Bedouin nomads, and succeeds in being blacklisted by politically hostile border officials of many of the world's countries.

Much more than a travelogue, *The World Commuter* teems with incident and strange encounter, combines history with anecdote and is a fascinating and dramatic account of one man's global passion.

'The clever mix of travelogue, history and anecdote makes for an entertaining and thought-provoking read.'
Geographical Magazine

'An enthralling read.'
The Railway Magazine

'Exciting and unusual . . . Life's never been dull for Christopher.'
The Weekly News

'Extraordinary . . . stranger than fiction.'
The Daily Express

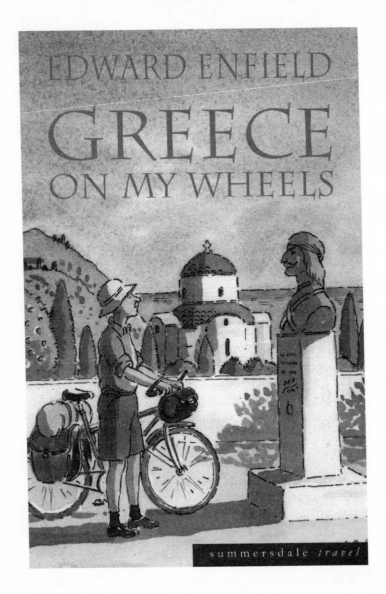

EDWARD ENFIELD

GREECE
ON MY WHEELS

summersdale *travel*

Greece on my Wheels
Edward Enfield

Two enchanting explorations of Greece by bicycle.

Mounted on his trusty steed, Edward explores the beauty and history of the Pelopponese in a travelogue that combines wit, charm and scholarship. Returning to Greece to follow in the footsteps of the Romantic poet Lord Byron, Edward's second trip sees him pedalling around the great historic sites of Epirus as he completes his own mini odyssey.

'displays genuine empathy with his surroundings, an infectious admiration for ancient Greek culture, and occasional flashes of wry wit, to provide a memorably satisfying read.'
The Bookseller

'full of humour and wonderful depictions of the wild beauty and fascinating people of Greece - all seen from the saddle of his trusty steed, no mean feat for a man approaching 70!'
The Oldie

'Enfield not only impresses - he informs and delights.'
Wanderlust Mag

'The most charming travelogue I've read this year. Mr Enfield (young Harry's father) takes the reader on a cycling tour, a history lesson and a literary safari that combines old world wit and charm with a sweeping breadth of knowledge. This volume should be on every creative writing course syllabus as an example of travel writing at its best'
Paul Blezard, *Oneword Radio*

www.summersdale.com